COMPETITION
IN THE
NATURAL GAS
PIPELINE INDUSTRY

COMPETITION
IN THE
NATURAL GAS
PIPELINE INDUSTRY

AN ECONOMIC POLICY ANALYSIS

EDWARD C. GALLICK

Westport, Connecticut
London

The views expressed herein are solely those of the author and are not intended to represent the position of the Federal Trade Commission, the Federal Energy Regulatory Commission, or any department or official of the United States government.

Library of Congress Cataloging-in-Publication Data

Gallick, Edward C.
    Competition in the natural gas pipeline industry : an economic policy analysis / Edward C. Gallick.
        p.   cm.
    Includes bibliographical references and index.
    ISBN 0-275-94346-1 (alk. paper)
    1. Gas industry—Government policy—United States. 2. Natural gas pipelines—Government policy—United States. 3. Competition—Government policy—United States. I. Title.
    HD9581.U5G23   1993
    388.5'6'0973—dc20   92-14536

British Library Cataloguing in Publication Data is available.

Library of Congress Catalog Card Number: 92-14536
ISBN: 0-275-94346-1

First published in 1993

Praeger Publishers, 88 Post Road West, Westport, CT 06881
An imprint of Greenwood Publishing Group, Inc.

Printed in the United States of America

The paper used in this book complies with the Permanent Paper Standard issued by the National Information Standards Organization (Z39.48-1984).

10 9 8 7 6 5 4 3 2 1

To my wife and son,
Linda and Jason,
for their belief in me
and in my work

CONTENTS

TABLES AND FIGURES

FIGURES

PREFACE

This book was written while the author was a senior economist with the Bureau of Economics at the Federal Trade Commission (FTC). It was completed in August 1989 and approved by the Bureau of Economics, by the Bureau of Competition, and by an outside reviewer. Given the policy implications of the analysis, however, it could not be released without the further review by each commissioner and his/her staff. For the next two and one-half years, the book was revised numerous times in an effort to narrow the policy implications of the study and meet the concerns of each commissioner. In late October 1991, the author was given permission to publish the book on his own. The author is currently the director of the Division of Competition Analysis in the Office of Economic Policy at the Federal Energy Regulatory Commission.

Hopefully, this book will make a contribution to the economics literature as well as to litigated and nonlitigated proceedings where competition or the exercise of market power is an important issue. First, the book suggests how to quantify the competitive effect of potential entry. The methodology is applied to the natural gas pipeline industry. Second, it is shown that any competitive analysis of the natural gas pipeline industry that ignores the competitive effect of potential entry is likely to suggest market power concerns where none, in fact, exist. Third, to the extent that federal regulation of the natural gas pipeline industry is based on the premise that current pipeline suppliers will exercise market power if allowed to set market-based rates, the reasonableness of this premise should be reconsidered by performing a competitive analysis of the market that includes the competitive effect of potential entry.

The research for this book was conducted in the mid-1980s when gas customers tended to purchase both gas and transportation from the pipelines (i.e., bundled sales). Purchasing patterns have changed in the 1990s: The current tendency is for customers to buy gas from producers and transportation from pipelines (i.e., unbundled sales). If a current pipeline supplier attempts to increase the price of delivered gas, the customer may be able to switch from sales service to transportation service on the pipeline and then search for cheaper, alternative gas supplies from a producer or marketer. It should be clear that this shift in purchasing patterns increases the alternatives available to customers and therefore strengthens the conclusions I reach about the competitiveness of city-gate markets.

This book takes a detailed look at one important and often neglected competitive factor in local natural gas markets: the extent to which local competition among pipelines is influenced by the potential entry of competitors. This entry can occur, for example, by building spurs from nearby pipelines. If such entry is relatively easy, then current suppliers would be constrained from raising prices above competitive levels because new firms would enter the market. Thus, potential entrants must be considered in any competitive evaluation of local natural gas markets. To prevent pipelines from setting prices above competitive levels, the Federal Energy Regulatory Commission (FERC) currently regulates the price at which natural gas can be sold by interstate pipelines and the entry or expansion of these pipelines. I find, however, that in most major markets, the ability of local dominant pipelines to raise prices may be limited by nearby suppliers that can enter the market relatively quickly. There are a fairly large number of pipelines located within 140 miles of most major markets. These pipelines may be able to profitably enter these major markets if anticompetitive pricing were to occur. If so, entry would tend to constrain prices to a competitive level. I conclude that once proper account is given to the role of entry, current price and entry regulations are costly and may by unnecessary in most localities.

Most past studies have focused on the number, or "concentration," of pipelines currently serving an area as an indicator of competitive conditions. I find that concentration measures that are used in analyzing the competitiveness of markets (i.e., the ability of incumbent firms to raise price above costs) are likely to underestimate competition if potential entry is ignored. Currently, most end-user markets for natural gas are served by only a very few pipelines. However, I find that most markets are significantly less concentrated when potential entrants are included.

I begin my analysis by identifying potential entrants and classifying markets by their level of concentration. To accomplish this, I define product markets, geographic markets, and potential entrants using the methodology described in the Department of Justice (DOJ) *Merger Guidelines* and in DOJ's 1986 study of oil pipeline regulation. The Guidelines are widely accepted in merger analysis, and the FTC and its staff give considerable weight to them in the "evaluation of horizontal mergers and in the development of the FTC's overall approach to horizontal mergers." See, for example, the "Federal Trade Commission Statement Concerning Horizontal Mergers," *Antitrust and Trade Regulation Report Special Supplement*, no. 1069, June 17, 1982; and *B. F. Goodrich Co.*, no. D9159 (March 15, 1988).

I find that for the majority of end-user markets in my sample, prices for natural gas might be set competitively by an unregulated market system. The data suggest that in many markets there would be several potential suppliers who could profitably enter if prices rose to noncompetitive levels. Thus, the number of incumbent firms and potential entrants make it unlikely that a firm or group of firms would be able to exercise market power and raise prices. If market power cannot be exercised in these major markets, then competition will serve as an effective regulatory mechanism.

My findings differ from earlier studies of natural gas pipelines, which generally concluded that some form of federal nationwide control of pipelines was needed in all destination markets. There are four reasons for these differences. First, the competitive effect of potential entry (largely ignored in earlier studies) is a focal point of my analysis. Second, most studies ignore the competitive impact of *intrastate* pipelines. My analysis, on the other hand, explicitly considers the major intrastate pipelines in the leading natural gas-producing states. Third, considerable care was taken to verify the independence of each pipeline competitor. I consider a pipeline to be an independent supplier only if it has alternative upstream sources of gas supplies and if it is not owned by another pipeline entity. Fourth, this is the first analysis to compile pipeline transmission data on such a disaggregated, geographical basis. Comprehensive data were developed and computerized on 208 local markets to analyze whether suppliers outside each of these markets are potential entrants. Given my cost estimates of constructing and operating a pipeline hookup, over 70 percent of the local markets are large enough to be served by potential suppliers within 140 miles of the market.

The approach I suggest, with its improved analysis, demonstrates that the number of current suppliers in the market may be a poor indicator of competitive conditions. Consequently, studies or analyses that fail to consider potential entry cannot provide economically sound recommendations on whether continued regulation is warranted.

My analysis of potential entry may also have applications that extend beyond the natural gas industry. Specifically, potential entry may be an important competitive factor in other industries, such as crude oil pipelines, refined petroleum products pipelines, and electric utility transmission. It should be remembered, however, that I do not offer a complete antitrust analysis of natural gas pipelines and its methodology would not yield a complete antitrust analysis of other markets. I take product markets as given and adjust concentration statistics for these markets to reflect potential entry, using the methodology described in the Merger Guidelines of the Department of Justice and the FTC "Statement Concerning Horizontal Mergers". I do not attempt to determine the exact product markets for antitrust purposes and do not analyze other factors that may facilitate or limit the ability of firms to engage in anticompetitive practices in concentrated markets.

ACKNOWLEDGMENTS

This book has benefitted from the wide variety of comments, suggestions, and efforts of many individuals both inside and outside of the Federal Trade Commission. First of all, I am grateful for the encouraging comments and suggestions of the outside reviewer. Within the Federal Trade Commission (as of August 1989), I would like to thank Keith Anderson, Denis Breen, David Dickey, Douglas Dobson, John Howell, John Morris, Paul Pautler, Charles Pidano, and Michael Wise for their comments on earlier drafts of this book. The complex computer programming requirements of the analysis were admirably performed by John Hamilton. I especially appreciate the time John took to understand the project and to continuously suggest ways to improve the analysis. Additional programming was provided by Richard Sogg. Excellent research assistance on each phase of the project was provided by Barbara Battle. Additional research assistance on specific projects was provided by Ernest Cowan, Delores Munson, Susan Painter, Carolyn Samuels, and Cheryl Williams. Word processing was ably performed by Betsy Zichterman. The pipeline map on the title page of Appendix B was creatively designed by Donald Cox.

I would like to thank former Federal Trade Commission staff who contributed to the book. The discussions and comments by Scott Harvey and Daniel Alger were always instructive. Nancy Cole was instrumental in developing the databases and provided the initial computer programming. Joseph Cholka drafted portions of Chapter 2 and computerized the data on supply contracts. Annette Shanklin performed all the word processing on numerous earlier drafts.

I would also like to recognize the helpful comments and assistance from Laurel Hyde and Frederick Lawrence of the Federal Energy Regulatory Commission and Joan Heinkel of the Energy Information Administration.

A special thanks goes to Paul Pautler whose continuous efforts to work with FTC commissioners and their advisors in an attempt to gain Commission approval for the publication of this work was greatly appreciated. John Hamilton's continued support and belief in this research provided me with encouragement at times when I thought the work would never be released for publication.

Lastly, I would like to thank John Hilke and Morris Morkre of the Federal Trade Commission for their support of this research and their technical assistance in preparing the manuscript for outside publication.

The form and substance of the book have been greatly improved as a result of the comments of the individuals mentioned above. Any remaining errors or shortcomings of the study are, however, the responsibility of the author.

COMPETITION
IN THE
NATURAL GAS
PIPELINE INDUSTRY

INTRODUCTION

INTRODUCTION

The Federal Energy Regulatory Commission (FERC) currently regulates the price at which natural gas can be sold by regulated interstate natural gas pipelines. Whether pipelines should be deregulated depends, to an important extent, on the competitive nature of the market. The key question is whether pipelines can successfully raise price (i.e., the transport fee) and reduce output if the market is deregulated. In most natural gas pipeline markets, there are a small number of current suppliers. Notwithstanding their structural characteristics, the extent of competition in such markets is determined by the same set of market responses found in any market.[1] Given the difficulty of obtaining data to estimate potential entry, however, the analysis of competition in pipeline markets is generally forced to ignore entry effects.

Opponents of deregulation argue that the unrestrained market power of pipelines in many local markets will introduce inefficiencies in the sale of natural gas.[2] Implicit in their arguments is a narrow view of competition: the number of *current suppliers*. The competitive effect of *potential entry* is largely ignored. These commentators would argue that without potential entry, it may be true that the net social cost of deregulation exceeds the costs of maintaining present regulation. Consequently, even if present regulation is inefficient, deregulation may represent an even more costly alternative. A fundamental issue, therefore, is whether potential entry is likely to exert such an insignificant competitive effect on the market that it can be ignored.[3]

THE SCOPE OF THE STUDY

The purpose of the study is to determine the extent to which potential entry might constrain the exercise of market power by natural gas pipelines if price and entry regulation is removed. Potential entrants are defined in the context of antitrust markets. That is, these markets are consistent with the Department of Justice (DOJ) Merger Guidelines.[4] The *smallest* group of products and geographic area that are subject to market power is an antitrust market.[5] Whether a group of suppliers has market power depends, to an important extent, on entry conditions and the size of the entry potential.

This study attempts to quantify the effects of potential entry on the market power of current suppliers. The selection of potential entrants therefore considers a number of factors (such as the size of the nearby supplier and the distance to the market) that are expected to affect the likelihood of collusion in a deregulated market. Thus, the analysis is not simply a study of how to adjust market concentration to account for potential entrants. However, several other structural characteristics (e.g., homogeneity of products and buyers, weak product substitutes, buyer market power, nonprice competition, vertical integration, cost structure of rivals, and product durability) that may change the incentive or ability of pipelines to collude are not analyzed.[6]

Studies of the horizontal structure of pipeline markets tend to over-estimate the market power of pipelines if the competitive effect of potential entry is ignored. That is, the possibility of entry by nearby pipelines may constrain the pricing and output decisions of incumbent pipelines. In my view, studies that fail to consider potential entry cannot provide economically sound recommendations on whether continued regulation is warranted. Consider two examples:

1. A 1984 study by David Mead[7] is a frequently cited work on natural gas pipelines. Mead finds that

in the absence of other considerations, the generally high levels of delivery capacity concentration would tend to indicate a large potential for pipeline monopoly power which might be exercised against distributors and end users in the absence of regulation.[8]

Thus, Mead concludes that in the short run, there is very little competition in delivery markets. What is surprising, however, is the policy implication that the potential for monopoly pricing depends completely on the ability of customers to switch to alternative fuels. In the long run, Mead believes that the competitive effect of alternative fuel switching will be moderate,[9] suggesting that markets may not be competitive--even in the long run. Yet without considering the competitive effect of potential entry, such a conclusion is highly tenuous.

2. In a recent study on competition in natural gas pipeline markets, Harry Broadman concludes:

The foregoing analysis suggests that, primarily as a result of economic and technical features endemic to the industry, gas pipelines inherently possess opportunities to exercise market power. Therefore, some form of regulatory oversight is desirable.[10]

Since Broadman believes that pipeline market power is "chronic," rather than transitory, he concludes that price regulation is warranted.[11] Granted, the large economies of scale in pipelining may limit the number of actual suppliers to a few. The number and size of current suppliers in a market (i.e., market concentration), however, is not a reliable indicator of the extent of competition in the market.

Thus, several major studies of competition in pipeline markets tend to reinforce the misconception that the market power of a pipeline is largely determined by the number of *current* suppliers.[12] In contrast, I attempt to show that it is the number of *potential* suppliers that matters.

Potential entry may be limited by a number of factors. In addition to price regulations, the ability or incentive to enter a new market or to serve a new customer is also influenced by nonprice regulations imposed by FERC, the Environmental Protection Agency (EPA), and state regulatory authorities. Consequently, an evaluation of the price and output effects of price deregulation will vary depending on whether entry, environmental, and storage regulations remain in force. This study evaluates the proposal to decontrol the price of natural gas pipeline transportation *given* that all associated nonprice regulations that restrict (1) expansion in current markets, (2) entry into new markets, and (3) utilization of underground storage facilities by pipelines and local distribution companies are eventually eliminated.[13]

It is assumed that regulatory approvals, operating permits, and other administrative requirements that delay entry in the short run (i.e., the immediate period) can be met within two years. Although pipelines are capable of constructing hookups to serve new markets within a relatively short period (e.g., six months), substantially more time is required to generate divertible throughput[14] or to increase the capacity (of some segments) of its trunk line to supply throughput to each new hookup. Thus, the length of time required for a pipeline to enter a new market is more likely to depend on available or divertible gas to feed the new pipeline hookup rather than by the time required to construct the hookup.[15]

This is primarily an intermediate-run study. The intermediate run is defined as a two-year period. The analysis therefore focuses on the market adjustments that occur within a two-year period following an announcement that natural gas price and entry regulations will be eliminated as of a given date. A two-year adjustment period enables nearby pipelines to divert excess trunk-line capacity and interruptible service capacity to new markets or to new customers in current markets. It also provides an opportunity for buyers and sellers to renegotiate some contracts and allows other contracts to expire.

The study considers the profitability of collusion by actual (i.e., current) suppliers, the ability of potential suppliers to undercut a cartel that does not include them, and the viability of any cartel that includes both current suppliers and potential entrants. In a majority of markets, the number of pipelines that must be included in a cartel that could profitably reduce output and raise prices is so large that the associated coordination and policing problems may well render the cartel ineffective, even in the intermediate run.

The longer the period of adjustment, the greater will be the available throughput, and the greater will be the threat of entry. The two-year adjustment period is initially assumed because, according to the Department of Justice's Merger Guidelines, ease of entry over a two-year period is a factor that may affect the market power of current suppliers.[16] The study also develops a long-run analysis to suggest the total competitive effect of potential entry.

In the long run, all supply contracts will expire. Absent regulation, nearby pipelines are able to enter new, higher-valued markets by simply *reallocating* the throughput from the expired contract to feed the new hookup. The expansion of trunk-line capacity may not be necessary. Such recontracting opportunities thereby enable nearby suppliers to *bid* for future contracts in new markets without maintaining excess capacity or interruptible sales in the present period. If the bid is accepted, lower-valued contracts can be renegotiated, or allowed to expire, until sufficient capacity is generated to meet the requirements of the new contract. Thus, a competitive bidding market for supply contracts is expected to provide a competitive constraint on actual suppliers. Poor performance by the supplier in the present is likely to result in the nonrenewal of the supply contract in the future.[17] In the long run, the competition in the bidding market will determine the competitive performance in the natural gas pipeline transportation market--despite the small number of actual suppliers.

The bias in the short-run analysis, which ignores potential entry, will be demonstrated by contrasting the short-run analysis with the intermediate-run analysis. One objective of the study is to demonstrate that any analysis of market structure based solely on the number of current suppliers is likely to understate the degree of competition that would exist absent FERC regulation. A more meaningful analysis of competition in the industry must adequately account for potential entry.

Granted, a group of colluding firms may possess market power in the short run, and a price increase may therefore be profitable. Without entry barriers, however, any short-run excess profit earned by the collusive group may be short-lived. In the longer run, nearby suppliers may be able to increase supply and offset the output reduction of the collusive group. If the present value of monopoly profits during the short run are less than the present value of the losses after new entrants bid away service contracts from the colluding group, monopoly pricing will not be a profit-maximizing strategy.[18] Thus, if pipelines maximize long-run profits and if potential entry is significant, short-run market power is unlikely to result in supra-competitive pricing.[19]

To summarize, the competitiveness of markets in three time periods is considered. (1) In the short run, the possibility for current suppliers to collude is the greatest. There are no potential entrants in the short run. (2) In the intermediate run, nearby suppliers are identified. Given two years to enter the market, however, all nearby suppliers cannot be considered potential entrants (e.g., they may have insufficient divertible gas to pose a competitive threat to the cartel). (3) In the long run, however, all nearby suppliers are potential entrants. The possibility of collusion is remote if the number of potential entrants is substantial.

In markets where monopoly power is of little or no concern, the efficacy of existing pipeline regulation can be reconsidered. For each market that is determined to be competitive, the justification for maintaining regulation can no longer be based on the prevention of competitive problems that may arise if deregulation occurs.

The policy implications of the study are relevant to the central deregulation issue of the natural gas pipeline industry (i.e., whether to adopt common or contract carriage or to maintain current regulation). It should be recognized, however, that any decision to eliminate price and entry regulations must also take into account the effect on competition of any remaining state and federal regulations. Whereas interstate pipelines are subject to federal regulation, intrastate pipelines and local distribution companies are regulated by the state. In addition, the decision to deregulate must also consider the effects of existing long-term contracts between the pipeline and upstream suppliers and between the pipeline and downstream buyers. The present study does not explicitly address these issues.[20]

It should also be noted that this study considers only delivery markets. Origin markets are not considered, given the time costs to develop the corresponding database. The same methodology could be applied to evaluate the extent of competition in origin markets.

PRINCIPAL FINDINGS

Without attempting a full antitrust analysis, I suggest that federal regulation in the less-concentrated markets[21] may produce few benefits. These larger markets, in which potential entry is feasible, account for 98 percent of the total output subject to federal control. In these "entry" markets, the number and size of the incumbent firms and potential entrants make it unlikely that a firm or group of firms would be able to exercise market power and raise prices. In comparison, the study conservatively estimates that FERC regulation in these markets costs taxpayers a total of $25.5 million per year and costs the private sector (i.e., FERC-regulated pipelines) $26.2 million. These costs do not include the indirect costs of regulation (i.e., the inefficiencies due to incorrectly setting the regulated price above or below the competitive market price), which are substantial.

I also find that 11 large local markets are relatively concentrated, even after adjusting for potential entrants within 140 miles of the market. I estimate that regulation in these 11 cities yields at most $3.0 million per year in the long-run benefits. These benefits, which take the form of larger volumes of delivered gas, are substantially less than the direct costs of regulation imposed on all U.S. taxpayers and FERC-regulated pipelines. In fact, I find that the social costs of federal regulation are more than 17 times larger than its associated benefits in these large concentrated markets.

Finally, 7 of the 11 most concentrated large markets are in Florida. Given that most of these markets are located in one state, I suggest that state regulation may be an alternative to federal regulation in these large markets.

In addition to these general findings, I specifically conclude the following:

1. A simple short-run analysis of pipeline concentration that does not consider potential entry would find almost all markets to be highly concentrated and indicative of possible anticompetitive concern. In the initial sample of 208 delivery markets, 60 percent of the markets (123/208) show a Herfindahl-Hirschman Index (HHI) of 10000 and all markets (208/208) show a HHI over 2500. The short-run analysis may be misleading, however, since it fails to consider the competitive effect of potential entry.

2. In the 148 largest markets, where entry is feasible, potential competition from nearby pipelines is a major competitive influence in the intermediate run. If nearby suppliers are given two years to plan the construction of a hookup (between their existing trunk line and the new market) and to switch service to higher-valued customers, then the number of potential entrants in most markets may be sufficient to prevent supracompetitive pricing. In 87 percent (129/148) of the local markets that otherwise appear to be highly concentrated, the ability of nearby pipelines to enter neighboring markets reduced market concentration below 2500 as measured by the HHI.

3. In the long run, the impact of potential competition on market concentration is even greater. In 93 percent (137/148) of those 148 markets that represent a potential anticompetitive concern (based on a short-run analysis), concentration falls below the Department of Justice 2500 level. Eighty-two percent of the markets fall below the 1800 level. Only 11 markets remain with a HHI over 2500.

4. Whether the remaining 11 large markets with high concentration would pose competitive problems in a deregulated environment is unknown. One possibility is that the majority of these markets are competitive in the long run because these markets are dominated by industrial and residential users who will eventually switch to alternative fuels if natural gas prices remain abnormally high.[22]

5. My examination of potential entry in natural gas markets suggests that in many instances, other studies that conclude *that markets would not be competitive if deregulated* are likely to be wrong.

THE ORGANIZATION OF THE STUDY

The study is developed as follows. Chapter 2 provides a brief description of the industry and a historical review of government regulation. Chapter 3 presents the basic methodology. A competitive response to a hypothetical price increase above cost is developed for three time periods: the short run, the intermediate run, and the long run. In the short run or immediate period, there are no potential entrants; competition is limited to current suppliers (Chapter 4). In the intermediate run, the existence of large nearby suppliers increases competition in the market. The intermediate run, which is defined as the two-year period following a price change, is the focal point of the study (Chapter 5). As the adjustment period is expanded, the long-run results (Chapter 6) are approached: All nearby suppliers are likely to become potential entrants. The bias in ignoring the competitive effects of potential entry can be seen by comparing the short-run results with the intermediate-run or long-run results.

The policy implications of the study are reviewed in Chapter 7.

THE NATURAL GAS INDUSTRY

This chapter provides a brief description of the natural gas industry. My intention is to note features of the industry that are especially relevant to the methodology and analysis of this study. The industry is comprised of three levels: production, transmission, and distribution. Although the analysis concentrates on the transmission of gas to local distribution centers, some understanding of the production and distribution levels is helpful.

Since one objective of this study is to provide evidence on the economic justification for federal price and entry regulations of pipelines, a brief review of the relevant regulations is also provided. A historical review of gas regulation reveals an inconsistency between regulations (or changes in regulations) at the wellhead and at the city gate. One consequence of such *ad hoc* regulation is to limit the ability of city-gate prices to efficiently adjust to changes in wellhead prices. In short, federal intervention has *created* gas shortages in some periods and surpluses in others.

THE INDUSTRY

Gas Production

Natural gas is a simple hydrocarbon that is gaseous when brought to the surface. Methane is the most common form of natural gas.[1] It is found by drilling into porous underground formations called reservoirs. Natural gas is generally produced from gas wells, but it is sometimes jointly produced with crude oil.[2] Small-diameter pipes (or gathering lines) are utilized to collect the gas from the producing wells in the field. In large gas fields, gathering lines deliver the gas and oil to field stations (or lease separators) for initial processing. At this point, natural gas is separated from oil and some of the heavier gas liquids, and water vapor is removed.[3]

Most gas requires some further processing at plants typically located near the field or pipeline. Before processing, the gas is generally referred to as wet natural gas because it contains heavier hydrocarbons such as ethane, propane, and butane. These liquid hydrocarbons are removed using such techniques as absorption, compression, and refrigeration.[4] Chemical processing is used to remove impurities, principally nonhydrocarbon gases such as hydrogen sulfide and carbon dioxide, which are highly corrosive. The processed gas is termed dry natural gas.[5]

Gas Transmission: The Pipeline System

The transmission of dry natural gas involves the acquisition and delivery of gas through long-distance pipelines. These high-pressure "trunk" lines are a very economical method of transporting gas from producing areas to local consumption markets. The throughput of a pipeline is proportional to its diameter and to its maximum operating pressure.[6] Therefore, the construction of larger-diameter pipeline systems results in greatly increased transmission capacities. Interstate pipeline networks, constructed of welded steel pipes up to 48 inches in diameter, deliver gas into nearly every state in the country.[7]

Compressor stations are installed at various intervals along a pipeline to maintain the gas pressure necessary to overcome any loss in pressure due to pipe friction and gravity, especially in mountainous regions.[8] In addition, compressor stations can also be installed to increase the flow rate. These compressors, fueled by natural gas taken from the pipeline, are the major variable cost of transporting natural gas.[9] Consequently, the cost of gas transportation is highly sensitive to the price of natural gas.

Generally, natural gas flows from field stations and processing plants into long-distance trunk lines at a steady rate.[10] This is because operating costs are lower for a constant rate of production. Since demand for gas is seasonal, many transmission companies and large distributors maintain storage facilities to accommodate these fluctuations in demand. Storage facilities located near the final market are often a substitute for both peak-load pipeline transmission capacity and peak production capacity.[11] Storage facilities located in producing areas serve to economize on production capacity. In addition, changes in the pressure of the pipeline system can also accommodate short-run changes in demand and thereby reduce the need for transmission capacity. In this way, both production and pipeline capacity can be designed and constructed to meet average seasonal peaks and still provide an efficient response to above-average peak-day demands.[12]

Natural gas pipeline companies have historically differed from oil pipeline companies in that gas pipelines are not common carriers.[13] Most gas pipeline companies perform the broker function between producers and end-users--in addition to their transmission function.[14] The primary business of gas pipelines is wholesaling (i.e., the sale of gas for resale). Since gas producers may only be able to sell to a few pipelines from any given field and since only one gas pipeline may sell to a local distributor or utility, the concern of some observers is that pipelines may possess substantial market power in the purchase and sale of natural gas.[15] A related issue is whether pipelines and local distribution companies (LDCs) will provide transportation services at competitive rates for large commercial and industrial customers who negotiate their own gas purchases directly with the gas producers.[16]

Gas Distribution

Interstate pipelines normally deliver gas through "city-gate" facilities. At the city gate, pipeline pressures are significantly reduced and an odorant is added to the gas as a safety precaution.[17] The odorant makes gas leakages in the transmission system or in the end-user's lines or appliances more easily detected.

Delivery of natural gas to end-users is normally provided by local distribution or utility companies. A distribution system consists of a network of smaller-diameter distribution piping, pressure-reducing valves, and meters.[18] Plastic pipe up to six inches in diameter is being used in the majority of new gas distribution installations.[19] The heat and line pressures are continuously monitored and regulated to provide constant and safe deliveries to residential and commercial users. Individual gas meters are installed at the point of delivery to measure the rate of consumption for billing purposes.

In addition to city-gate sales, pipelines also make sales to other pipelines and to industrial customers. Pipelines are interconnected in ways that allow gas to be transferred from one pipeline to another. In this way, gas can be shifted between regions in response to changes in demand or supply. These sales are referred to as "off-system" sales.[20] Another type of sale also occurs before the city gate. Large industrial users and *electric* utilities[21] often construct their own low-pressure hookups to a trunk pipeline. Such direct sales by the pipeline at various points along their system are called direct "main line" sales. Unlike all other pipeline sales, the price for main line sales is usually a market price.[22] It is not subject to FERC regulation because they are not sales for resale.[23]

Many industrial users and utility companies have invested in dual-fuel capability.[24]   That is, these users have the option of substituting an alternative fuel to operate their power plants. As a result, industrial gas users are highly sensitive to changes in the price of natural gas and to changes in the price of substitute fuels.

This brief description of the natural gas industry is intended to provide the reader with a simplified overview of the industry to better understand the analysis to follow. More technical aspects of the industry will be provided in connection with the issues examined in subsequent chapters.

REGULATION AND THE DEVELOPMENT OF THE NATURAL GAS INDUSTRY

The purpose of this section is to provide a historical review of government participation in the natural gas industry. Specific attention is given to those regulations that have created gas shortages or surpluses in local delivery markets. Although the discussion may appear to focus on regulation and deregulation at the wellhead, our primary concern is with the ultimate effect of regulation--which is to limit the ability of the delivered price of gas to fully reflect the real (or social) costs of gas to end-users. An analysis of the historical record suggests that government intervention has hindered the efficient allocation of resources in natural gas markets.

Local Synthetic Gas Markets

Since the emergence of the gas industry in the early nineteenth century, some form of government intervention has existed.[25] The first gas companies distributed *synthetic gas* for local consumption. Synthetic gas was extracted from coal, oil, and other substances through controlled burning. Local regulations recognized the notion of a *natural monopoly* aspect of gas production, transmission, and distribution.[26] On this basis, gas companies were granted charters or local monopolies to serve local areas.   Gas companies petitioned for the right of eminent domain (to build pipelines on public and private property) and for franchises (exclusive service areas). In return, the gas companies were subject to rate or price regulation, safety standards, and the requirement to provide service to all customers. These local regulations became statewide with the introduction of public service commissions and public utility commissions. The first commission was established in New York, in 1907. The jurisdiction of these state regulatory agencies was constitutionally limited to *intrastate* commerce.

The Market for Natural Gas

In the 1920s, three events stimulated the development of the natural gas industry. First, the advantages of burning natural gas instead of its synthetic counterpart were recognized. Second, large gas and oil fields were discovered in regions far from the local urban markets. Third, technological advances in the extraction and transmission of natural gas created the opportunity to transport gas over long distances. As local sources in the Appalachian region became depleted, advances in pipeline construction permitted longer-distance transmission. Major interstate pipelines were constructed during the latter part of this decade. Since these pipelines crossed state borders, they were exempt from local and state regulation. Throughout this period, federal courts held that individual states lacked jurisdiction over the interstate transmission of natural gas.

The Public Utility Holding Company Act of 1935

The pipeline building boom of the early 1920s connected the gas-producing regions of Louisiana, Oklahoma, and the Texas panhandle with the consuming areas in the Midwest (Chicago, Indianapolis, St. Louis, and others).[27] A contributing factor to this growth was the popular form of business organization known as the holding company. The holding companies provided a mechanism for generating the necessary capital for the financing of long-distance pipeline construction and for the building of local distribution networks. Holding companies resulted in vertical integration. Under vertical arrangements, one company could control the production, transmission, and distribution facilities for a particular natural gas market. Some holding companies were also horizontally integrated, owning both gas utility and electric utility companies in the same city. Public concern over the trend toward integration resulted in the passage of the Public Utility Holding Company Act of 1935 (PUHCA). Under this act, the Security and Exchange Commission (SEC) was granted regulatory powers over firms owning at least 10 percent of the stock of a gas or electric company. More precisely

the act directed the SEC to supervise the restructuring and divestiture of corporations to yield "single coordinated systems confined in operations to single areas or regions . . ." The act, in effect, called for an end to the excesses in vertical, horizontal, and geographic integration. Specifically, it forbade most affiliations between electric and gas companies that were not municipally owned and whose operations crossed state lines.[28]

Integrated companies either voluntarily chose to spin off vertically related companies or to permit the SEC to oversee the divestiture of their natural gas related assets.

The ultimate effect of the PUHCA was to produce a divestiture wave in the natural gas industry. Holding companies split into smaller firms organized along industrial or regional lines. For instance, Columbia Gas and Electric separated into two firms, one electric and one gas, and the new gas company was also ordered to spin off its Panhandle Eastern pipeline system. Likewise, Standard Oil of New Jersey was forced to spin off its large gas pipelines and distributors. Cities Service, on the other hand, divested along geographic lines. Its New England utilities and southern operations were made independent entities while its midwestern operations retained the original Cities Service name. Altogether, 15 years after the passage of the PUHCA, holding company control over interstate gas pipeline mileage fell from 80 percent to 18 percent.[29] The reduction in vertical integration, however, was followed by the use of long-term contracts that contained features such as take-or-pay and minimum bill provisions.[30]

The Natural Gas Act of 1938

The divestitures created an industry in which gas purchasers (the local utility companies and industrial users) were physically and organizationally separate from gas producers (the oil and gas fields). The interstate pipelines were the middlemen between consumers and producers. These long-distance pipelines were in a position to purchase low-valued gas from numerous gas and oil producers (a substantial quantity was still being flared, or burned, at the wellhead) and to transport this gas to the final consumer, where it was more highly valued. However, the next federal intervention into the natural gas industry attempted to restrict the behavior of interstate pipelines.

In 1938, the Natural Gas Act (NGA) was passed. This law enabled the Federal Power Commission (FPC) to set rates on gas delivered by interstate pipelines and to grant exclusive service areas or franchises. In other words, no one could build a gas pipeline into a market already served by a gas pipeline--unless the FPC first approved the construction. The federal government therefore controlled interstate pipeline *entry* and the delivered price of gas (at the city gate). The intent of the NGA was to encourage the pipeline to pass the low price of wellhead gas on to the customer. The NGA specifically exempted the drilling and gathering of natural gas from regulation and strictly focused on the *transmission* of natural gas. Presumably, the large number of producers was expected to ensure competitive prices at the wellhead.[31]

Federal Regulation at the Wellhead

The 1950s brought a different political climate as reflected in the Supreme Court's reinterpretation of the NGA in the 1954 decision *Phillips Petroleum Co. v. Wisconsin*. The Court inferred that the congressional intent was to regulate wellhead prices. The FPC began to set the wellhead price of natural gas sold to interstate pipelines. The FPC used a cost-of-service[32] approach in setting both the wellhead price and the tariff on gas delivered by pipelines.

Gas Shortages and the Natural Gas Policy Act of 1978

During the 1970s it became apparent that the supply and demand of natural gas at the wellhead were in constant disequilibrium. During periods of high gas demand, shortages began to appear in the interstate gas markets.[33] One of the reasons for this shortfall in interstate gas deliveries was that gas was flowing into the intrastate market. Intrastate pipelines in the gas-producing states could outbid their *interstate* rivals for gas throughput because *intrastate* prices were not regulated. As late as June 1974, the "national ceiling price [for interstate gas] was still only half the price Texas and Louisiana producers were receiving for intrastate sales."[34] The low price of regulated interstate gas offered little incentive to producers to drill for more gas but, at the same time, encouraged consumers to use more gas. To alleviate the shortage, LDCs imposed moratoriums on new gas customers and forced curtailments of service on "low-priority" customers.

The shortages of natural gas during the winter of 1977 culminated in the passage of the Emergency Natural Gas Act. This temporary law enabled the FPC to waive certain price ceilings and transmission requirements. At approximately the same time, the FPC was replaced by the FERC (Federal Energy Regulatory Commission), whose responsibility it was to oversee all the previous duties of the FPC and, in addition, to assume the regulation of oil pipelines.

Shortly thereafter, in 1978, Congress passed the Natural Gas Policy Act (NGPA) and the Power Plant and Industrial Fuels Use Act (FUA). The intent of these laws was to reduce the gas shortage at the wellhead by removing the price differences between intrastate and interstate gas and to provide incentives for oil and gas producers to drill for more natural gas.[35,36]

The NGPA enabled FERC to divide gas at the wellhead into 26 categories. Each category had its own price structure, with escalator clauses and a timetable for eventual deregulation. All prices were initially based on the then-current price of oil, or about $15 per barrel. Although all gas prices rose, the increase varied depending on the category of gas. For example, prices on *old* gas continued to be based on vintage and location, prices of *new* gas (produced after 1977) were allowed to vary with oil prices and the general price level, and prices of *deep* gas (produced from wells over 15,000 feet deep) were completely deregulated.[37]

The two acts (NGPA and FUA) also attempted to redistribute the low-cost gas from industrial to residential users. Title 2 of the NGPA provided for "incremental pricing" provisions that tended to shift the new, high-cost gas toward the industrial user and away from the residential user. The FUA "off-gas" provisions reduced access to gas by industrial users in general (i.e., boiler users) and reduced access by electric utilities in particular.[38]

Another response to the shortfalls in gas deliveries was the so-called self-help program initiated by FERC. This program allowed industrial users to contract directly with gas producers for supply, since the transactions did not involve "sale-for-resale" gas. Industrial users could then contract with pipelines for transportation service from the wellhead. The effect of the self-help program was to exempt these industrial supply contracts from wellhead price regulation. Until this ruling, pipelines acted as private carriers buying in the field and selling to end-users. Now, users could purchase directly from producers and then negotiate with a pipeline to carry the gas for a simple transmission fee. Likewise, pipelines could now carry gas for other pipelines. The central role of the pipeline as a middleman began eroding.[39]

The net effect of these regulations was to raise the price of natural gas. As more gas flowed into local delivery markets, the shortages were eliminated.

The Gas Surplus of the 1980s

The second Organization of Petroleum Exporting Countries (OPEC) oil crisis (1979-80) together with the increase in the general price level caused another round of price increases in oil and natural gas. Given the incentives of higher wellhead gas prices, producers drilled, discovered, and supplied more gas and oil. The pipelines contracted for the newly available (deregulated) deep gas and regulated new gas, locking in long-term supplies at relatively high prices.[40] The higher prices of new and deep gas were blended in (averaged) with the older, low-cost gas, raising the average price of delivered gas to the customer. For instance, "the U.S. city average residential rate increased some 24 percent from October 1981 to October 1982."[41]

Consumer response to these higher city-gate prices was predictable. Consumers substituted cooler homes and home insulation for the more expensive natural gas. For instance, the 1981 natural gas usage per household was the lowest since 1959.[42] "By the end of 1982, many observers held that the average price of natural gas met or exceeded its market clearing price."[43]

The rapid increase in OPEC prices was short-lived, however, and the price of crude oil began to fall around the end of 1982. Reflecting market conditions, the price of deregulated wellhead gas also began to decline.[44] Without regulation, the reduced price of gas at the wellhead would have resulted in a decline in the delivered price of gas (at the city gate). Given government intervention (and the market responses to government intervention), the delivered city-gate price failed to respond to the decline in the price of wellhead gas.

Since federal regulation set artificially low wellhead prices during the 1970s, wellhead producers tended to allocate gas on a nonprice basis. To assure minimum supplies of gas, pipelines agreed to higher take-or-pay requirements. Take-or-pay clauses require a pipeline to pay for some fixed percentage of gas whether or not the pipeline takes delivery at the wellhead. By 1982, however, pipelines were faced with a 10 percent decline in sales, and the take-or-pay requirement forced pipelines to take gas they could not sell.[45]

Take-or-pay requirements between the pipeline and the wellhead producer were usually associated with "minimum bill" requirements between the pipeline and the LDC.[46] Minimum bills require LDCs to purchase stipulated amounts of gas from a pipeline during the contract period.[47] Thus, the pipeline's minimum take was satisfied by negotiating a corresponding minimum bill with large customers such as LDCs. By 1984, however, the excess supply of gas at the wellhead was substantial, and FERC realized that the regulated price at the city gate was too high.[48] In contrast to the gas shortages experienced in the 1970s, the industry now faced a substantial surplus of natural gas.

FERC rulings on purchased-gas adjustment (PGA) clauses further impeded the ability of the city-gate price to respond efficiently to changes in wellhead prices. PGAs, established in the mid-1970s, allow a pipeline (usually semiannually) to automatically pass on higher gas acquisition costs. The PGA allowance was important in the 1970s as interstate pipelines searched for alternative supply sources to alleviate gas shortages (most alternative supplies, such as liquified natural gas, were significantly more expensive). The PGA, however, created a perverse incentive system. As city-gate prices rose to market-clearing levels, the quantity of gas sold declined, and the average cost of service increased (due to high fixed costs). Pipelines attempted to recover these cost increases by passing through the higher price of the most recently acquired gas.[49] These higher prices, of course, continued to push city-gate prices upward.

FERC responded by allowing LDCs to renege on their minimum bill commitments with pipelines.[50]   Consequently, in an attempt to promote more efficient pricing at the city gate, FERC placed many pipelines on the edge of financial ruin.   Pipelines were still legally bound to meet their minimum takes but lost their right to force LDCs to accept their minimum bill obligations.   Pipelines reduced purchases to minimum allowable quantities, attempted to sell the gas to other pipelines, and initiated legal action to extricate themselves from take-or-pay provisions.   Estimates of pipeline losses vary, since some contracts allowed future purchases of gas to offset past deficiencies in pipeline "takes" from a wellhead.   FERC finally accepted an estimate of pipeline take-or-pay obligations at $7 billion.   On average, pipelines were able to "buy out" their liability for about 20 cents on the dollar.[51]

To summarize, government intervention in the natural gas industry is one factor contributing to the substantial shortages and surpluses experienced over the last 20 years.   The regulation of interstate pipelines without corresponding intrastate pipeline regulation together with the regulation at the wellhead encouraged producers to sell gas in intrastate gas markets and created the gas shortages experienced in interstate markets during the 1970s. Partial deregulation at the wellhead in addition to the PGA allowances contributed to the elimination of these gas shortages.

The changes in regulation that contributed to the elimination of the gas shortages in the 1970s, however, created surpluses in the 1980s.   In late 1982, the decline in crude oil prices led to a decline in the wellhead price of gas. The city-gate price, however, failed to respond to the fall in wellhead prices. The PGA allowances permitted pipelines to pass through the higher price of new gas.   Further, the regulated prices on old contracts with producers contained fixed escalator clauses unresponsive to downturns in current market conditions. As a result, the high city-gate prices provided a false signal to producers to maintain high rates of production.   As gas customers reduced their consumption, LDCs could not meet their minimum bill obligations to purchase gas. The mounting surplus of gas led FERC to revoke the minimum bill requirements.   In an attempt to make city-gate prices more responsive to changes in wellhead prices, FERC imposed potentially large losses on pipelines that remained obligated to producers under take-or-pay agreements.

THE METHODOLOGY

INTRODUCTION

The purpose of this chapter is to outline the basic methodology used in this study. To simplify the exposition, the more complex or technical aspects of the methodology are presented in subsequent chapters where an issue is initially encountered and analyzed. Since the study considers three time periods (i.e., short, intermediate, and long runs), the methodology common to all three periods is explained in this chapter.

This study estimates the effects of potential entry on market concentration. Thus, the initial steps involve defining the product market, the geographic market, and the concentration measure. One contribution of the study lies in its use of antitrust concepts to identify potential entrants and its ability to quantify the impact of entry on concentration. Since the ability to enter a market depends, in part, on the length of the adjustment or time period, three "runs" are considered. Each of these principal components of the methodology is discussed below.

THE RELEVANT ANTITRUST MARKET

We identify antitrust markets by identifying the *smallest* group of products and area subject to market power. To determine the product and geographic market, we consider whether a group of perfectly colluding suppliers (i.e., a *hypothetical monopolist*) could profitably raise the price of natural gas 5 to 10 percent above cost without inducing consumers to switch to alternative products or suppliers.[1] Thus, the market definition considers (1) the substitution among competing products in the same geographic area[2] and (2) the substitution among suppliers of the same product in different geographic areas. This process is essentially an attempt to examine the "residual demand" facing producers in a particular region.[3]

The determination of the geographic market considers the "residual demand" facing the group of perfectly colluding suppliers.[4] In geographic space, the residual demand specifies the quantity of a homogeneous product demanded from the group of suppliers as a function of the price they set. At each possible price, the residual demand equals the market demand minus the quantity supplied by all other firms (those excluded from the group). Thus, explicit assumptions or estimates must be made about the elasticity of the competitive fringe supply, the elasticity of market demand, and the size of the colluding group of pipeline suppliers.[5]

If products are not homogeneous, the residual demand analysis must be expanded to determine the relevant product. In product space, the residual demand equals the market demand for a group of products (facing all suppliers in the area) minus the quantity of those products supplied by sellers outside the colluding group.[6] If the product in question has no strong substitutes, however, the market demand is a good proxy for the residual demand.[7]

The Relevant Product Market

Natural gas is a relatively homogeneous product. Federal standards require that gas volumes be reported on a pressure base of 14.73 pounds per square inch absolute pressure (psia) and a temperature base of 60 degrees Fahrenheit.[8] This is the pressure required by most residential appliances and industrial applications. More importantly, pipeline gas meets the federal standard, which is also the industry standard.[9] Thus, despite the different origins and initial impurities of gas, processed gas can be treated as a homogeneous product. Interstate and intrastate pipelines, gas fields, storage facilities, and foreign suppliers of LNG therefore deliver the same quality gas.

The relevant product for this study is delivered natural gas. Long-distance pipelines buy gas at the wellhead or from other pipelines and sell either to local distribution companies or directly to industrial customers.[10] The difference between the pipeline's buying and selling prices is the transport fee explicitly or implicitly charged for the transmission service. What matters to the user, however, is the total delivered price.[11]

Alternative modes of transporting natural gas are generally cost prohibitive. Insignificant amounts of natural gas are moved by truck, water carriers, and rail.[12] For long-distance transportation into local delivery markets, transmission system pipelines have no good substitutes. Although it is technologically possible to convert petroleum product and crude oil pipelines to the transportation of natural gas, one only occasionally finds petroleum pipelines that are both severely underutilized and located where they are useful for natural gas transmission.

Since the demand for gas transportation is a derived demand for natural gas, substitutes for natural gas reduce the demand for gas transmission service. The question, then, is whether natural gas is a separate product. The likelihood of consumers shifting to substitute products in response to a small but significant and nontransitory increase in price is difficult to quantify for the market as a whole. The demand for energy has two major components: residential/commercial demand and industrial demand. Residential and commercial users are generally served by an LDC. These customers use the energy provided by natural gas primarily for space heating, water heating, and cooking.[13] The primary fuel alternatives to natural gas are electricity and distillate fuel oil.[14]

Residential Demand

In the residential sector, several econometric studies suggest that the market demand elasticity of natural gas is less than one. Table 3.1 reports the findings of eight residential demand studies. With the exception of the Joskow and Baughman study, all the market demand elasticity coefficients (column 3) have an absolute value less than .70. Such low elasticity coefficients imply that substitution away from natural gas and into alternative fuels such as electricity and oil is limited in the residential sector. It is also apparent that the cross-elasticity coefficients (e.g., measuring the responsiveness of electricity use to changes in the price of natural gas) shown in columns 4 and 5 are also low.[15] On this basis, we can conclude that substitution of electricity or fuel oil for natural gas is insufficient to cause one to broaden the definition of the relevant product market in the residential sector.

Industrial Demand

The industrial market for natural gas consists of four largely independent segments: boilers, utilities, process heat, and petrochemicals. Both manufacturers and utilities purchase fuel for boilers, and over half of all industrial boilers now in use have dual-fuel capacity and can switch from oil to gas, depending on their relative prices.[16] Equally important, almost all

Table 3.1

Natural Gas
Market Elasticity and Cross-Elasticity Estimates
from Residential Demand Studies

Study	Data Used	Elasticities		
		Own	Electricity	Oil
Joskow and Baughman (1976)	Cross-section/ time series: 1968-72	-1.01	0.170	0.190
Barnes, et al. (1982)	Cross-section: 1972-73	-0.682	-----	----
Balestra and Nerlove (1966)	Cross-section/ time series: 1957-62	-0.630	-----	----
Gurbacz (1983)	Cross-section:	-0.462[+] -0.343[++]	0.206[+++] 0.037[*][+++]	---- ----
Danielson[**] (1977-78)	Aggregate time series: 1947-74	-0.415	-----	-0.172
Beirlein et al. (1981)	Cross-section/ time series for the Northeast: 1967-77	-0.353	0.174	-0.126

Table 3.1 (Continued)

Study	Data Used	Elasticities		
		Own	Electricity	Oil
Blatten-berger et al. (1983)	Time series/ Cross-sectional: 1961-74	-0.333	0.327	-----
DOE/EIA (1979)	Aggregate time series: 1985 projected	-0.272	0.072	0.008

+   January (peak)
++   July (trough)
+++ All substitutes are combined.
*   Not significant at .05 level.
**   Aggregates residential and industrial data.

boilers that now run on natural gas can, at a nominal cost, be quickly altered to use fuel oil.[17] Each segment and its corresponding substitute fuels are summarized in Table 3.2.

The market demand elasticity for natural gas in industrial uses is also relatively low. In seven recent studies, the highest short-run elasticity coefficient is -.52, estimated by Pindyck (1979). However, since long-run elasticities allow for the decrease in energy use as well as for interfuel substitution, which assumes constant energy use, long-run elasticities are expected to be larger than the corresponding short-run (or partial) elasticities.[18] Thus, we consider the long-run elasticity to represent a more reliable indicator of the relevant product market. Although the possibility of interfuel substitution is greater in industrial uses than in residential uses, most econometric studies find that the industrial demand elasticity is less than one, regardless of the application. As shown in Table 3.3, five of the seven long-run elasticity estimates (column 3) have an absolute value substantially less than one; the range is -.39 to -1.47.

Overall, the evidence on substitute fuels in the industrial sector is insufficient to include fuel oil and natural gas in the same product market. In addition, since a primary concern of this study is the competitive effects of pipeline deregulation in residential markets, where fuel switching is most limited, natural gas is considered a separate product for the purpose of this study.

The Relevant Geographic Market

The smallest relevant market to evaluate the economic effects of pipeline deregulation is local in nature. On the demand side, residential and commercial users are clustered in and around major cities and industrial users are often located within a relatively short distance of a city. Unlike petroleum products, natural gas is extremely costly to transport by truck. Unless the price were to fall dramatically in a nearby area, it would not be profitable to buy gas in a nearby area and then truck it into the consuming area. Further, the high costs of storing natural gas makes storage a weak alternative for most residential and industrial users. Although storage is a substitute for pipeline capacity in meeting peak demand, the typical buyer cannot maintain an inventory of natural gas during peak periods while searching for lower-cost suppliers. Under these conditions, a small increase in the local market price of delivered gas is unlikely to induce the user to purchase outside the consuming area in order to acquire a cheaper source of supply.

If we view LDCs as brokers for residential customers, the demand analysis outlined above remains essentially unchanged. Consider a natural

Table 3.2

Natural Gas and Substitute Fuels
in Industrial Applications

Industrial Markets	Alternative Fuels
1. petrochemical segment:	fuel oil and gas liquids
2. process heat segment:	electricity and distillate fuel oil
3. boiler segment:	coal, residual fuel oil, and distillate fuel oil
4. utility segment:	coal and nuclear power for baseload generation; fuel oil for peaking purposes

Table 3.3

Natural Gas
Market Elasticity and Cross-Elasticity
Estimates from Industrial Demand Studies

Study	Data Used	Elasticities			
		Own	Oil	Coal	Electricity
Halvorsen (1977)	Cross-section state data: 1971	-1.470	1.030	0.280	0.350
Atkinson and Halvorsen (1976)	Cross-sectional for power plants only: 1972	-1.430	0.760	0.450	-----
Joskow and Baughman (1976)	Aggregate time series: 1950-72	-0.810	0.750	0.750	0.730
Pindyck (1979)	Cross-section/ time series: 1959-73	-0.670	-0.880	1.500	-0.430

Table 3.3 (Continued)

Study	Data Used	Elasticities			
		Own	Oil	Coal	Electricity
Beirlein et al. (1981)[*]	Cross-section/ time series for the Northeast: 1967-77	-0.606	0.312	-----	0.186[*]
Danielson[**] (1977-78)	Aggregate time series: 1949-74	-0.415	-0.172	-----	-----
DOE/EIA (1979)	Aggregate time series: 1985 projected	-0.389	0.043	0.012	0.103

[*] Not significant at .05 level.
[**] Aggregates residential and industrial area.

gas delivery market absent price and entry regulations. Residential customers must buy their gas from the LDC. Pipelines are assumed to know which service areas are supplied by each LDC. Therefore, if the pipeline has market power, it can effectively price discriminate between markets even if both markets are served by the same LDC.[19] This assumption is reasonable because the LDC is unable to buy extra gas at one location and transport it to another area without the supplier recognizing the arbitrage operation.[20] Consequently, if the LDC is to receive gas at one location, it must identify the gas requirements for each of its service areas.

On the supply side, each independent supplier in the market must invest in a long-distance transmission pipeline to meet his delivery commitments. Sellers are unable to deliver gas from one area to another without a high-pressure transmission hookup between the areas. Although a distant pipeline can contract with another pipeline for transportation services to make a local delivery (e.g., an off-system sale or an exchange delivery), the ability to deliver gas would be dependent on another pipeline. Because such deliveries only represent a competitive supply response given the cooperation of another pipeline, they do not influence our definition of the relevant market.

Although *independent* nearby suppliers may be able to enter the market given (1) sufficient time to acquire the necessary state, federal, and environmental approvals, (2) sufficient time to construct a spur line into the new market, and (3) sufficient time to generate divertible throughput to feed the new hookup, the time required to meet all these conditions is too long (i.e., over one year) to consider these suppliers to be in the market in the short run.[21] Pipeline companies are therefore either in or out of a market, depending on whether they do or do not have a hookup in the current period.[22]

If the relevant geographic market is considered to be an area in which a group of incumbent suppliers could profitably raise price above cost without inducing customers to obtain supply outside the geographic area or without inducing nearby suppliers to serve the area (for approximately one year),[23] then the market is local. In our view, both demand and supply factors suggest that the relevant geographic market can be approximated by each major city and its immediate surrounding area.[24] It is on this basis that we define local markets to be Metropolitan Statistical Areas (MSAs). All our data are therefore compiled on a MSA or county basis.[25,26]

THE HERFINDAHL-HIRSCHMAN INDEX

Once the product and geographic market or markets are defined (i.e., given the relevant antitrust market), the competitive analysis focuses on how well the *actual group* of colluding suppliers approximates the behavior of the *hypothetical monopolist*. The profitability of the colluding group will depend on a number of factors, including the competitive effect of potential entry.

The next step is to measure concentration in each relevant antitrust market. High concentration is often considered a necessary but insufficient condition for the existence of collusive behavior among large firms, absent regulation. Since the colluding group must reduce output in order to raise price and maximize profits, the colluding group will be forced to include any firm that can offset the planned output reduction of the cartel. Thus, only firms (or groups of firms acting jointly) with the ability to offset the anticipated output reduction by the colluding group are considered as possible colluders.[27] Since the output reduction represents a substantial portion of the initial competitive output, membership in the colluding group will tend to be limited to the larger firms in the market. Given that potential entrants may also pose a competitive threat to the cartel if excluded, they too may gain admission. Consequently, the success of the colluding group will depend, in part, on its ability to enforce the joint profit-maximizing price and output on each member. As the number of colluding firms increases, so does the incentive to cheat on the collusive price.[28]

A market concentration measure is utilized to provide a crude index of the likelihood of successful coordination or collusion among the colluding group of gas suppliers.[29] The larger the number of firms in the cartel, the less valuable is any firm's share in the joint profit of the cartel and the greater is the incentive of each member to undercut the cartel price and expand output.[30] Thus, the higher the concentration index, the more likely that the colluding suppliers can agree on and enforce the output and price changes necessary to maximize their joint profit.[31]

The specific concentration measure utilized in this study is the Herfindahl-Hirschman Index, (HHI).[32] The HHI is calculated by summing the squares of the individual market shares of all the firms in the market. A market, for example, consisting of four firms with market shares of 45 percent, 30 percent, 20 percent, and 5 percent has a HHI of 3350 (= 2025 + 900 + 400 + 25). The HHI rises as the number of firms decreases and the largest firms gain market share and attains its highest value of 10000 in the case of a single seller or monopolist.[33]

The selection of the HHI over other concentration measures (e.g., the four-firm concentration ratio) is based, to a large extent, on its greater sensitivity to the likelihood of dominant firm behavior in local natural gas markets. First, a concentration index that places greater weight on larger firms than smaller firms is more sensitive to the concern that natural gas markets may be dominated by one or two suppliers.[34] The pricing policy of a dominant firm, for example, will vary directly with its market share. In markets with less than four suppliers, therefore, the HHI is superior to the four-firm concentration index, which ignores relative size. Second, the HHI explicitly accounts for fringe firms and potential entrants. Thus, smaller firms which may jointly pose a competitive threat to a dominant firm are incorporated in the HHI. In contrast, the four-firm concentration measure arbitrarily ignores all firms except the top four.[35]

POTENTIAL ENTRANTS: THE DISTANCE AND SIZE TESTS

In the short run, the HHI is based solely on the market share of each colluding firm and the market share of each fringe supplier. In the intermediate run, however, allowance must be made for potential entrants. As will be explained below, potential entrants are "nearby suppliers" who are large enough to pose a threat to the cartel if excluded. In addition to this *size requirement*, nearby suppliers must also be located close enough to the market to make a pipeline hookup economically feasible. The latter requirement is called the *distance requirement*. Thus, only nearby suppliers who meet both the size and distance requirements are considered potential entrants.[36]

Similarly, existing suppliers in a market are not presumed to be part of the colluding group. Since each incumbent supplier does not necessarily pose a competitive threat to the collusive group, incumbent suppliers must meet the same two conditions that nearby suppliers must meet to gain admission into the cartel.[37] Current suppliers, or groups of current suppliers, who fail to meet these conditions are treated as fringe suppliers. These small suppliers are allowed to sell all the transportation service they want at the cartel price. The cartel maximizes profit based on its own firm demand curve, which equals the market demand minus fringe supply.

Since the HHI will incorporate only suppliers who meet the distance and size tests, the remainder of this chapter examines the distance and size requirements in more detail. (Some of the more technical aspects will be presented in Chapter 5.)

Distance from the Local Market

To be included in the market, a potential supplier must be sufficiently close to the market to make the construction of the pipeline hookup profitable. The more distant the supplier, the longer and more costly the required hookup, and the less profitable the investment, *ceteris paribus*. Given the distance to the nearby market, the potential supplier is assumed to compare the unit transport fee necessary to yield a competitive return on investment to the expected increase in the price of delivered gas in the nearby market. If the transport fee is less than the price increase, the supplier is considered a potential entrant, assuming that the size requirement is also met.[38]

The time required to construct a pipeline hookup is quite short. The proposal to construct the Ozark Gas Transmission System, for example, allowed only for a three-month construction period. The proposed pipeline system included 285 miles of 20-inch transmission line and 170 miles of 4-inch, 6-inch, 8-inch, and 10-inch lateral lines with an estimated capacity of 170,000 Mcf per day.[39] Construction actually took about six months: from early August 1981 to late January 1982. Transportation services began on March 1, 1982.[40]

The Size of the Potential Entrant

A potential entrant represents a competitive threat to a colluding group if it is able to offset the output reduction that maximizes the monopoly profit of the cartel. Unless the cartel can reduce output below the competitive level, it will not earn supracompetitive profits (i.e., it will be totally ineffective). If a 5 to 10 percent price increase above cost represents the minimum price increase to warrant public concern,[41] the question is whether nearby suppliers exist with the capacity to offset the corresponding output reduction. The size of a potential entrant therefore determines the ability or capacity of the nearby supplier to offset the output reduction of the colluding group, thereby preventing the colluding group from raising the price 5 to 10 percent above its costs.

LENGTH OF ADJUSTMENT PERIOD

The ability of a nearby supplier to meet the size requirement varies with the length of the adjustment or time period. Three adjustment periods are considered in the study: short, intermediate, and long runs. For each period or "run," the following factors are considered: (1) interruptible sales, (2) access to underground storage facilities, and/or (3) contracts approaching termination and subject to renewal. Let us consider each possibility in turn.

Interruptible Sales

Pipelines are designed to operate at full capacity during seasonal peaks.[42] Gas purchasers (e.g., LDCs) pay demand charges to the pipeline to reserve space in its line, even if no gas is taken. Generally, the total contract demands of pipeline customers equal the capacity of the pipeline. It is possible, however, that an LDC may experience a reduction in its demand for gas during the contract period and therefore be willing to reduce its contract demand if it were given the opportunity. In this case, the nearby pipeline would be able to divert some deliveries into a new market, without adding capacity to the main line.[43]

If a pipeline consistently services interruptible customers during peak periods, this implies that some customers who are paying demand charges, to reserve space in the line, are not using all their reserved space.[44] Customers who are not using the full capacity on which they are paying demand charges may be willing to reduce their contract demand.[45] This reduction in contract demand by old customers would enable the pipeline to negotiate new contracts with customers in the new service area. Empirically, however, it is a difficult task to quantify this possibility for pipeline expansion on a pipeline-by-pipeline basis.[46] Nevertheless, for a sample of pipelines, we estimate annual divertible deliveries for each nearby pipeline based on its highest peak day interruptible sales.[47]

Underground Storage

The competitive effects of underground storage facilities in local transportation markets are generally ignored in pipeline studies.[48] The present study may represent the first attempt to take account of this competitive factor. Although a complete analysis of underground storage is beyond the scope of this study, we take account of the possibility that the profitability (or success) of a colluding group may be limited, to some extent, by nearby underground storage operators.

If underground storage operations have excess or divertible capacity or can readily expand their capacity,[49] the number and size of potential entrants into local delivery markets during peak demand periods may be substantially underestimated if such operations are ignored. A pipeline that is fully utilized during the peak season may nevertheless be able to provide gas that can be used to meet peak season demands by delivering gas in off-peak periods to storage facilities that could potentially serve nearby markets.

A crude measure of the competitive effect of underground storage is obtained if we treat the storage operation as if it were a nearby pipeline. Thus, if it meets the size and distance entry requirements imposed on nearby pipelines, it will be admitted into the colluding group.[50]

Contract Terminations

The third alternative means for a nearby supplier to divert gas into a new market or to a new customer is not to renew contracts that are approaching expiration. The corresponding pipeline capacity can then be used to bid for more valuable customers. Based on an Energy Information Administration (EIA) sample of pipeline contracts, the standard length of resale supply contracts is 10 years[51] with a maximum *remaining* life of five years.

The ability of nearby suppliers to meet the size requirement will depend, in part, on their ability to divert gas into the new market. For service currently under contract, what matters is remaining contract life--not length of contract. If five years remain on a ten-year contract, for example, the pipeline is able to contract to supply new customers in five years. The maximum remaining life of resale contracts in the EIA sample is five years. Thus, at least 20 percent of the supplier's capacity is available at the end of the first year, and 40 percent is available within two years.

POTENTIAL ENTRY INTO MORE THAN ONE MARKET

If a nearby pipeline meets the size and distance requirements as discussed above, the pipeline is considered to be a potential entrant. If, however, the pipeline can enter only one of several possible new markets, the potential entrant exerts a competitive influence on all markets only as long as it remains a potential entrant (i.e., as long as it does not enter any one of the markets). Under these conditions, a collusive group of suppliers would form expectations about the likelihood of entry by the nearby firm. The output expansion of the potential entrant in each specific market would be weighted by the probability of entry. Cartels operating in different markets, however, may form different expectations on the likelihood of entry into a given market and may also disagree on which markets the nearby pipeline will enter. Developing a model which specifies a cartel's reaction function which explicitly considers the probability of potential entry is beyond the scope of this study.

Instead, we estimate a simple probability of entry in the intermediate run. Since most pipelines are potential entrants to several markets, we initially compare the number of markets in which each pipeline could potentially enter *simultaneously* to the total number of markets in which it is a potential entrant. This ratio is referred to as the entry ratio.[52] For example, a pipeline that could potentially enter any two of ten markets within 100 miles of its existing transmission system has an entry ratio of 20 percent at the 100-mile range.

Given that pipelines are expected to bid for contracts to serve nearby

LDCs, the question becomes, In how many markets must the pipeline submit bids in order to win higher-valued service contracts sufficient to fully utilize available divertible gas? Assuming that operating and construction costs of pipelines within the same region do not significantly differ, we expect that the chance of submitting a winning bid (i.e., the "win" ratio) equals the total number of markets divided by the total number of bids from potential entrants and current suppliers. If there are six markets with 20 bids from potential entrants and 10 bids from current suppliers, for example, a "representative" pipeline would expect to win one out of every five bids. Thus, a pipeline that could simultaneously serve 20 percent of its potential entry markets[53] is expected to bid in all of its nearby markets. More generally, any profit-maximizing pipeline with an entry ratio greater than or equal to the win ratio will bid in all of its potential entry markets.[54]

ESTIMATING POTENTIAL ENTRY: ALTERNATIVE ASSUMPTIONS

To summarize, the ability of a nearby pipeline to qualify as a potential entrant is based on four requirements. Since each requirement is an approximation, we consider two distinct sets of entry requirements:

1. *Highly restrictive requirements*--requirements that tend to reduce the number of potential entrants and increase the HHI in the market, and
2. *Moderately restrictive requirements*--requirements that tend to increase the number of potential entrants and reduce the HHI.

The highly restrictive entry requirements are the following:

1.1 The residual demand curve of the colluding group is of constant elasticity;
1.2 The capacity to expand is based on lower-bound estimates of interruptible deliveries, supply contract expirations, and excess capacity in underground storage facilities;
1.3 The win ratio is greater than the regional average win ratio; and
1.4 The distance from the local market is based on the upper-bound estimates of (a) pipeline construction costs and (b) operating and maintenance costs, and on the lower-bound estimates of (c) annual throughput or volume and (d) the current market price of delivered gas.

As will be explained in the next chapter and Appendix C, the first requirement that the residual demand of the colluding group is of constant elasticity (rather than linear) determines a larger output reduction for the profit-maximizing cartel. This larger output reduction, however, increases the minimum size of a potential entrant. The second requirement is more straightforward. Given that high and low estimates of interruptible deliveries, contract expirations, and excess underground storage capacity can be computed, the highly restrictive entry requirements incorporate the lower-bound estimate of deliveries, contract expirations, and storage. If each pipeline assumes a win ratio greater than the regional average, it will not bid in some markets that it could actually serve. Thus, the first three requirements make it more difficult for nearby suppliers to meet the *size requirement* for entry. The fourth requirement, which relates to the *distance requirement* for entry, can be interpreted similarly. For example, if all nearby suppliers are treated as if they were exactly 140 miles away from the new market, the estimates of construction and operating costs will be high for those suppliers who are less than 140 miles from the market.

The moderately restrictive entry requirements are the following:

2.1 The residual demand curve is linear;

2.2 The capacity to expand is based on the upper-bound estimates of interruptible deliveries, supply contract expirations, and excess capacity in underground storage facilities;

2.3 The win ratio equals the industry average;[55] and

2.4 The distance from the local market is based on the lower-bound estimates of (a) pipeline construction costs and (b) operating and maintenance costs, and on the upper-bound estimates of (c) annual throughput and (d) the current market price of delivered gas.

A GROUP OF POTENTIAL ENTRANTS

The colluding group should include all potential entrants who either individually or jointly have the ability to undercut the collusive price. One major short-run limit on the number of competitors is likely to be the lack of divertible throughput. Nearby suppliers who cannot meet the size requirement on their own, however, may be able to joint venture with other small suppliers to generate the minimum quantity of throughput to undercut the collusive price. In fact, one nearby small supplier may be able to joint venture with more distant suppliers and jointly pose a competitive threat to the colluding group. The possibility of such joint venture arrangements tends to increase the number of potential entrants and makes collusion more difficult to sustain.

Since entry by a group of suppliers who cannot meet the size requirement on their own cannot be unambiguously determined, we are unable to consider this form of potential entry. As explained earlier, our analysis of potential entry requires an estimate of the number of markets that each potential entrant can enter *simultaneously*. The number of markets that a group of suppliers can enter simultaneously when some of the joint venturers are also potential entrants in other markets depends on the specific order in which each joint venturer will enter markets. The ability of a joint venture to enter a market will therefore be conditional on the entry preference of each individual joint venturer. Estimating the conditional probability of entry by a joint venture is beyond the scope of this study. Consequently, our estimate of potential entry is conservative, since entry by joint ventures is not considered.

OTHER COMPETITIVE FACTORS

The ability of the market to limit cartel pricing will also depend on a number of other competitive factors. This study explicitly considers the independence of each supplier, subsidiary relationships among pipelines, intrastate suppliers, and foreign suppliers.

Most of the major interstate pipelines obtain their gas supplies at wellheads located in gas-producing regions of the United States. A 1984 EIA study of 20 major interstate pipelines, for example, found that 17 of the 20 major pipelines acquired over 60 percent of their supply from three or more gas-producing areas, including both onshore and offshore areas.[56] We consider such pipelines to be independent in the sense that their decision to enter a market is not dependent on obtaining gas supplies from any single supplier. In addition, the EIA study found that pipelines that purchase 25 percent or more of their gas from other pipelines contracted with three or more suppliers. Pipelines that acquire their throughput from another pipeline but have at least one alternative supplier are also considered independent competitors. If, on the other hand, a pipeline is dependent on another pipeline for its total supply, it is treated as a subsidiary of its supplier.

The competitive behavior of a pipeline with its own independent gas supplies, however, may still be restrained if its organizational structure is not also independent of other pipelines. Consequently, pipelines owned by other pipelines are assumed not to compete with one another. If the parent pipeline and one or more of its subsidiary pipelines serve the same market, they are treated as a single competitor (i.e., their output is combined).[57]

No attempt is made to analyze joint venture agreements to determine the managing and controlling owners. Instead, we treat joint ventures as if they were subsidiaries of the largest nearby joint venturer. The market share of a joint venture is therefore added to the market share of a wholly owned pipeline if two conditions are met: namely, if (1) both pipelines serve the same market and (2) the wholly owned pipeline is also owned by one of the joint venturers. As a result, the HHI may be overestimated in markets that are served (or potentially served) by the joint venture *and* by another pipeline that is also owned by one of the joint venturers.[58]

Intrastate pipelines near local markets may also represent potential entrants. The major intrastate pipelines in the principal gas-producing states are therefore factored into our analysis. The same size and distance requirements that interstate suppliers must meet to qualify as potential entrants are applied to intrastate suppliers. Intrastate suppliers who pose a competitive threat to the cartel are assumed to gain admission.

The competitive effect of natural gas imports into a local market may also constrain the colluding group. Foreign gas producers, utilizing ocean tankers, provide domestic gas users with another alternative source of supply. As a result, any attempt by the colluding group to increase price above cost is expected to result in a greater loss of sales. Markets that have the capability to receive foreign gas are therefore expected to be more competitive, *ceteris paribus*.

Since the foreign suppliers we consider deliver to liquified natural gas (LNG) terminals (receiving stations for LNG shipments via ocean tankers), we consider only domestic markets that can be reached directly by ocean tanker. Thus, for these markets, foreign suppliers are current suppliers (i.e., the distance requirement is already met). Because of the lack of data needed to evaluate the size requirement, we consider the two extreme cases: The size requirement is *or* is not met. The first case tends to increase the number of potential entrants, reduce market shares, and lower the corresponding HHI. The opposite effects are implicit in the second case.

MEASURE OF OUTPUT AND THE HHI CALCULATION

Sales are used to measure the size of actual and potential pipeline suppliers in the market. The fundamental reason for preferring sales to capacity is that for our purposes, the output measure must relate to the local market. The ability of a colluding group to raise price above cost will depend, to an important extent, on the size *and* location of pipelines. The pipeline's total system capacity is not available to serve every local market along its trunk line. Whereas total capacity is difficult, if not impossible, to allocate across the numerous local markets, sales in each market are known.

In the short run, only current suppliers are in the market. The size of the market and the size of each current supplier is measured by sales. As will be explained in Chapter 4, only those current suppliers with sales large enough to meet the size requirement are considered colluding firms. All other suppliers are considered fringe suppliers.

In the intermediate run, potential entrants have no current sales in the market. Given the combined sales of the colluding group of current suppliers, however, the minimum size necessary to threaten the cartel (if denied admission) can be determined. Chapter 5 will explain how the divertible gas supplies of nearby pipelines are used to determine whether the nearby supplier meets the size requirement. Nearby suppliers who fail to meet the size requirement are not potential entrants in the intermediate run. In the long run, however, all gas is divertible and therefore all nearby suppliers are potential entrants.

The existence of potential entrants reduces the likelihood that the collusive group will be profitable. Given its demand curve, the group produces that level of output that maximizes profit. This joint profit-maximizing level of output is therefore independent of the number of members in the group. Consequently, as the number of potential entrants increases, the same profit-maximizing level of output for the colluding group must be maintained. If the cartel is successful in maximizing profits initially, each cartel member will expect to receive a smaller profit share as membership in the cartel expands. As a result, the incentive to undercut the cartel price increases with membership, since the cost of cheating (i.e., the size of each member's share of cartel profits) decreases.

The HHI is used as a crude measure of the coordination and policing costs of maintaining the colluding group given potential entry. Unlike the standard HHI analysis, however, each supplier included in our HHI estimate is large enough to eliminate the profits of the colluding group (at prices 5 to 10 percent over cost) if excluded from the group. Alternatively stated, each individual colluder is large enough to completely offset the profit-maximizing output reduction of the cartel. Thus, these large suppliers are an important determinant of the HHI.

Given the economies of scale in pipeline construction and operation, it is not necessary that each potential entrant actually enter the market. The colluding group may prefer to pay some members not to produce. In terms of the incentive to cheat on the collusive agreement, however, it is "as if" each colluding member is given an equal share of output.[59] Thus, the market share of each *colluding firm* is the average market share of the *colluding group* (i.e., the sum of the market shares of all current suppliers who become colluders is divided by the number of colluders). The HHI is therefore computed on the average market share of each colluding firm plus the individual market shares of each fringe firm.[60] The HHI computation is explained more fully in the next chapter.

THE SHORT RUN

COMPETITION IN THE SHORT RUN

In the short run, there is no adjustment period to provide nearby rivals with an opportunity to respond to a cartel price. Only those pipelines that utilize their own transmission lines to currently sell in the market are relevant. Thus, potential entrants (i.e., nearby pipelines that could construct a hookup and divert gas into the market in question) are ignored. On the other hand, intrastate pipeline deliveries into the market from gas fields within the state and imports from foreign gas suppliers can affect the profitability of collusive behavior in the short term. Although these alternative sources of supply have been largely ignored in earlier studies, we consider whether such suppliers are likely to gain admission into the collusive group.

Thus, all current suppliers (interstate and intrastate pipelines and foreign suppliers) are tested to determine whether they are sufficient in size to undercut a local cartel if denied membership.[1] Current suppliers who cannot meet the size requirement will be grouped together and retested. Once the number of colluding suppliers is determined, the HHI can be computed.

Pipelines that pass through a local market but make no deliveries are ignored in this period of analysis. The short run does not allow sufficient time for a nondelivering pipeline to secure the necessary operating permits and approvals to install a tap or terminal and begin new service. Equally important, the pipeline is unlikely to have sufficient excess capacity or divertible gas to meet short-run peaks in demand. It takes time for supply contracts to expire and for the pipeline to substitute higher-valued customers for lower-valued customers. For these reasons, such "pass-through" pipelines are distinguished from current suppliers. In our view, the time requirements for pass-through pipelines to enter a market are more similar to those for nearby pipelines in the intermediate run.   Pass-through pipelines are therefore treated as nearby pipelines.

COMPILATION OF MARKET CONCENTRATION DATA

The first phase of the data compilation is accomplished in two steps. Since the smallest area of analysis is an MSA, the counties within each MSA were initially identified from a map published in 1979 by the U.S. Department of Commerce.[2]   Changes in the number or the composition of MSAs since 1979 are made and reported by the Office of Management and Budget (OMB). Thus, the second step is to update the 1979 listing based on the OMB revisions.[3] Appendix A lists all the MSAs by state.

The second phase of the data compilation is to locate each major pipeline that delivers into an MSA. Our primary data source was the 1982 Natural Gas Pipeline Map published by Pennwell.[4] In addition to the U.S. and Canadian map, special regional maps of the Texas Gulf, Louisiana, and Oklahoma provided the necessary detail to differentiate among the complex pipeline networks in each of these regions.

The third and most complex phase is to develop a pipeline deliveries dataset on an MSA basis.[5] The data source for pipeline deliveries is the *FERC Form 2: Annual Report of Major Natural Gas Companies (Class A and Class B)*.[6] One reason why this data source is not more widely used is that it does not report transactions on any consistent geographical basis. For each FERC pipeline in our dataset, we attempted to assign each individual delivery to an MSA or to a county outside an MSA. In filling out FERC Form 2, however, pipelines sometimes list several destinations but only report a single volume for the combined deliveries.   Such deliveries, commonly referred to as "to various points" (TVP) deliveries, make it difficult to assign every delivery to a specific MSA (or county).   TVP deliveries were usually posted to the state and were not included in the MSA or county delivery datasets.[7]

Table 4.1 lists all the pipelines who filed a FERC Form 2.[8] LDCs without transmission lines are deleted from the sample, since our primary concern is whether independent pipelines (i.e., pipelines with alternative sources of gas supply including gas fields) can collude.[9] Similarly, interstate (FERC) pipelines without alternative sources of supply are also deleted from the pipeline sample. On the other hand, LDCs with transmission lines are often supplied by major interstate pipelines that do not serve a given market. In this case, the LDC is considered a current supplier. In addition, major intrastate and foreign suppliers (imports) are added to the sample.[10]

Table 4.1

Pipelines Filing a FERC Form 2 in 1983

---

1. Alabama-Tennessee Natural Gas Co.
2. Algonquin Gas Transmission Co.
3. ANR Pipeline Co.
4. Arkansas Oklahoma Gas Co.
5. Arkla, Inc.
6. Associated Natural Gas Co.
* Bazzle Gas Co.
* Black Marlin Pipeline Co.
* Canyon Creek Compression Co.
* Capitol Oil Co., Inc.
7. Carnegie Natural Gas Co.
* Chandeleur Pipeline Co.
8. Colorado Interstate Gas Co.
9. Columbia Gas Transmission Corp.
10. Columbia Gulf Transmission Co.
11. Commercial Pipeline Corp.
12. Consolidated Gas Supply Corp.
13. Consolidated System LNG Co.
14. Crab Run Gas Co.
15. Distrigas of Massachusetts Corp.
16. East Tennessee Natural Gas Co.
17. Eastern Shore Natural Gas Co.
18. El Paso Natural Gas Co.
19. Enserch Corp.
20. Equitable Gas Co.
21. Florida Gas Transmission Co.
22. Gas Transport, Inc.
23. Granite State Gas Transmission, Inc.
24. Great Lakes Gas Transmission Co.
* Great Plains Natural Gas Co.
* Indiana Utilities Corp.
25. Inland Gas Co.
* Interstate Power Co.
* Iowa-Illinois Gas & Electric Co.
26. Kentucky-West Virginia Gas Co.

Table 4.1 (Continued)

27. KN Energy Co.
 * Lawrenceburg Gas Transmission Corp.
 * Louisiana-Nevada Transit Co.
28. Michigan Consolidated Gas Co.
29. Michigan Gas Storage Co.
 * Michigan Power Co.
30. Mid-Louisiana Gas Co.
31. Midwestern Gas Transmission Co.
 * Mississippi Gas Corp.
32. Mississippi River Transmission Corp.
33. Montana-Dakota Utilities Co.
34. Mountain Fuel Supply Co.
35. National Fuel Gas Distribution Corp.
36. National Fuel Gas Supply Corp.
37. Natural Gas Pipeline Company of America
38. North Penn Gas Co.
39. Northern Natural Gas Co.
40. Northwest Central Pipeline Corp.
41. Northwest Pipeline Corp.
42. Ohio River Pipeline Corp.
 * Orange & Rockland Utilities, Inc.
43. Pacific Gas Transmission Co.
44. Pacific Interstate Offshore Co.
45. Pacific Interstate Transmission Co.
46. Pacific Offshore Pipeline Co.
47. Panhandle Eastern Pipeline Co.
 * Pennsylvania & Southern Gas Co.
 * Raton Natural Gas Co.
48. Ravencliff Fuel Supply Co.
49. Ringwood Gathering Co.
50. Shenandoah Gas Co.
 * South County Gas Co.
51. South Georgia Natural Gas Co.
 * South Penn Gas Co.
52. Southern Natural Gas Co.

Table 4.1 (Continued)

53. Southwest Gas Corp.
 * Sunflower Pipeline Co.
54. Tenneco, Inc.
55. Texas Eastern Transmission Corp.
56. Texas Gas Pipeline Co.
57. Texas Gas Transmission Co.
58. Trailblazer Pipeline Co.
59. Transcontinental Gas Pipeline Corp.
60. Transwestern Pipeline Co.
61. Trunkline Gas Co.
62. Trunkline LNG Co.
63. Union Gas System, Inc.
 * Union Light, Heat, and Power Co.
64. United Cities Gas Co.
65. United Gas Pipeline Co.
66. Valero Interstate Transmission Co.
67. Valley Gas Transmission, Inc.
68. Washington Gas Light Co.
69. West Lake Arthur Corp.
70. West Texas Gathering Co.
71. Western Gas Interstate Co.
 * Wheeler Gas, Inc.
72. Wyoming Interstate Gas Co.

* Denotes local distribution company deleted from the sample.

Despite the different types of suppliers into a market, the delivery data were generally limited except for FERC pipelines. On this basis, we restricted our sample of markets (i.e., our reference markets) to those that currently received deliveries from interstate FERC pipelines. Thus, only 208 of the 314 MSAs in Appendix A could be included in our market sample.[11] In each reference market, however, we included the delivery information for all types of suppliers.

An extensive computerized database was developed from (1) the *pipeline profile,* which lists the pipeline name and number, parent-subsidiary relationships, whether a FERC Form 2 was filed, whether the pipeline is intrastate, and total U.S. deliveries by type of delivery[12]; (2) the *market profile,* which lists each MSA name and number and its affiliated census region; (3) the MSA-specific *delivery records* for each pipeline; and (4) the *distance records* between MSAs and between MSAs and counties outside the MSA. The distance records are used to identify nearby pipelines.

EMPIRICAL FINDINGS

Following the steps outlined in our methodology, the market shares of current independent suppliers were first computed. Before the delivery records for each current supplier can be aggregated into meaningful market concentration measures, ownership interrelations among the pipelines must be identified and eliminated. If two pipelines delivering into the same MSA, for example, are subsidiary companies wholly owned by the same parent company, the two subsidiaries are not likely to compete against one another. In the case of wholly owned subsidiary pipelines, therefore, the deliveries of each subsidiary pipeline into the same MSA are aggregated and treated as a joint operation.[13] In most instances, the two related pipelines approach one another from different geographic areas. As a result, their interdependence affects only the market in which they meet.

Appendix B contains the standard market share data based on current, MSA-specific sales. For each local market (MSA), only current pipelines with independent sources of supply are listed.[14] If a delivering pipeline is solely dependent on another pipeline for its supply, it is treated as if it were a subsidiary of the other pipeline. Subsidiary relationships are denoted with an asterisk (*), and the market share of the parent entity is listed. The "detail of subsidiaries" lists each subsidiary, its deliveries, and the percentage of the parent's deliveries in the market. In Boston, Massachusetts, for example, Tenneco owns Granite State but only 25 percent [= (23,816,349 Mcf)/(95,439,795 Mcf)] of Tenneco's deliveries in the Boston MSA are from Granite State. The remaining 75 percent of the deliveries are from additional transmission lines owned by Tenneco.

Given the small market shares of a number of suppliers, it is clear that many current suppliers are not large enough to pose a competitive threat to a colluding group if denied membership. However, if some of these "fringe" suppliers acted jointly, they may be large enough to gain admission into the colluding group. As a result, the HHIs reported in Appendix B may underestimate the short-run competitive effect of small suppliers.

To reduce this bias, the minimum size of a recalcitrant supplier sufficient to prevent the cartel from setting a profit-maximizing price 5 to 10 percent above the competitive level was calculated. As demonstrated in Appendix C, if members of the colluding group supply more than 66.6 percent of the competitive output, the cartel can set a threshold price 5 to 10 percent above the competitive level, and all other current suppliers will be excluded from the cartel in the short run.[15] On the other hand, if a current supplier or group of current suppliers can supply at least 33.3 percent of the current market output, it can credibly threaten and gain admission into a cartel whose members initially supplied 66.6 percent of the competitive output. In this case, suppliers with less than a 33.3 percent market share are considered too small to gain admission into the colluding group.

Thus, given the percentage of the monopolized market supplied by the colluding group, the corresponding minimum size necessary to gain admission into the cartel is also known. Suppliers or groups of suppliers who are too small are therefore treated as fringe suppliers. Since the market is comprised of potential colluders and fringe suppliers, the market share of each fringe supplier is also factored into the HHI computations.

Local markets are expected to be highly concentrated in the short run, since the colluding group will consist of only one or two current suppliers. Since each colluding supplier is assumed to share equally in the cartel's output and profit, the market share of each colluder is the average market share of the colluding group. For example, if two current competitors with market shares of 50 percent and 30 percent, respectively, form a collusive group, they jointly control 80 percent of the current market. Given the assumption that the two colluders share the market equally, each colluder is allocated a 20 percent share of the total competitive output in the monopolized market, or a 40 percent share in the current market. Since a third firm's current market share of 20 percent is insufficient to fully offset the cartel's profit-maximizing reduction of current market output from 80 percent to 40 percent (i.e., a 40 percent reduction in current output), it is too small to pose a threat to the cartel. It is therefore considered a fringe supplier in the short run. Assuming no other fringe firms, the HHI is 3600.[16]

In the short run, the HHI reflects the current output controlled by the colluding group in addition to the output of each fringe supplier. Thus, the market power of a colluding group of current suppliers will vary inversely with the size of the fringe supply. The HHI is sensitive to the disparity between the market shares of potential colluders and fringe suppliers.[17]

Table 4.2 reports the distribution of Herfindahl indices for each of the 208 local delivery markets in the lower 48 states. To facilitate comparisons, the individual MSA markets are classified into one of the nine census regions. Appendix D lists the states within each census region; the MSAs within each state are listed in Appendix A. In the New England region, for example, there are six MSAs (accounting for 50 percent of the MSAs in the region) that are served by only one pipeline (i.e., with a HHI of 10000). The column totals (bottom line of Table 4.2) show that with the exception of 16 markets, including seven markets in the West South Central Region, all the MSAs show a HHI of at least 5000. All 208 markets report a HHI over 2500.

A HHI threshold value of 2500 is used by the Department of Justice to determine whether a pipeline destination market is so concentrated that a pipeline might have substantial market power.[18] The threshold value of 2500, instead of the 1800 threshold used to indicate highly concentrated markets in the DOJ's "Merger Guidelines", is warranted, according to the DOJ, because the index is used to determine whether pipeline regulation is appropriate--not whether a merger is likely to lead to the exercise of market power. Since regulation is costly, the consumer must either bear the costs of regulation necessary to prevent the exercise of market power or bear the costs of market power. Although a HHI of 2500 may indicate a higher degree of market power than a HHI of 1800, the question is whether the additional costs of monopoly pricing, implicit in the increase in the HHI from 1800 to 2500, is less than the costs of continued regulation. Thus, the use of a HHI of 2500 recognizes that pipeline regulation is costly.[19] We therefore consider a HHI of 2500 or less to indicate that a colluding group with four or more *equal-sized members* is too large to establish and enforce a monopoly price and earn supracompetitive profits.[20]

The HHI distribution in Table 4.2 is consistent with Mead's findings. Mead finds that in almost 90 percent of the natural gas delivery markets in his study, four-firm concentration averages at least 90 percent.[21] Thus, the distribution of concentration ratios by market is extremely skewed to the right. In our analysis, which uses the HHI instead of the four-firm concentration index, the HHI distribution is also skewed toward high levels of concentration with all markets reporting a HHI over 2500. A HHI of 2500 is equivalent to a cartel with four equal-size members.[22] The corresponding four-firm concentration would be 100 percent. Thus, despite the differences in methodology, the results of our short-run analysis are not significantly different from Mead's. The generalized nature of our methodology, however, enables us to develop the corresponding analysis for the intermediate run and the long run.

Table 4.2

HHI Distribution by Census Regions

(based on number of potential colluders plus fringe suppliers)

from: to:	0-1800	1801-2500	2501-2999	3000-3999	4000-4999	5000-5999	6000-6999	7000-7999	8000-8999	9000-9999	10000	TOTAL
New England	0	0	0	0	1	1	2	0	2	0	6	12
Mid-Atlantic	0	0	1	0	2	3	2	0	0	3	10	21
East North Central	0	0	0	0	0	4	1	1	0	6	20	32
West North Central	0	0	0	0	1	1	0	1	1	1	19	24
South Atlantic	0	0	0	1	0	2	1	1	1	3	31	40
East South Central	0	0	0	1	1	2	0	0	1	3	12	20
West South Central	0	0	0	0	7	3	4	3	3	6	12	38
Mountain	0	0	0	0	1	0	0	3	1	1	8	14
Pacific	0	0	0	0	0	0	0	1	0	1	5	7
TOTAL	0	0	1	2	13	16	10	10	9	24	123	208

LIMITATIONS OF THE SHORT-RUN ANALYSIS

Since the short-run analysis does not consider potential entry, it underestimates the number of members that are likely to gain admission into the cartel and consequently underestimates the coordination and policing problems facing the colluding group. The magnitude of this omission is suggested as follows. For each market in question, we identify three types of nearby suppliers:

1. pipelines that traverse or "pass through" (PT) the market but make no deliveries,
2. pipelines that pass through a nearby market (NPT) but make no deliveries in that market or in the market in question, and
3. pipelines that make deliveries to a nearby market (NDL) but do not pass through or make deliveries to the market in question.

For each market in our sample, Appendix E identifies each of the three types of nearby suppliers with the prefix PT, NPT, or NDL. Current suppliers are listed without a prefix. For example, in Abilene, Texas, there is only one current supplier (Enserch Corp.) and one pass-through supplier (Western Interstate). Within 100 miles, however, there are five suppliers who deliver to nearby markets and six additional suppliers who pass through nearby markets. In addition, there are two more suppliers within 121-140 miles of the Abilene market. It is immediately apparent that in almost every market, the number of nearby suppliers is substantial and greatly exceeds the number of current suppliers.

If these nearby pipelines can profitably construct a pipeline hookup into the market in question and quickly divert sufficient gas supplies to feed the hookup, they may be able to limit the market power of the colluding group of current suppliers if excluded from the group. Under these conditions, the number of current suppliers in the market would not provide a reliable indication of the extent of competition in the market.

The critical flaw in the short-run analysis, therefore, is that it tends to overestimate the expected success of collusive behavior and raises a competitive concern when, in fact, the market may be competitive. Even if a market is highly concentrated in the short run, the entry threat provided by nearby suppliers may limit the ability of a cartel to significantly raise price over cost.[23] What should matter from a policy point of view is whether markets are "open" or "closed" to potential entrants.[24]

The fundamental question, then, is how to determine whether the distance and size of the nearby pipeline is sufficient to make the pipeline a potential entrant. The answer to this question is the subject of the next two chapters. Chapter 5 addresses the question for the intermediate run, and Chapter 6 considers the long run.

THE INTERMEDIATE RUN

INTRODUCTION

Despite the large number of pipelines within 100 to 140 miles of most markets, these nearby pipelines have no time to enter a market in the short run. In this chapter, we consider whether nearby pipelines can become potential entrants within a two-year period, the length of the intermediate run. There are two requirements: The nearby pipeline must be able to construct an economically viable hookup from its trunk line to the market, and the nearby pipeline must be able to divert sufficient gas to feed the new pipeline hookup. These two requirements will be referred to as the distance requirement and the size requirement, respectively. Suppliers who require more than two years to meet the size requirement are excluded in the intermediate run.[1]

THE DISTANCE REQUIREMENT

Conceptually, the pipeline makes an investment in the new pipe and compressors to transport gas from its main line to the new market area. In the first year, the investment is made and the hookup is completed.[2] After the construction phase, natural gas is delivered to the new market and the pipeline incurs maintenance and operating costs that extend over the useful life of the hookup. The question is, What is the transport fee required to earn a competitive rate of return on the pipeline hookup?

The Required Transport Fee

The transport fee (t^*) necessary to rationalize the pipeline hookup is estimated as follows. We compute the transport fee necessary to generate an annual cash flow equal to the annualized expenses of the hookup. The major expense categories are (1) amortized construction cost expenses, (2) maintenance and operating expenses, and (3) taxes.[3] Each of these expenses is estimated as follows.

The construction cost of the hookup is estimated from a sample of *actual* diameter-length specifications of pipeline construction projects filed with FERC. Since 20-24-inch-diameter pipe is sufficient to serve the average metropolitan area, we compiled a sample of all projects between 20 inches and 24 inches in diameter.[4] Table 5.1 reports the 30 pipeline projects (under 200 miles in length) that were completed between 1979 and 1985. Although the hookup length varies over a wide range of 4 miles to 185 miles, the diameter of the hookup is limited to 20-24 inches. Four small underwater projects constructed in the Gulf of Mexico were excluded because the costs of underwater construction is not representative of construction on land.[5]

Expected construction costs are estimated using regression analysis on all the projects listed in Table 5.1. Construction costs are expected to be determined largely by pipeline diameter and length. The two independent variables are expressed in logarithms to capture the economies of scale in pipeline construction.[6] More specifically, the increases in construction costs are expected to decline in response to equal increments in pipeline length.[7] Our best estimate of construction costs on a 100-mile hookup is $12.8 million.[8] For our cash flow analysis, however, we need to find the corresponding annual amortized cost. Depending on the useful life of the pipeline hookup, a high estimate of amortized construction costs per year (I_H) is $0.94 million and a low estimate (I_L) is $0.74 million.[9]

Operating and maintenance costs for a large sample of pipelines are reported in DOE/EIA, *Statistics of Interstate Natural Gas Pipeline Companies*.[10] Table 5.2 lists the operating and maintenance costs of the smaller pipelines in the EIA sample that report deliveries to one or more of our markets or to nearby counties.[11] The weighted average annual cost of maintenance and operating expenses is $207,310 per 100 miles.[12] Using regression analysis on the same sample, a higher estimate of $354,500 is obtained.[13] The regression approach seems more reliable, since the average length of the pipeline sample (824 total miles, including field lines) is substantially longer than 140 miles, the length of the longest hookup we consider. If there are economies of scale in operating pipelines, the average cost approach is likely to overestimate the economies associated with a 140-mile hookup. Accordingly, we consider $354,500 per 100 miles to represent

Table 5.1

Pipeline Construction Projects: 1978-84
(20-24 inch diameter)

Docket Number (CP)	Company	Length of Pipeline	Diameter of Pipeline	Construction Cost	Total Cost per Mile	Date of Commission Order	Date of Completion
83-193	Mountain Fuel R	39.70	20	12,653,114	318,718		1985
84-145	Northwest Central	5.30	20	1,049,140	197,951		1985
83-376	El Paso Nat. Gas	7.50	20	1,848,258	246,434		1985
84-223	Transcontinental	5.05	24	8,204,212	1,624,596		1985
Morgan*	N.A.	25.40	20	7,402,299	291,429	1st Qtr 84	N.A.
Morgan*	N.A.	185.00	24	22,052,682	119,204	1st Qtr 84	N.A.
83-392	Northern Natural	8.50	24	3,338,391	392,752		1984
81-408	ANR Pipeline	10.10 6.90 7.10	20 20 20	2,855,468 2,100,095 2,256,774	282,720 304,362 317,856		1984
83-131	Northern Natural	3.50	24	4,342,391	1,240,683		1984
81-44	Columbia Gas Trans.	24.70	20	9,567,000	387,328	9/10/82	6/7/83
81-326	Mountain Fuel Supply	38.50	20	8,099,551	210,378	4/30/82	1/18/83

Table 5.1 (Continued)

Docket Number (CP)	Company	Length of Pipeline	Diameter of Pipeline	Construction Cost	Total Cost per Mile	Date of Commission Order	Date of Completion
81-433	Columbia Gas	67.10	24	39,279,325	585,385		1983
81-257	Columbia Gulf & Tenn. Gas	10.10	22	7,427,200	735,366	7/13/82	12/11/82
80-343	Southwest Gas Corp.	61.01	20	16,721,766	274,082	3/9/81	11/17/82
81-179	Consolidated Gas Trans.	20.27	24	9,601,970	473,704	7/24/81	8/4/82
81-210	Texas Gas Trans.	32.23	20	15,964,894	495,343	6/30/81	1/23/82
79-374	Southern Natural Gas	31.25	20	9,211,753	294,776	7/30/81	1/1/82
80-209	ANR Pipeline	27.20	20	21,653,403	796,081		1982
81-144	Columbia Gas Trans.	61.60	24	33,210,720	539,135	6/5/81	12/23/81
79-337	El Paso Natural Gas	19.60	20	5,763,856	294,074	6/22/81	10/1/81
80-218	Transcontinental & United Gas	14.29	24	13,405,041	938,071	7/24/80	9/24/81
80-119	ANR Pipeline	19.30 / 23.90	24 / 24	18,391,495 / 20,976,764	952,927 / 877,689		1981 / 1981
80-40	Colorado Interstate Gas	51.80	24	16,662,178	321,664	6/2/80	9/26/80

Table 5.1 (Continued)

Docket Number (CP)	Company	Length of Pipeline	Diameter of Pipeline	Construction Cost	Total Cost per Mile	Date of Commission Order	Date of Completion
74-316	ANR Pipeline	15.30	24	7,605,042	497,062	8/25/79	8/25/80
76-500	Northwest Central Pipeline	113.00	20	22,706,696	200,944	9/1/78	11/8/79
		136.50	20	26,425,672	193,595	9/1/78	11/8/79
78-143	Consolidate Gas Trans.	19.10	24	10,712,691	560,874	4/12/78	10/4/78
	TOTALS	1,090.80		381,489,481			

Source: U.S. Federal Energy Regulatory Commission, Pipeline Company Proceedings, Docketed Matters. Federal Energy Regulatory Commission, Office of Pipeline; and Producer Regulation Staff Report, *Cost of Pipeline and Compressor Station Construction Under Natural Gas Act Section 7(c) for the Years 1980 through 1983; 1981-1984; and 1982-1985;* Washington, D.C.

* Morgan (1985), p. 82.

Table 5.2

Pipeline Maintenance and
Operating Expenses, 1983
(diameter under 30 inches)

Pipeline	Length[1] (miles)	Field Lines[2] (miles)	Total Expenses[3]
1. Ala.-Tenn. Nat.Gas	315	1	1,531,407
2. Arkansas-Okla.Gas	380	172	380,300
3. Associated Natural	602	0	231,377
4. Carnegie Natural Gas	257	918	2,130,202
5. Consolidated Sys. LNG	200	0	293,705
6. Eastern Shore Nat. Gas	247	0	600,609
7. Equitable Gas	478	1,637	5,518,513
8. Gas Transport, Inc.	41	68	539,685
9. Granite State Gas Trans.	57	0	141,741
10. Inland Gas	136	394	448,355
11. Kentucky W.Va. Gas	28	2,078	1,238,829
12. Montana-Dakota Utilities	3,096	1,026	13,042,703
13. National Fuel Gas Distr.	923	339	683,772
14. North Penn Gas	571	300	662,546
15. Ringwood Gathering	43	249	78,340
16. Shenandoah Gas	79	0	81,549
17. So. Georgia Natural Gas	767	0	1,831,902
18. Southwest Gas	1,454	6	4,155,335
19. Valero Transmission	273	226	864,709

Table 5.2 (Continued)

Pipeline		Length[1] (miles)	Field Lines[2] (miles)	Total Expenses[3]
20.	Washington Gas Light	353	0	2,059,178
21.	West Texas Gathering	59	68	25,226
22.	Western Gas Interstate	243	53	1,059,762
TOTALS		10,602	7,535	37,599,745

[1] *Source*: DOE/EIA (1984d), Appendix H, "Physical Quantity Statistics, as of December 31," Pipeline Transmission Lines.

[2] *Source*: DOE/EIA (1984d), Appendix H, Pipeline Field plus Storage Lines.

[3] *Source*: DOE/EIA (1984d), Appendix E, "Gas Operations and Maintenance Expenses, December 31."

our best estimate of expected maintenance and operating costs (E).[14]

In addition to covering construction, maintenance, and operating costs, revenues must also meet the corporate tax liability associated with the pipeline hookup. The tax base depends on revenues net of all expenses, including depreciation.[15]   For simplicity, we assume the maximum corporate tax rate of 46 percent for the 1983 tax year.

A high and a low estimate of the revenues required to yield a competitive rate of return on the pipeline hookup can now be computed. Using the best estimates of E = \$0.35 million, tax rate = 46 percent, and I_L = \$0.74 million (with an implicit project life of 30 years), the corresponding required annual revenues (R_L) are \$1.35 million.[16]   On the other hand, the higher cost estimate of I_H = \$0.94 million (with the implicit project life of 20 years) determines a higher estimate (R_H) of \$1.56 million in annual revenues necessary to yield a competitive rate of return on the pipeline investment.

Given the required revenues to construct the hookup (R), the next step is to estimate the expected volume or throughput of the new hookup (V). The expected volume of the hookup will be some percentage of current market sales (Q). If the potential entrant bid to supply one-half of the market, for example, then V = .5Q. Given R and V, the transport fee required to earn a competitive return on the pipeline investment (t^*) can be determined. If $t^* < t^{**}$, the maximum allowable transport fee, the hookup will be profitable.

Alternatively, given R and t^{**}, V^* is the minimum volume in the market that is sufficient to justify construction and operation of a 100-, 120-, or 140-mile pipeline hookup. Potential entry can be considered only in the subset of the 208 markets in our sample where $V > V^*$.

The Maximum Transport Fee (t^{**})

The problem at hand is to identify which of the 208 markets are large enough to permit nearby sellers to enter if the price were to increase by 5 to 10 percent. We therefore want to determine V^*, the minimum volume necessary to earn a competitive return on the hookup.[17]   Markets with a V equal to or greater than V^* will allow suppliers within 140 miles to meet the distance requirement. For V^* to be the profit-maximizing output of the colluding group, however, the current market V must equal $2V^*$. (Appendix C explains why the colluding group will supply one-half the competitive output.) Thus, in small markets, where $V < 2V^*$, nearby suppliers may bid to supply the entire market.[18]   Since $V^* = R/t^{**}$ and since R is known, we now estimate t^{**}.

If nearby suppliers (with sufficient divertible gas) are profit maximizers, they will bid to supply the market if $p > t^*$, where p is the *price increase* of natural gas delivered to the city gate. Even if a colluding group of pipelines control one or more transmission paths into the market, any attempt to exercise monopoly power in transmission will be limited by alternative suppliers of delivered gas. This is because the demand for transportation is derived from the demand for delivered gas. The demand for delivered gas depends on the price of alternative fuels. Hence, the profit-maximizing transport fee equals the price of alternative fuel (e.g., fuel oil) at the point of consumption (or burner tip) minus the price of gas at the wellhead.[19] If the pipeline has monopoly power, however, it could increase the price of delivered gas, which includes the price of the gas purchased at the wellhead.[20] For our sample of markets, the lowest price of delivered gas is \$3.41 in Arkansas markets and the highest price is \$5.87 in North Dakota markets.[21]

Thus, if the colluding group of current suppliers attempts to increase the delivered price of gas by 10 percent, the expected price increase would range from a low of \$0.34 per Mcf in Arkansas markets to a high of \$0.59 per Mcf (thousand cubic feet) in North Dakota markets. Hence, $t^{**} = p^* = \$0.34$, where p^* denotes the smallest increase in the city-gate price in the market sample, represents the highest t that can be charged in the market.[22]

Given $R_H = \$1.56$ million and $t^{**} = \$0.34$, the corresponding V^* is 4.59 Bcf (billion cubic feet) for a 100-mile hookup.[23] Using the same methodology, the V^* associated with a 140-mile hookup is 5.56 Bcf. Since we want to consider whether suppliers within 140 miles of the market constrain the exercise of monopoly power, we use the V^* for a 140-mile pipeline hookup.[24] The sales or current V in each of the largest 148 markets in our original sample of 208 markets equal or exceed 5.56 Bcf. Thus, 60 markets (208 - 148) are too small to consider potential entry.[25] All suppliers within 140 miles of the largest 148 markets, however, meet the distance requirement.[26]

Markets that are large enough to accept a 140-mile pipeline hookup will be called *entry markets*. That is, suppliers within 140 miles of an entry market know that the market is large enough to yield at least a competitive return on the hookup if the market price increases by 5 to 10 percent. However, the nearby supplier must be able to divert sufficient throughput from other markets to feed the new hookup (i.e., meet the size requirement). Thus, without additional information about the size of the nearby supplier, an entry market implies only that the distance requirement is satisfied. Given that the nearby supplier meets the size requirement, however, an entry market implies that both the distance and size requirements have been met. This distinction should be clear in the specific context of the analysis.

One hundred forty-eight of the 208 markets in our original sample are entry markets. It is important to note that although the subset of entry markets accounts for only 71.2 percent of the 208 markets, it represents 98.7 percent (7.5/7.6 Tcf, trillion cubic feet) of the corresponding output. Thus, a finding that most of the entry markets are either competitive or non-competitive is significant because it describes 98.7 percent of total output.

In brief, assuming a 5 to 10 percent price increase in all markets and using the high cost estimates of constructing and operating the longer hookup of 140 miles, we still find that entry is possible in the largest 148 markets. If the actual volume in a market exceeds $2V^*$, the profit-maximizing output of the colluding group would exceed V^*, and a price increase of less than 10 percent would be required to justify the pipeline hookup. For example, if the current market $V = 4V^*$, the colluding group would supply $2V^*$, and only a 5 percent price increased would be necessary to yield a given R. This is the case in the overwhelming majority of the 148 entry markets.

These larger markets are called entry markets because it is profitable for suppliers within 140 miles of any such market to construct a pipeline hookup if the market price is expected to increase by 5 to 10 percent.[27] Furthermore, if these nearby suppliers can also obtain the necessary divertible gas to serve the market, they are potential entrants.

THE SIZE REQUIREMENT

To be a potential entrant in the intermediate run, nearby suppliers must be able to *divert* gas from current customers to the new market within a two-year period. Thus, even if the pipeline operates at full capacity during peak demand periods, it can still substitute service among customers.[28] We consider two sources of divertible gas: supply contract expirations and interruptible service contracts.

Contract Expirations

Although 20-year contracts between the pipeline and its major customers were once the industry standard, the length of these supply contracts has declined dramatically over the last 25 years. Perhaps more importantly, the remaining life of these contracts (i.e., the difference between the expiration date and today's date) is even shorter.

We analyzed a large sample of supply contracts originally reviewed by EIA.[29] Four pieces of information from each EIA contract summary form were entered into a computer file: (1) date of contract, (2) effective (starting) date of contract, (3) expiration date of contract, and (4) type of sale. Table 5.3 summarizes the data on contract length and remaining life for the 1,247 contracts in our sample.[30]

The EIA data show that the actual length of all three types of contracts has been steadily declining since 1963. The widespread belief that actual contract length is about 20 years is empirically supported only in the pre-1968 periods (Table 5.3, Age Categories V and VI); it has no empirical basis after 1968. In fact, the actual length of most of the recent (Age Category I) contracts is less than ten years.[31]

Since our concern is with the ability of the pipeline to divert gas from current to new customers, however, the data on remaining contract life are more relevant. What matters is the *remaining* obligation to deliver gas under current contracts, not the actual length of the contract. For example, if a pipeline must deliver to a customer for one more year on a 20-year contract, this gas is divertible after one year. The fact that the contract was negotiated 19 years ago provides little or no useful information. Accordingly, the remaining life of the same EIA sample of contracts was computed and reported in Table 5.3. The average remaining life on 1983 sales-for-resale contracts, which include the sales to LDCs, is 5.6 years.[32]

The average remaining contract length is misleading, however, because it includes long-term contracts that are not being renewed. Since contract length has steadily declined over the last 20 years, 20-year contracts are being replaced by substantially shorter term contracts. This evidence suggests that contracts with a remaining life greater than the average remaining life are not being renewed. For resale contracts in Age Category I, only six contracts have a remaining life greater than five years. If all 186 Category I contracts are combined, the maximum remaining life is five years (with the exception of the same six contracts). In addition, a recent study by Broadman (1986, p. 122) finds that actual contract length has declined from 15-20 years to 1-5 years. Thus, the maximum actual contract length (and the maximum remaining contract length) in recent contracts is no more than five years. This evidence suggests that the steadily declining trend in contract length found in Table 5.3 can be extended to the present. Given Broadman's finding and the five-year maximum remaining contract life on most Age Category I contracts, we use five years as our best estimate of the maximum contract life on standard contracts negotiated after 1983.

Assuming that all existing standard contracts have a maximum remaining life of five years and all new standard contracts have an actual life of five years or less,[33] at least one-fifth, or 20 percent, of each pipeline's delivery obligations expire annually. Given that the intermediate run is defined as a two-year period, we estimate that contract expirations in the intermediate run enable pipelines to divert 40 percent of their annual sales to new markets.

Table 5.3

Length of Representative Contracts
(in years)

Age Category[1]		Actual Length[2]			Remaining Length[3]		
		Resale	*Indus.*	*Trans.*	*Resale*	*Indus.*	*Trans.*
I.	(1/1/83 - 12/31/83)	9.57 (33)	4.30 (6)	0.97 (147)	5.57	0.45	0.21
II.	(1/1/78 - 12/31/82)	10.42 (280)	4.88 (68)	5.91 (167)	4.45	1.10	1.87
III.	(1/1/73 - 12/31/77)	11.83 (50)	3.60 (28)	14.81 (30)	1.09	0.02	3.79
IV.	(1/1/68) - 12/31/72)	16.92 (231)	10.10 (24)	17.66 (15)	1.86	0.26	2.90
V.	(1/1/63 - 12/31/67)	19.08 (48)	12.83 (51)	23.86 (4)	0.34	0.28	1.70
VI.	(before 1/1/63)	18.93 (22)	19.85 (40)	18.47 (3)	0.00	0.07	0.00

Note: The number in parenthesis is the number of observations used in each calculation. Actual and Remaining Lengths are computed on the same sample.

[1] Based on effective date or starting date of the contract.

[2] *Actual Length* is the difference between the expiration date and the effective date of the contract.

[3] *Remaining Length* is the difference between the expiration date and July 1, 1987.

Interruptible Deliveries

Some customers, usually with sources of alternative fuel, negotiate lower gas prices in exchange for interruptible service. Evidence that interruptible customers are consistently served during peak periods suggests that absent regulation, current holders of firm service rights, or entitlements, would reduce their commitments for firm service. If markets are deregulated, however, capacity brokering, as well as capacity releasing, would be possible. Customers attempting to avoid a price increase by their current suppliers could simply outbid lower-valued-firm customers currently served by nearby pipelines. Interruptible sales at peak are therefore used as one indication of a pipeline's ability to obtain gas supplies to enter new markets.[34]

Peak interruptible sales can be estimated from the FERC Form 2 in two ways. One approach is to compute the percentage of *peak day deliveries to interruptible customers* to *total peak day deliveries* from aggregated peak day data.[35] Use of the peak day data assumes that industrial users always contract for interruptible service and residential users do the opposite. Consequently, if some industrial users negotiate firm service, interruptible deliveries will be overestimated. On the other hand, if some LDCs contract for supplemental interruptible service, interruptible service is under-estimated. Given that these biases are in opposite directions, the estimate is expected to be a reasonable approximation. Since peak day deliveries in any one year may vary due to random events, the percentage of interruptibles is computed for the highest peak day deliveries in 1982, 1983, and 1984. The weighted average is 13.14 percent.

Another method of estimating peak day interruptible deliveries is to tabulate the disaggregated peak day transactions reported on two FERC schedules: Sales for Resale, and Main Line and Industrial Sales.[36] Dividing total peak day interruptibles by total peak day deliveries (for both residential and industrial users) produces an alternative estimate. The weighted average peak day interruptibles for 1982, 1983, and 1984 is 9.54 percent of total peak day deliveries. This estimate is biased downward because peak day interruptibles are not always reported. Nevertheless, to avoid overestimating divertible gas and underestimating the HHI, the lower estimate of interruptibles is used. For computational purposes, we round to the nearest whole percentage point or 10 percent.

To summarize, divertible gas in the intermediate run is estimated at 50 percent of annual deliveries. Eighty percent of divertible gas is due to contract expirations, and the remaining 20 percent is due to interruptible service contracts. A nearby pipeline satisfies the size requirement if its total divertible gas equals or exceeds the minimum output necessary to threaten a group of colluding suppliers. If a nearby supplier meets both the distance and the size requirements, the supplier is a potential entrant.

POTENTIAL ENTRANTS

The Linear Demand Case

All the nearby suppliers to each of the 148 entry markets in our sample were examined to determine whether they met the distance and size requirements. Appendix E lists all nearby pipeline suppliers. In addition, underground storage facilities that owned and operated pipelines were also considered.

As already explained, nearby suppliers can construct a 140-mile pipeline hookup into a market if the expected price is 5 to 10 percent above the current price. Whether suppliers within 140 miles of the market are potential entrants will therefore depend on their ability to obtain the necessary throughput for the new hookup. We estimate that over a two-year period, nearby suppliers can generate a volume of divertible gas equal to 50 percent of annual deliveries.

Next, the entry markets for each potential entrant must be identified. Each supplier starts with a divertible gas account equal to 50 percent of its annual deliveries. If 50 percent of the current market output is necessary to threaten the colluding group of current suppliers,[37] a nearby pipeline can enter any market if its divertible gas is equal to or greater than 50 percent of the market output.[38]

One concern of the potential entrant, however, is that his bids to supply a market always remain credible. That is, the LDC or customer will expect that if the pipeline is awarded a supply contract, the pipeline will be able to meet its contractual obligations. This may require the pipeline to construct a hookup as long as 140 miles and to obtain the required divertible gas within a two-year period. A potential entrant who fails to deliver on a contract will lose credibility, and all subsequent bids in any market will be severely discounted or ignored.[39] As a result, the potential entrant must determine the number of markets that it can enter simultaneously.

To illustrate the dilemma facing a potential entrant in two or more markets, consider a pipeline with the following characteristics: (a) located within 140 miles of 11 markets, (b) a potential entrant in ten equal-sized markets, and (c) able to generate sufficient divertible gas to enter two markets simultaneously. If the probability of submitting a winning bid is 10 percent, the pipeline expects to win one out of every ten bids and is capable of supplying two of the ten markets. Hence, the potential entrant could bid in all ten entry markets. If, on the other hand, the win ratio increases to 33 percent, the pipeline expects to win three out of ten bids. Consequently, the pipeline must reduce its bids to six markets since he can only supply two [i.e., $(.33)(6) = 2$]. Otherwise, the pipeline is likely to overbid: three of the ten bids are likely to be accepted but only two markets can be supplied. The eleventh market is irrelevant since the pipeline is not a potential entrant in that market.

To generalize the entry response of the potential entrant, we define the potential entry ratio (ER) as the subset of potential entry (PE) markets that can be entered *simultaneously* (s) to the total number of PE markets (n), entered one at a time. Given the probability of submitting a winning bid or the win ratio (WR), the potential entrant will bid in all PE markets if, and only if, ER is equal to or greater than WR.[40] If WR exceeds ER, the potential entrant is assumed to enter the subset of markets that can be entered simultaneously.[41]

Operationally, we initially compute the ER for each potential entrant. On a market-by-market basis, we then begin counting the number of potential entrants or bidders in each of our 148 entry markets.[42] As each potential entrant is included in a market, any related subsidiary or parent pipeline that is also a potential entrant in the same market is excluded. Thus, we are careful to include only one "family member" in each market.

The win ratio (WR) is based on the total number of markets relative to the total number of bids[43] in each region. Since all potential entrants own and operate pipelines, we assume that given two years to plan the project, the costs of constructing and operating a 140-mile hookup between existing trunk lines and the new market are roughly the same for all potential entrants in any given region. Thus, if there are 100 bids in a region that includes 20 markets, the WR is .20 (= 20/100). Our best estimate of the WR for all 148 markets is 20.53 percent, with a low of 9.06 percent and a high of 40.00 percent. Table 5.4 reports the WRs by census region. Since there may be significant transaction costs associated with overbidding, bidders are assumed to adjust the average WR to reduce the probability of such an outcome. We therefore use the average WR (20.53 percent) plus two standard deviations (18.10 percent) to determine a cost-adjusted WR of 38.63 percent.[44] Thus, there is only a 5 percent chance that a potential entrant will overbid. For computational purposes, we use a WR of 40 percent.[45]

Increasing the WR tends to reduce the number of bidders[46] and to increase the market concentration ratio. Pipelines with an ER > WR are assumed to bid in all of their PE markets. In contrast, pipelines with an ER < WR are assumed to only bid in the subset of PE markets that they can enter simultaneously. For example, given WR = .30, a pipeline with ten PE markets will bid in all ten markets if, and only if, his ER is greater than or equal to .30. If s = 3 and ER = .30 (= 3/10), the pipeline will bid in all ten markets. If ER < WR, however, the pipeline is assumed to bid only in the three markets that can be entered simultaneously. In our example, an increase in WR from .30 to .40 will, therefore, reduce the number of bids from ten to three. Consequently, market concentration will tend to increase

Table 5.4

Win Ratios by Census Region

	Census Region	Number of Markets	Win Ratio *(percent)*
1.	New England	10	18.87
2.	Mid-Atlantic	17	24.29
3.	East North Central	23	15.13
4.	West North Central	19	17.92
5.	South Atlantic	23	26.44
6.	East South Central	15	13.04
7.	West South Central	25	9.06
8.	Mountain	12	20.00
9.	Pacific	4	40.00
	Totals	**148**	**20.53**

with increases in WR. A decrease in ER can be interpreted similarly.

The competitive effect of potential entry in reducing the market power of current suppliers is suggested by the HHI adjusted for potential entry. Without allowing for potential entry (i.e., in the short run), the HHI exceeds 2500 in each of the original 208 markets (see Table 4.2). Thus, the HHI must also exceed 2500 in the largest 148 markets in which entry is feasible. The HHI for each of these 148 entry markets is therefore computed for potential entrants located within 100 miles, 120 miles, and 140 miles of each market.[47] The corresponding HHI distributions are reported in Tables 5.5, 5.6, and 5.7. The three principal findings in the intermediate run are the following:

1. If potential entrants within 100 miles of the market are recognized (Table 5.5), the HHI falls below 2500 in 81 percent of the entry markets (120/148). Thus, over 80 percent of those entry markets that represented a potential anticompetitive concern based on a short-run analysis appear to be competitive in the intermediate run.
2. Furthermore, since suppliers within 120 miles of the market are also potential entrants, the number of entry markets below the HHI threshold of 2500 is more correctly estimated at 127, or 86 percent (Table 5.6).
3. Since the number of competitive markets increases only by two as the maximum hookup length is expanded from 121 miles to 140 miles,[48] potential entrants located more than 120 miles from the market do not appear to exert a substantial influence in the market in the intermediate run.[49]

We consider these findings to be quite reliable because they are relatively insensitive to large changes in our four major assumptions. More specifically:

a. If the remaining life of supply contracts is increased from five to ten years, the number of entry markets with a HHI < 2500 falls by 11;[50]
b. If there were no interruptible service contracts, the HHI distribution in Table 5.7 does not significantly change;
c. If potential entrants expect their chances of winning a bid (WR) to increase or decrease by 50 percent, the number of competitive markets changes only by four;[51] and
d. A reduction in the length of the hookup from 140 miles to 100 miles (or 28.57 percent) reduces the number of entry markets below HHI = 2500 by nine (or 7 percent).[52]

These results do not include imports of liquified natural gas (LNG). In 1983, only four MSAs received imported natural gas deliveries.[53] Although the volume of imports into New York and Los Angeles is insignificant, the possibility of receiving additional imports at these locations serves as another source of potential competition. Small current deliveries may

Table 5.5

HHI Distribution by Census Regions (≤100 miles)
Linear Demand
Divertible Gas: 50% and Win Ratio: .40

from: to:	0- 1800	1801- 2500	2501- 2999	3000- 3999	4000- 4999	5000- 5999	6000- 6999	7000- 7999	8000- 8999	9000- 9999	10000	TOTAL
New England	3	5	0	1	0	1	0	0	0	0	0	10
Mid-Atlantic	15	2	0	0	0	0	0	0	0	0	0	17
East North Central	20	2	0	1	0	0	0	0	0	0	0	23
West North Central	9	4	0	5	0	1	0	0	0	0	0	19
South Atlantic	8	2	0	5	0	3	0	0	0	0	5	23
East South Central	15	0	0	0	0	0	0	0	0	0	0	15
West South Central	24	1	0	0	0	0	0	0	0	0	0	25
Mountain	3	6	0	0	0	2	0	0	0	0	1	12
Pacific	0	1	0	0	0	3	0	0	0	0	0	4
TOTAL	97	23	0	12	0	10	0	0	0	0	6	148

Table 5.6

HHI Distribution by Census Regions (≤120 miles)
Linear Demand
Divertible Gas: 50% and Win Ratio: .40

from: to:	0-1800	1801-2500	2501-2999	3000-3999	4000-4999	5000-5999	6000-6999	7000-7999	8000-8999	9000-9999	9000-10000	TOTAL
New England	5	5	0	0	0	0	0	0	0	0	0	10
Mid-Atlantic	11	6	0	0	0	0	0	0	0	0	0	17
East North Central	22	0	0	1	0	0	0	0	0	0	0	23
West North Central	9	6	0	3	0	1	0	0	0	0	0	19
South Atlantic	8	4	0	3	0	4	0	0	0	0	4	23
East South Central	15	0	0	0	0	0	0	0	0	0	0	15
West South Central	24	1	0	0	0	0	0	0	0	0	0	25
Mountain	4	6	0	1	0	1	0	0	0	0	1	12
Pacific	0	1	0	1	0	2	0	0	0	0	0	4
TOTAL	98	29	0	8	0	8	0	0	0	0	5	148

Table 5.7

HHI Distribution by Census Regions (≤140 miles)
Linear Demand
Divertible Gas: 50% and Win Ratio: .40

from: to:	0- 1800	1801- 2500	2501- 2999	3000- 3999	4000- 4999	5000- 5999	6000- 6999	7000- 7999	8000- 8999	9000- 9999	10000	TOTAL
New England	5	5	0	0	0	0	0	0	0	0	0	10
Mid-Atlantic	13	4	0	0	0	0	0	0	0	0	0	17
East North Central	22	0	0	1	0	0	0	0	0	0	0	23
West North Central	10	6	0	3	0	0	0	0	0	0	0	19
South Atlantic	10	3	0	4	0	4	0	0	0	0	2	23
East South Central	15	0	0	0	0	0	0	0	0	0	0	15
West South Central	25	0	0	0	0	0	0	0	0	0	0	25
Mountain	6	4	0	1	0	1	0	0	0	0	1	12
Pacific	0	1	0	1	0	2	0	0	0	0	0	4
TOTAL	106	23	0	9	0	7	0	0	0	0	3	148

therefore affect the pricing decisions of interstate pipelines, especially in a deregulated environment.[54] The decline in gas prices since 1983, however, makes LNG imports relatively costly sources of supply. The reliance on LNG suppliers in the future is therefore uncertain.

The Constant Elasticity Case

If the colluding group of current suppliers is subject to a constant elasticity demand curve instead of a linear demand curve, a larger percentage of current market output[55] is necessary to gain admission into the colluding group. As explained in Appendix C, 65 percent of current output is required to enter the colluding group. With the larger size requirement, some potential entrants in the linear demand case may be too small to pose a threat to a colluding group. As the number of bidders in the market declines, the possibility of anticompetitive behavior may increase.

The HHI for each of the 148 entry markets is therefore recomputed using the larger size requirement. Table 5.8 shows the HHI distribution for potential entrants within 140 miles of the market. The number of entry markets with a HHI < 2500 decline by only two percent (from 129 to 126 markets) relative to the corresponding HHI distribution in Table 5.7, the linear demand case.[56]

The constant elasticity case therefore adds little to our analysis. Furthermore, for WR > ER, the number of bidders in the market is grossly underestimated regardless of the demand elasticity.[57] The slightly higher number of competitive markets in the linear demand case tends to partially offset the substantial downward bias in the ER. For both reasons, we consider only the linear demand case in the remainder of this study.

CONCLUSION

Our analysis suggests that potential entry is an important restraint on the exercise of market power in the largest 148 markets. That is, a number of nearby suppliers could construct and operate a 140-mile hookup (within a two-year period) in response to a 5 to 10 percent price increase by collusive incumbent firms. In addition, most of these suppliers could generate sufficient divertible gas to feed their new hookup in the intermediate run and earn at least a competitive return on their investment.

Any one of these potential entrants is large enough to offset the profit-maximizing output reduction by the colluding group of current suppliers.[58] If the colluding group is expanded to include such potential entrants, the group is likely to become so large that it will be unable to maintain a

Table 5.8

HHI Distribution by Census Regions (≤140 miles)
Constant Demand Elasticity
Divertible Gas: 50% and Win Ratio: .40

from: to:	0- 1800	1801- 2500	2501- 2999	3000- 3999	4000- 4999	5000- 5999	6000- 6999	7000- 7999	8000- 8999	9000- 9999	10000	TOTAL
New England	4	6	0	0	0	0	0	0	0	0	0	10
Mid-Atlantic	12	4	0	0	0	1	0	0	0	0	0	17
East North Central	22	0	0	1	0	0	0	0	0	0	0	23
West North Central	10	6	0	3	0	0	0	0	0	0	0	19
South Atlantic	9	3	0	5	0	4	0	0	0	0	2	23
East South Central	15	0	0	0	0	0	0	0	0	0	0	15
West South Central	24	1	0	0	0	0	0	0	0	0	0	25
Mountain	6	4	0	0	0	1	0	0	0	0	1	12
Pacific	0	0	0	2	0	2	0	0	0	0	0	4
TOTAL	102	24	0	11	0	8	0	0	0	0	3	148

collusive price 5 to 10 percent above cost and capture the corresponding monopoly profits over a two-year period. The size of the group will be so large that individual colluding members will have an incentive to cheat on the collusive price by offering a lower contract price in an attempt to win a contract to serve a substantial portion of the market. Competition in these markets is expected to be even stronger in the long run, since all suppliers within 140 miles of the market are potential entrants in the long run.

The analysis assumes, however, that price and entry regulation is suspended. A major restraint on potential entry in the intermediate run may take the form of regulatory approvals (and operating permits) to enter and exit[59] markets. Despite this qualification, Section 311 of the Natural Gas Policy Act (NGPA) of 1978 and Part 284 of FERC's regulations may provide an opportunity to substantially reduce the regulatory requirements to construct a pipeline hookup. On June 30, 1988, for example, Transco requested FERC approval to establish initial rates for transportation service on its newly constructed 124-mile Mobile Bay pipeline system. Transco completed construction without additional FERC approval, citing Section 311 and Part 284 as sufficient authority for construction.[60] Although Transco was fined for failing to satisfy environmental requirements, it provides evidence of how Section 311 can promote entry. According to INGAA (1988), 56 percent of gas delivered to market in 1987 moved under the authority of NGPA Section 311 or Orders 436/500.

In any event, if the regulatory approval process can be completed within two years, there is reason to believe that partial price deregulation in the natural gas pipeline industry will not result in monopoly pricing in the vast majority of entry markets. Deregulation of these 148 entry markets would deregulate 98.7 percent of the total output of our original sample of 208 markets.[61]

THE LONG RUN

COMPETITION IN THE LONG RUN

In the intermediate run, only those nearby suppliers who can meet two conditions within a two-year period are potential entrants and therefore members of the colluding group. A nearby supplier must be able to (1) construct a pipeline hookup into the new market (i.e., meet the distance requirement) and (2) divert sufficient gas into the new market to undercut the colluding group if denied admission (i.e., meet the size requirement). Nearby suppliers who fail to meet either one of the above conditions are excluded from the colluding group.

In the long run, however, all nearby suppliers who meet the distance requirement are potential entrants. The inability of some suppliers to meet the size requirement in the intermediate run does not exist in the long run. Existing contracts can be renegotiated or allowed to expire. If necessary, trunk-line capacity can be increased. Thus, pipelines are assumed to have sufficient divertible throughput to service new entry markets or new customers in the long run. Similarly, storage operations, intrastate suppliers, and foreign suppliers can also expand service to accommodate any shortages in peak demand periods.

Potential entrants are assumed to bid for supply contracts before building a pipeline hookup into a new market or acquiring an existing hookup.[1] The competitive issue, therefore, is whether *rival bidders* can successfully collude to raise the contract price over cost and share in the excess profits. From an economic perspective, potential entrants are therefore more correctly viewed as potential bidders.

Competition in natural gas delivery markets takes place in the bidding market for gas service. LDCs, for example, can solicit bids in the *present* to provide service in the *future*. Any nearby pipeline interested in the customer and/or market area is free to submit a bid, including a plan to expand service to the LDC if its bid is accepted. Thus, a pipeline does not have to currently serve the market in order to bid for future business.

If the bidding market is highly competitive, the resulting supply contracts are also competitive.[2] The observation that only one pipeline (the winning bidder) currently serves a market is therefore no indication of substantial market power (or monopoly profits). What matters is whether the current supplier was "forced" by rivals to offer a competitive supply contract (i.e., at a price equal to cost).[3]

Analogous to the intermediate run, each potential entrant (bidder) expects to share equally in the collusive profits. Consequently, the greater the number of bidders, the lower the expected profit per bidder, and the greater the incentive to cheat on a collusive bid. The ability of the bidding cartel to control its members is measured by the HHI. The lower the HHI, the less likely that the cartel will be able to prevent recalcitrant members from undercutting the cartel price and expanding output.[4]

EMPIRICAL FINDINGS

Nearby suppliers who failed to meet the size requirement in the intermediate run must be admitted into the colluding group in the long run. Although these suppliers need more than two years to divert sufficient gas into the market to undercut the cartel if excluded, the additional time is implicit in the long run. Hence, all nearby suppliers are potential entrants in the long run. A complete listing of all nearby *pipeline* suppliers in each market (MSA) is provided in Appendix E. In addition, underground storage operators that are not owned by nearby pipelines also represent potential entrants into markets within 100, 120, and 140 miles.[5] These underground storage operators are included in our analysis.

Revised HHI distributions were computed assuming that all current and nearby suppliers are admitted into the colluding group. Although the long run provides sufficient time to construct a hookup of any length, such a hookup may not be cost-justified. That is, the expected profitability of the hookup does not significantly increase with the time allowed for its construction. A more important determinant of the rate of return on the hookup is the (expected) delivered price of natural gas. Consequently, if a hookup is expected to be unprofitable in the short run (i.e., given the current market price and given the supplier's current expectation of future prices), it is expected to remain unprofitable in the long run.[6] We therefore continue to consider 100-, 120-, and 140-mile hookups--even in the long run.

The principal finding is that in an overwhelming majority of the 148 entry markets,[7] there is a significant potential for competition. The number of potential bidders (entrants) within 100 miles of each market is so large that the HHI falls to 2500, or below in 89 percent (130/148) of these markets. The HHI distribution is shown in Table 6.1. Furthermore, this finding does not vary significantly with respect to the distance from the market. At the 120- and 140-mile distances, about 92 percent (136/148) of all entry markets show a HHI of 2500 or less. See Tables 6.2 and 6.3.

Thus, a colluding group of all bidders[8] within 100 miles of the market is so large that it is not likely to prevent price cutting by some members. The likelihood of successful "bid rigging" among such large suppliers is extremely remote.[9] On this basis, we conclude that the elimination of price and entry regulations is unlikely to promote monopoly pricing in *most* entry markets.

A stronger conclusion that deregulation is appropriate in *all* entry markets is justified only if the potential welfare loss from monopoly pricing in the highly concentrated markets (i.e., the benefit of regulation) is significantly less than the direct cost of regulating all markets.[10] We therefore attempt to estimate the potential net welfare loss in each entry market if deregulated. The sum of these potential losses is then compared to the direct cost savings from deregulation.[11] If the aggregate potential losses in the highly concentrated entry markets are less than the combined annual direct savings in current expenditures on gas pipeline regulation by (a) the public sector (i.e., FERC) and (b) the private sector (i.e., FERC-regulated pipelines), we can conclude that deregulation on the federal level is appropriate in all 148 entry markets. That is, if federal regulation merely serves to reduce the possibility of monopoly pricing in entry markets located in one or two states, the public and private costs of federal pipeline regulation in all entry markets across the United States may not be socially warranted.

The first step is to identify those entry markets with high concentration.

ENTRY MARKETS WITH HHI > 2500

Florida Entry Markets

Although the HHI typically falls below 2500 when potential entrants within 100 miles of the market are considered, the HHI remains extremely high in a few markets. Table 6.1 shows that six entry markets are served by a single supplier.[12] Five of the six markets are in the South Atlantic census region. The South Atlantic region also shows relatively high concentration

Table 6.1

HHI Distribution by Census Regions (≤100 miles)
(based on number of bidders)

from: to:	0-1800	1801-2500	2501-2999	3000-3999	4000-4999	5000-5999	6000-6999	7000-7999	8000-8999	9000-9999	10000	TOTAL
New England	9	0	0	1	0	0	0	0	0	0	0	10
Mid-Atlantic	17	0	0	0	0	0	0	0	0	0	0	17
East North Central	22	0	0	1	0	0	0	0	0	0	0	23
West North Central	11	4	0	3	0	1	0	0	0	0	0	19
South Atlantic	10	6	0	0	0	2	0	0	0	0	5	23
East South Central	15	0	0	0	0	0	0	0	0	0	0	15
West South Central	25	0	0	0	0	0	0	0	0	0	0	25
Mountain	6	3	0	2	0	0	0	0	0	0	1	12
Pacific	0	2	0	2	0	0	0	0	0	0	0	4
TOTAL	115	15	0	9	0	3	0	0	0	0	6	148

Table 6.2

HHI Distribution by Census Regions (≤120 miles)
(based on number of bidders)

from: to:	0- 1800	1801- 2500	2501- 2999	3000- 3999	4000- 4999	5000- 5999	6000- 6999	7000- 7999	8000- 8999	9000- 9999	10000	TOTAL
New England	10	0	0	0	0	0	0	0	0	0	0	10
Mid-Atlantic	17	0	0	0	0	0	0	0	0	0	0	17
East North Central	22	0	0	1	0	0	0	0	0	0	0	23
West North Central	12	4	0	2	0	1	0	0	0	0	0	19
South Atlantic	12	4	0	0	0	3	0	0	0	0	4	23
East South Central	15	0	0	0	0	0	0	0	0	0	0	15
West South Central	25	0	0	0	0	0	0	0	0	0	0	25
Mountain	7	4	0	0	0	0	0	0	0	0	1	12
Pacific	0	3	0	1	0	0	0	0	0	0	0	4
TOTAL	120	15	0	4	0	4	0	0	0	0	5	148

Table 6.3

HHI Distribution by Census Regions (≤140 miles)
(based on number of bidders)

from: to:	0- 1800	1801- 2500	2501- 2999	3000- 3999	4000- 4999	5000- 5999	6000- 6999	7000- 7999	8000- 8999	9000- 9999	10000	TOTAL
New England	10	0	0	0	0	0	0	0	0	0	0	10
Mid-Atlantic	17	0	0	0	0	0	0	0	0	0	0	17
East North Central	22	0	0	1	0	0	0	0	0	0	0	23
West North Central	13	5	0	1	0	0	0	0	0	0	0	19
South Atlantic	13	3	0	1	0	4	0	0	0	0	2	23
East South Central	15	0	0	0	0	0	0	0	0	0	0	15
West South Central	25	0	0	0	0	0	0	0	0	0	0	25
Mountain	7	4	0	0	0	0	0	0	0	0	1	12
Pacific	0	3	0	1	0	0	0	0	0	0	0	4
TOTAL	122	15	0	4	0	4	0	0	0	0	3	148

in two additional markets (i.e., a HHI of 5000 or more). Thus, 39 percent of the markets (7/18) with a HHI over 2500 are in the South Atlantic. Table 6.4 lists those markets in the South Atlantic with only one or two current and nearby suppliers (within 100 miles of each market). All seven of these markets are located in Florida. Considering all five consuming sectors (i.e., residential, commercial, industrial, transportation, and public utilities),[13] Florida accounts for 1.82 percent of total consumption in the U.S.[14] If we consider only those sectors that are unable to switch to alternative fuels and therefore most subject to monopoly pricing (i.e., residential and commercial users with lower demand elasticities), only 0.65 percent of total U.S. residential and commercial consumption is affected.[15] Thus, consumption of natural gas in Florida is minimal relative to total U.S. consumption. If the price elasticity of demand is low, we would not expect the social costs of a price 5 to 10 percent above cost to be substantial.[16,17]

Non-Florida Entry Markets

Unlike the Florida markets, the remaining 11 entry markets with a HHI over 2500 show no definite pattern. As shown in Table 6.5, these markets are geographically distributed over five census regions. The MSA-specific sales in each market are also reported in Table 6.5.

Whereas some suppliers cannot meet the size requirement in the intermediate run, all gas is divertible in the long run. In the long run, therefore, all nearby suppliers have sufficient divertible gas. On this basis, we consider all suppliers within 140 miles of an entry market to be potential entrants in the long run.

If suppliers within 140 miles of the market are considered potential entrants, the HHI falls to 2500 or below in all entry markets except four. In all four markets, there are no potential suppliers within 101 to 140 miles. Consequently, the HHI does not change. The four markets are identified in Table 6.5 with an asterisk (*).

Potential Welfare Losses

The same methodology utilized to determine relevant, antitrust markets allows us to estimate the potential social loss of a price increase 5 to 10 percent above cost. The basic specifications of the model are the following:

1. analysis is confined to natural gas delivered to a LDC, municipality, or industrial user;

Table 6.4

South Atlantic Markets with HHIs Over 2500
(South Atlantic census region)

Entry Market	HHI	Sales (Mcf)	Price per Mcf[*] (1983)	(1986)
1. Gainesville	5000	11,758,519	3.43	2.65
2. Jacksonville	5000	14,067,369	3.43	2.65
3. Lakeland-Winter Haven	10000	17,595,821	3.43	2.65
4. Miami-Hialeah	10000	14,990,044	3.43	2.65
5. Orlando	10000	26,201,254	3.43	2.65
6. Tampa	10000	15,593,375	3.43	2.65
7. West Palm Beach	10000	5,848,108	3.43	2.65
Total		106,054,490		

Note: Table includes suppliers within 100 miles; there are no additional supplies between 101 and 140 miles (except for West Palm Beach, which has a HHI of 3333 at 140 miles).

[*] *Source:* DOE/EIA (1985b), Table 21: "Volume and Average Price of Gas Purchased from Interstate Pipelines, Intrastate Pipelines, and/or Distributors, by Type of Purchase, 1983"; EIA/DOE (1987), Table 27: "Average City Gate Price by State."

2. supply is infinitely elastic in the relevant range;[18]
3. market demand is linear with a finite elasticity; and
4. the current suppliers in the market produce the competitive level of output.

The model is presented graphically in Figure 6.1. The intersection of the market demand curve (DD) and the market supply curve (P_1S) at point E determines the competitive price (P_1) and output (Q_1). Real resources are efficiently allocated in the natural gas market because the value of these resources in their current use (implicit in the vertical distance between any given output and the corresponding point on the *demand curve*) equals their opportunity cost or value in their next best alternative use (implicit in the vertical distance between any given output and the corresponding point on the *supply curve*). That is, at output Q_1, the marginal social benefit of all inputs employed in the delivery of natural gas just equal their marginal social costs, Q_1E.

The evaluation of the consequences of a price increase above cost generally considers two welfare effects.[19] These effects and their corresponding areas in Figure 6.1 are

1. the redistribution effect (area b), and
2. the net welfare loss (area c).

The measure of consumer welfare (i.e., consumer surplus) is the area under the demand curve (DD) and above price. At P_1, consumer surplus equals areas a + b + c. A price increase from P_1 to P_2 reduces consumer welfare by areas b + c.

The loss to consumers, however, does not all represent a net welfare loss (or loss to the economy) because part of the loss to consumers is offset by gains to suppliers. The gain to suppliers is measured by the increase in producer surplus (i.e., the increase in the area over the supply curve, P_1S, and below the price). The increase in price to P_2 therefore increases producer surplus by area b.

Hence, the price increase will result in a net welfare loss equal to area c [= (b + c) - b]. Area c is often referred to as the net welfare loss because it measures the net loss to the economy due to the reduction in consumption.

The net welfare loss is estimated as follows: Using Figure 6.1, we see that area c equals $[(P_2 - P_1) (Q_1 - Q_2) (1/2)]$.[20] If the colluding group is expected to raise price by 5 percent above cost, $(P_2 - P_1) = .05P_1$. Assuming a market demand price elasticity of 1.0, $(Q_1 - Q_2) = .05Q_1$.[21] The net welfare loss therefore equals c = $(.05P_1)(.05Q_1)(.5)$.

Given P_1 and Q_1, area c can be determined for each market. Since 1983 is our sample year, we use the 1983 price of natural gas purchased from

Table 6.5

Non-Florida Markets with HHIs over 2500

Entry Market	HHI	Census Region[+]	Sales (Mcf)	Price per Mcf[++] (1983)	(1986)
1. N. Bedford-Fall River-Attleboro, MA	3333	New England	18,057,330	4.48	3.59
*2. Wausau, WI	3333	East N Cen	13,326,593	4.48	3.85
3. Des Moines, IA	3333	West N Cen	29,554,920	4.11	3.30
*4. Duluth, MN-WI	3333	West N Cen	12,868,473	4.17	3.31
5. Sioux City, (IA-NE)	3333	West N Cen	9,823,222	4.11	3.30
6. Sioux Falls, SD	5000	West N Cen	7,385,285	4.27	3.61
*7. Boise City, ID	10000	Mountain	21,947,620	4.52	3.18

Table 6.5 (Continued)

Entry Market	HHI	Census Region[+]	Sales (Mcf)	Price per Mcf[++] (1983)	(1986)
8. Las Cruces, NM	3333	Mountain	5,785,730	3.90	2.83
9. Reno, NV	3333	Mountain	6,749,761	5.72	3.19
*10. Medford, OR	3333	Pacific	5,567,637	4.12	3.13
11. Van-couver, WA	3333	Pacific	7,620,274	4.18	3.15
Total			136,686,845		

Note: Table includes suppliers within 100 miles.

* HHI over 2500 including suppliers, if any, within 140 miles.

[+] N Cen = North Central

[++] *Source:* See Table 6.4.

Figure 6.1

The Welfare Effects of Raising Price 5 to 10 Percent Above Cost

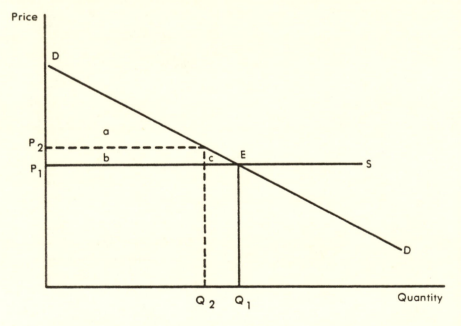

interstate and intrastate pipelines. The prices for Florida and non-Florida markets are shown in Tables 6.4 and 6.5, respectively.[22] The 1986 prices are also reported to show that although our sample year is nine calendar years from the present, prices have tended to decline since 1983. Using the current lower prices would therefore result in lower net welfare losses.[23]

The potential welfare losses are shown in Table 6.6. For a 10 percent increase in price, the largest potential welfare loss in all entry markets is $4.8 million per year.[24] The individual losses are shown in column 2. This estimate, however, excludes suppliers between 101 and 140 miles of the market. If we include those more distant suppliers, the total welfare loss falls to $3.0 million due mainly to a reduction in welfare losses in non-Florida markets from $3.0 million to $1.2 million (as shown by comparing columns 2 and 4). We believe that suppliers within 140 miles of the market must be included[25] and therefore the $3.0 million estimate is more appropriate.

Given the estimated welfare losses from monopoly pricing, the next step is to compare these losses with the corresponding direct benefits of deregulation. These benefits take the form of regulation costs that will no longer be incurred (i.e., direct cost savings). The costs of *regulation* are therefore the benefits of *deregulation*. Let us consider the costs of regulation.

Real resources employed in regulation represent a cost to society. The opportunity cost of these resources (i.e., the value in their highest alternative use) can be approximated by the expenditures required to keep them in their current use (i.e., regulation of natural gas pipelines). Thus, if markets are deregulated, both public and private expenditures on pipeline regulation could be saved. This cost savings represents a potential social benefit of deregulation.

Perhaps more importantly, if the regulated prices of natural gas are not the same prices that would be determined in an unregulated environment, the resulting price distortions also represent a social cost of regulation. If the regulated price in a market is too high, for example, the quantity of gas demanded will be too low and too few resources will be employed in the market. The social costs of such price distortions could be substantial. In any given market, there is no difference between a regulated price that is 5 to 10 percent above the competitive price and a collusive (or monopoly) price that is 5 to 10 percent above cost. One fundamental difference between price distortion effects of regulation and collusive pricing, however, is that current regulation affects all 148 markets whereas the potential for collusive pricing is found in only 11 entry markets.

Our estimate of the social costs of regulation is extremely conservative, since it considers only actual expenditures by the federal government and by FERC-regulated pipelines on natural gas pipeline regulation. Our estimate

Table 6.6

Potential Welfare Losses
(in dollars per year)

| Entry Markets | 10 Percent Price Increase | | |
| | Suppliers within: | | |
(1)	*100 miles* (2)	*120 miles* (3)	*140 miles* (4)
Florida Markets			
1. Gainesville	201,659	201,659	201,659
2. Jacksonville	241,255	241,255	241,255
3. Lakeland	301,768	301,768	301,768
4. Miami-Hialeah	257,079	257,079	257,079
5. Orlando	449,352	449,352	449,352
6. Tampa	267,426	267,426	267,426
7. West Palm Beach	100,295	100,295	100,295
Florida Markets Subtotals	1,818,834	1,818,834	1,818,834

Table 6.6 (Continued)

Entry Markets	10 Percent Price Increase		
	Suppliers within:		
	100 miles	*120 miles*	*140 miles*
(1)	(2)	(3)	(4)
Non-Florida Markets			
1. N. Bedford, MA	404,484		
2. Wausau, WI	298,516	298,516	298,516
3. Des Moines,	607,354		
4. Duluth, MN-WI	268,308	268,308	268,308
5. Sioux City, (IA-NE)	201,867	201,867	
6. Sioux Falls, SD	157,676	157,676	
7. Boise City, ID	496,016	496,016	496,016
8. Las Cruces, NM	112,822		
9. Reno, NV	193,043		
10. Medford, OR	114,693	114,693	114,693
11. Vancouver, WA	159,264		
Non-Florida Markets Subtotals	3,014,043	1,537,076	1,177,533
ALL MARKETS	**4,832,877**	**3,355,910**	**2,996,367**

does not include the indirect costs of regulation (i.e., the price distortion effects), and it ignores the public and private costs of state pipeline regulations. Given these assumptions, direct public expenditures on natural gas pipeline regulation were estimated at $25.5 million for fiscal year 1982.[26] Direct private expenditures for 1983 totaled $26.2 million.[27] Thus, we conservatively estimate the direct costs of regulation at $51.7 million per year.

We find that all three welfare loss estimates shown in Table 6.6 are substantially less than the direct costs of regulation. Thus, even if the potential welfare loss is estimated at $4.8 million instead of $3.0 million, it is significantly less than the $51.7 million annual savings in regulation costs.[28] On this basis, we conclude that the benefits of deregulation in 93 percent of the entry markets (= 137/148) more than offset the *potential* welfare losses from monopoly pricing in the remaining 11 entry markets.[29] Deregulation of all 148 entry markets will increase social welfare by nearly $50 million annually (= $51.7 - $3.0 million). Although our sample year is 1983, the same conclusion is supported in 1988 as long as private expenditures on natural gas pipeline regulation have not been significantly reduced.[30]

Although some observers may consider the redistribution of income from consumers to pipelines a cost of deregulation, allowance for this consumer loss is more than offset by the price distortion effects of regulation. For a 10 percent price increase over cost, the potential (consumer) redistribution losses (area b in Figure 6.1) in the 11 markets total $54.0 million annually.[31] If regulated prices are only 10 percent above the level determined in deregulated markets, however, the corresponding redistribution losses due to regulation in the 148 markets total $2,822 million annually.[32] Thus, if consumer losses are considered, the indirect costs of regulation are even greater.[33]

To the extent that consumer losses relate to the redistribution of income, however, such losses are difficult to assess objectively. These losses to the consumers of natural gas are gains to the consumers who own the pipelines. On what basis can it be concluded that consumers are worse off? To avoid interpersonal comparisons (i.e., a $1 loss to one consumer group is more valuable than a $1 loss to another), we focus on the *net* social losses of regulation. Our estimate of $50.0 million per year represents a real loss to the economy--a loss to taxpayers and to FERC-regulated pipelines that is not offset by gains to any sector of the economy.

THE POLICY CHOICE

INTRODUCTION

The principal finding of this study is that potential entry is likely to provide a significant competitive restraint on monopoly power if natural gas entry markets were to be decontrolled. Although the majority of these markets may be served by only one or two suppliers, the number of potential entrants is generally so large that any attempt by current suppliers to collude to raise the market price is likely to fail. That is, if current suppliers attempted to set a supracompetitive price, most LDCs and other large users could turn to potential entrants for new service. Even if this new evidence on potential entry is interpreted conservatively, some form of deregulation is likely to be warranted.

POLICY OPTIONS

Complete Federal Decontrol in Entry Markets

Based on our sample of 148 entry markets, a strong case for complete federal deregulation in entry markets can be made based on the following preconditions:

1. The price of delivered gas is expected to increase by 5 to 10 percent;
2. Nearby pipelines can profitably construct 140-mile pipeline hookups;
3. Nearby pipelines are able to divert 50 percent of current deliveries into new markets;
4. The win ratio is 40 percent; and

    5. The HHI of 2500 is the appropriate threshold to evaluate whether the market power of current suppliers is sufficient to warrant continued regulation.

In our view, the above preconditions are more restrictive than necessary. Recall how each precondition was determined. (1) The price of delivered gas is based on the lowest price in our sample ($3.41 per Mcf in Arkansas markets) rather than on the weighted average price of all markets ($4.23). As a result, the 5 to 10 percent price increase determines a lower expected price of delivered gas, which, in turn, discourages pipeline hookups into new markets. (2) Construction of 140-mile hookups appears to be profitable despite the use of a shorter useful life of the pipeline hookup (10 or 20 years) instead of the corresponding longer life (30 years). (3) Divertible gas is underestimated, since it excludes exchange deliveries.[1] Further, the remaining life of supply contracts is based exclusively on the pipeline's longest-term customers, namely, LDCs. If transportation contracts are included, their substantially shorter remaining life would also increase the volume of divertible gas.[2] Consequently, our underestimate of divertible gas acts to reduce the number of markets that a potential entrant can enter simultaneously (i.e., the ER ratio). (4) The use of a lower ER ratio together with a high win ratio (a 40 percent cost-adjusted ratio instead of the average win ratio of 20.5 percent across all census regions) tends to reduce the number of bidders in each market. (5) The 2500 HHI threshold is used because it is the HHI value suggested in the U.S. Department of Justice study (1986). An analysis of the proper threshold may find that a HHI threshold higher than 2500 is appropriate.[3]

Although we systematically use those assumptions that make the case for decontrol difficult to support, the number of potential entrants in the intermediate run is sufficient to reduce the HHI to 2500 or less in 87 percent of the 148 entry markets in our sample. Furthermore, delivery data limitations in the intermediate-run analysis raise a strong possibility that the long-run findings are obtainable in the intermediate run.[4] Thus, over 93 percent of the entry markets may not pose a competitive problem absent regulation. In the 11 markets with HHIs over 2500, the possibility of competitive problems, if any, is centered on the 7 Florida markets.[5] Therefore, state regulation rather than federal regulation may be appropriate.

In our view, current federal regulation is not an efficient response to a state problem. The social costs of federal regulation in all 148 entry markets are substantially greater than the benefits in the 11 entry markets that remain highly concentrated after allowing for potential entry.[6] The annual benefits of approximately $3.0 million in the form of a higher volume (or a lower regulated price) of delivered gas in 11 markets (Table 6.6) are overwhelmed by the $51.7 million in annual direct regulation costs borne by taxpayers and FERC-regulated pipelines in all markets.[7] On this basis, one could readily conclude that federal regulation of entry markets is not socially desirable.

Limited Federal Decontrol in All Markets

Despite our efforts to underestimate rather than to overestimate potential entry, proponents of continued regulation could take exception to our use of a HHI threshold of 2500 to indicate whether continued regulation is warranted. Although a HHI threshold greater than 1800 may be justified, it might be argued that without additional evidence an 1800 HHI may be closer to the appropriate threshold than a HHI of 2500. Since the 1982 Merger Guidelines were published, the DOJ has brought almost no cases where the HHI was below 1800.[8]

The number of entry markets that may potentially raise competitive concerns more than doubles with the lower HHI threshold of 1800. Although the number of Florida entry markets with HHIs over 1800 remains at 7, the number of non-Florida entry markets increases from 4 to 19. Absent federal control, there exists a potential for welfare losses in excess of $1 million per year in five different states.[9] In contrast, only the state of Florida is similarly affected if a 2500 HHI threshold is used. Although the welfare costs of complete deregulation are still substantially less than the social costs of continued regulation,[10] it might be argued that some form of federal control is more efficient than increased state control.

In addition, our analysis of potential entry has been limited to the 148 entry markets in our original sample of 208 markets. Although the remaining 60 smaller markets account for only 1.3 percent of the output,[11] it is possible that the current suppliers in these markets possess significant market power. Allowing for a possible welfare loss associated with a price increase of 10 percent in these 60 markets increases the total welfare loss from 3.0 to 5.4 million per year.[12] Relative to the annual direct regulation costs of $51.7 million, however, the potential welfare losses in the 208 markets are not sufficient to justify continued federal regulation. Nevertheless, since these smaller markets are geographically distributed across several states, it might be argued that some form of federal control may be preferred to additional state control.

One alternative is limited federal regulation. The policy guideline might be that federal control will remain unchanged only in regions (or markets) where competition is weak.[13] In markets where significant market power cannot be exercised, however, "light-handed" regulation might be approved. In these markets, prices could be market-determined subject to some price cap. In this way, the social costs of regulation in the majority of entry markets, which are competitive, could be avoided. Additional analysis of the remaining entry markets and the 60 smaller markets should be undertaken on a case-by-case basis.[14] A substantially smaller appropriation for federal regulation could then be targeted for the remaining markets.

A FINAL QUALIFICATION

Our analysis of potential entry is based on the 1983 sample year. Recent changes in the industry including (1) lower city-gate prices, (2) additional pipeline mergers, (3) the increase in transportation service (i.e., the tendency of customers to buy gas directly from producers and to contract with pipelines for transportation), and Order Nos. 636 and 636A could alter the policy choice.[15] Ideally, our methodology could be applied to a more recent year (e.g., 1990) to verify that our findings are not substantially altered. It is my understanding that FERC is analyzing a number of competitive issues relating to the transportation and sale of natural gas in both origin and destination markets.

Appendix A

MSAs CLASSIFIED BY STATE

State	MSA
Alabama (10)	Anniston
	Birmingham
	Columbus (GA-AL)
	Dothan
	Florence
	Gadsen
	Huntsville
	Mobile
	Montgomery
	Tuscaloosa
Arizona (2)	Phoenix
	Tucson
Arkansas (6)	Fayettesville-Springdale
	Fort Smith (AR-OK)
	Little Rock-North Little Rock
	Memphis (TN-AR-MS)
	Pine Bluff
	Texarkana (TX-AR)

MSAs Classified by State

State	MSA
California (22)	Anaheim-Santa Anna
	Bakersfield
	Chico
	Fresno
	Los Angeles-Long Beach
	Modesto
	Oakland
	Oxnard-Ventura
	Redding
	Riverside-San Bernadino
	Sacramento
	Salinas-Seaside-Monterey
	San Diego
	San Francisco
	San Jose
	Santa Barbara-Santa Maria-Lompoc
	Santa Cruz
	Santa Rosa-Petaluma
	Stockton
	Vallejo-Fairfield-Napa
	Visalia-Tulare-Porterville
	Yuba
Colorado (6)	Boulder-Longmont
	Colorado Springs
	Denver
	Fort Collins-Loveland
	Greeley
	Pueblo
Connecticut (4)	Bridgeport-Stamford-Norwich-Danbury
	Hartford-New Britain-Middletown-Bristol
	New Haven-Waterbury-Meriden
	New London-Norwich
Delaware (1)	Wilmington (DE-NJ-MD)

MSAs Classified by State

State	MSA
Florida (20)	Bradenton
	Daytona Beach
	Fort Lauderdale-Hollywood-Pompano Beach
	Fort Myers
	Fort Pierce
	Fort Walton Beach
	Gainsville
	Jacksonville
	Lakeland-Winter Haven
	Melbourne-Titusville-Palm Bay
	Miami-Hialeah
	Naples
	Ocala
	Orlando
	Panama City
	Pensacola
	Sarasota
	Tallahassee
	Tampa-St. Petersburg-Clearwater
	West Palm Beach-Boca Raton-Delray Beach
Georgia (7)	Albany
	Athens
	Atlanta
	Augusta (GA-SC)
	Chattanooga (TN-GA)
	Macon-Warner Robins
	Savannah
Idaho (1)	Boise City
Illinois (13)	Aurora-Elgin
	Bloomington-Normal
	Champaign-Urbana-Rantoul
	Chicago
	Davenport-Rock Island-Moline (IA-IL)

MSAs Classified by State

State	MSA
Illinois *(continued)*	Decatur
	Joliet
	Kankakee
	Lake County
	Peoria
	Rockford
	Springfield
	St. Louis (MO-IL)
Indiana (14)	Anderson
	Bloomington
	Cincinnati (OH-KY-IN)
	Elkhart-Goshen
	Evansville (IN-KY)
	Fort Wayne
	Gary-Hammond
	Indianapolis
	Kokomo
	Lafayette
	Louisville (KY-IN)
	Muncie
	South Bend-Mishawaka
	Terra Haute
Iowa (7)	Cedar Rapids
	Des Moines
	Dubuque
	Iowa City
	Omaha (NE-IA)
	Sioux City (IA-NE)
	Waterloo-Cedar Falls
Kansas (3)	Lawrence
	Topeka
	Wichita

MSAs Classified by State

State	MSA
Kentucky (4)	Clarksville-Hopkinsville (TN-KY) Huntington-Ashland (WV-KY-OH) Lexington-Fayette Owensboro
Louisiana (8)	Alexandria Baton Rouge Houma-Thibodaux Lafayette Lake Charles Monroe New Orleans Shreveport
Maine (3)	Bangor Lewiston-Auburn Portland
Maryland (4)	Baltimore Cumberland (MD-WV) Hagerstown Washington (DC-MD-VA)
Massachusetts (5)	Boston-Lawrence-Salem-Lowell-Brockton New Bedford-Fall River-Attleboro Pittsfield Springfield Worcester-Fitchburg-Leominster
Michigan (11)	Ann Arbor Battle Creek Benton Harbor Detroit Flint Grand Rapids Jackson

MSAs Classified by State

State	MSA
Michigan *(continued)*	Kalamazoo Lansing-East Lansing Muskegon Saginaw-Bay City-Midland
Minnesota (5)	Duluth (MN-WI) Fargo-Moorhead (ND-MN) Minneapolis-St. Paul (MN-WI) Rochester St. Cloud
Mississippi (3)	Biloxi-Gulfport Jackson Pascagoula
Missouri (5)	Columbia Joplin Kansas City St. Joseph Springfield
Montana (2)	Billings Great Falls
Nebraska (1)	Lincoln
Nevada (2)	Las Vegas Reno
New Hampshire (2)	Manchester-Nashua Portsmouth-Dover-Rochester
New Jersey (10)	Allentown-Bethlehem (PA-NJ) Atlantic City Bergen-Passaic Jersey City

MSAs Classified by State

State	MSA
New Jersey *(continued)*	Middlesex-Somerset-Hunterdon
	Monmouth-Ocean
	Newark
	Philadelphia (PA-NJ)
	Trenton
	Vineland-Millville-Bridgeton
New Mexico (3)	Albuquerque
	Las Cruces
	Santa Fe
New York (13)	Albany-Schenectady-Troy
	Binghamton
	Buffalo
	Elmira
	Glens Falls
	Nassau-Suffolk
	New York
	Niagara Falls
	Orange County
	Poughkeepsie
	Rochester
	Syracuse
	Utica-Rome
North Carolina (9)	Asheville
	Burlington
	Charlotte-Gastonia-Rock Hill (NC-SC)
	Fayetteville
	Greensboro-Winston-Salem-High Point
	Hickory
	Jacksonville
	Raleigh-Durham
	Wilmington

MSAs Classified by State

State	MSA
North Dakota (2)	Bismarck Grand Forks
Ohio (14)	Akron Canton Cleveland Columbus Dayton-Springfield Hamilton-Middletown Lima Lorain-Elyria Mansfield Parkersburg-Marietta (WV-OH) Steubenville-Weirton (OH-WV) Toledo Wheeling (WV-OH) Youngstown-Warren
Oklahoma (4)	Enid Lawton Oklahoma City Tulsa
Oregon (4)	Eugene-Springfield Medford Portland Salem
Pennsylvania (13)	Altoona Beaver County Erie Harrisburg-Lebanon-Carlisle Johnstown Lancaster Pittsburgh Reading

MSAs Classified by State

State	MSA
Pennsylvania (*continued*)	Scranton-Wilkes-Barre
	Sharon
	State College
	Williamsport
	York
Rhode Island (1)	Providence-Pawtucket-Woonsocket
South Carolina (5)	Anderson
	Charleston
	Columbia
	Florence
	Greenville-Spartanburg
South Dakota (2)	Rapid City
	Sioux Falls
Tennessee (4)	Jackson
	Johnson City-Kingsport-Bristol
	Knoxville
	Nashville
Texas (27)	Abilene
	Amarillo
	Austin
	Beaumont-Port Arthur
	Brazoria
	Brownsville-Harlingen
	Bryan-College Station
	Corpus Christi
	Dallas
	El Paso
	Fort Worth-Arlington
	Galveston-Texas City
	Houston

MSAs Classified by State

State	MSA
Texas *(continued)*	Killeen-Temple
	Laredo
	Longview-Marshall
	Lubbock
	McAllen-Edinburg-Mission
	Midland
	Odessa
	San Angelo
	San Antonio
	Sherman-Denison
	Tyler
	Victoria
	Waco
	Wichita Falls
Utah (2)	Provo-Orem
	Salt Lake City-Ogden
Vermont (1)	Burlington
Virginia (6)	Charlottesville
	Danville
	Lynchburg
	Norfork-Virginia Beach-Newport News
	Richmond-Petersburg
	Roanoke
Washington (9)	Bellingham
	Bremerton
	Olympia
	Richland-Kennewick-Pasco
	Seattle
	Spokane
	Tacoma
	Vancouver
	Yakima

MSAs Classified by State

State	MSA
West Virginia (1)	Charleston
Wisconsin (11)	Appleton-Oshkosh-Neenah Eau Claire Green Bay Janesville-Beloit Kenosha La Crosse Madison Milwaukee Racine Sheboygan Wausau
Wyoming (2)	Casper Cheyenne
Total MSAs	314

Notes: MSAs which traverse more than one state are assigned to that state which incorporates the greatest population of the MSA.

MSAs in Alaska and Hawaii are excluded.

Appendix B

STANDARD MARKET SHARE REPORT

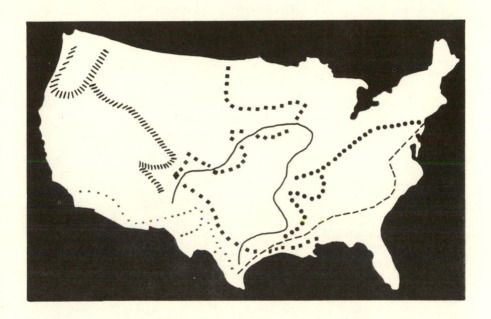

An explanation of the construction and use of this appendix is provided in Chapter 4, subsection "Compilation of Market Concentration Data" and subsection "Empirical Findings." Deliveries are defined as sales for resale, industrial sales, and transportation for others. Intrastate pipeline deliveries are not reported due to confidentiality commitments with intrastate suppliers. Pipeline names may be truncated due to space limitations. See Appendix E for the complete pipeline name.

ABILENE, TX
PIPELINE	DELIVERIES	MARKET SHARE
Enserch Corp.	81,109	1.0000
TOTALS	81,109	HHI 10000

ALBANY, GA
PIPELINE	DELIVERIES	MARKET SHARE
South Georgia Nautura	4,967,411	1.0000
TOTALS	4,967,411	HHI 10000

ALBANY–SCHENECTADY–TROY, NY
PIPELINE	DELIVERIES	MARKET SHARE
Consolidated Gas Supp	19,147,561	1.0000
TOTALS	19,147,561	HHI 10000

ALEXANDRIA, LA
PIPELINE	DELIVERIES	MARKET SHARE
Arkla Inc.	5,953,186	0.7962
Trunkline Gas Co.	58,861	0.0079
Tenneco Inc.	28,830	0.0039
United Gas Pipeline C	1,435,851	0.1920
TOTALS	7,476,728	HHI 6709

ALLENTOWN–BETHLEHEM (PA–NJ)
PIPELINE	DELIVERIES	MARKET SHARE
Columbia Gas Transmis	1,627,589	0.0415
Transcontinental Gas	37,566,254	0.9585
TOTALS	39,193,843	HHI 9204

AMARILLO, TX
PIPELINE	DELIVERIES	MARKET SHARE
Western Gas Interstat	2,791,198	0.0931
Colorado Interstate G	27,187,380	0.9069
TOTALS	29,978,578	HHI 8311

ANDERSON, IN
PIPELINE	DELIVERIES	MARKET SHARE
Panhandle Eastern Pip	2,529,479	1.0000
TOTALS	2,529,479	HHI 10000

ANDERSON, SC
PIPELINE	DELIVERIES	MARKET SHARE
Transcontinental Gas	4,484,284	1.0000
TOTALS	4,484,284	HHI 10000

ANNISTON, AL
PIPELINE	DELIVERIES	MARKET SHARE
Southern Natural Gas	5,396,069	1.0000
TOTALS	5,396,069	HHI 10000

ATHENS, GA

PIPELINE	DELIVERIES	MARKET SHARE
Transcontinental Gas	3,159,437	1.0000
TOTALS	3,159,437	HHI 10000

ATLANTA, GA

PIPELINE	DELIVERIES	MARKET SHARE
Southern Natural Gas	94,302,026	0.7512
Transcontinental Gas	31,234,081	0.2488
TOTALS	125,536,107	HHI 6262

AUGUSTA (GA-SC)

PIPELINE	DELIVERIES	MARKET SHARE
Southern Natural Gas	39,322,816	1.0000
TOTALS	39,322,816	HHI 10000

AUSTIN, TX

PIPELINE	DELIVERIES	MARKET SHARE
Enserch Corp.	62,631	0.1351
United Gas Pipeline C	400,879	0.8649
TOTALS	463,510	HHI 7663

BALTIMORE, MD

PIPELINE	DELIVERIES	MARKET SHARE
Columbia Gas Transmis	79,334,834	1.0000
TOTALS	79,334,834	HHI 10000

BATON ROUGE, LA

PIPELINE	DELIVERIES	MARKET SHARE
United Gas Pipeline C	8,956,003	0.9908
Northern Natural Gas	83,065	0.0092
TOTALS	9,039,068	HHI 9818

BATTLE CREEK, MI

PIPELINE	DELIVERIES	MARKET SHARE
Panhandle Eastern Pip	15,716,299	1.0000
TOTALS	15,716,299	HHI 10000

BEAUMONT-PORT ARTHUR, TX

PIPELINE	DELIVERIES	MARKET SHARE
Enserch Corp.	2,573,316	0.6128
Tenneco Inc.	56,379	0.0134
Texas Gas Pipeline Co	1,558,487	0.3711
Valley Gas Transmissi	11,010	0.0026
TOTALS	4,199,192	HHI 5135

BEAVER COUNTY, PA

PIPELINE	DELIVERIES	MARKET SHARE
Columbia Gas Transmis	3,819,976	0.4717
Tenneco Inc.	4,278,203	0.5283
TOTALS	8,098,179	HHI 5016

BENTON HARBOR, MI

PIPELINE	DELIVERIES	MARKET SHARE
ANR Pipeline Co.	30,727,709	0.9990
Panhandle Eastern Pip	31,218	0.0010
TOTALS	30,758,927	HHI 9980

BERGEN-PASSAIC, NJ

PIPELINE	DELIVERIES	MARKET SHARE
Tenneco Inc.	15,790,849	1.0000
TOTALS	15,790,849	HHI 10000

BILLINGS, MT

PIPELINE	DELIVERIES	MARKET SHARE
Montana-Dakota Utilit	1,591,802	1.0000
TOTALS	1,591,802	HHI 10000

BILOXI-GULFPORT, MS

PIPELINE	DELIVERIES	MARKET SHARE
Tenneco Inc.	230,769	0.0279
United Gas Pipeline C	8,031,731	0.9721
TOTALS	8,262,500	HHI 9457

BINGHAMTON, NY

PIPELINE	DELIVERIES	MARKET SHARE
Columbia Gas Transmis	582,485	0.3063
Consolidated Gas Supp	1,319,470	0.6937
TOTALS	1,901,955	HHI 5751

BIRMINGHAM, AL

PIPELINE	DELIVERIES	MARKET SHARE
Southern Natural Gas	43,398,240	1.0000
TOTALS	43,398,240	HHI 10000

BISMARCK, ND

PIPELINE	DELIVERIES	MARKET SHARE
Montana-Dakota Utilit	326,204	1.0000
TOTALS	326,204	HHI 10000

BOISE CITY, ID

PIPELINE	DELIVERIES	MARKET SHARE
Northwest Pipeline Co	21,947,620	1.0000
TOTALS	21,947,620	HHI 10000

```
BOSTON-LAWR.-SALEM-LOW.-BROCK.,MA
          PIPELINE              DELIVERIES           MARKET SHARE

*Tenneco Inc.                 95,439,795                0.5715
 Algonquin Gas Transmi        38,124,132                0.2283
 Distrigas of Massachu        33,421,531                0.2001
          TOTALS             166,985,458                HHI     4188
                                               PCT. OF
DETAIL OF SUBSIDIARIES        DELIVERIES        PARENT DEL.  PARENT

Granite State Gas Tran        23,816,349        24.95%  Tenneco Inc.

BRADENTON, FL
          PIPELINE              DELIVERIES           MARKET SHARE

 Florida Gas Transmiss          2,569,488               1.0000
          TOTALS                2,569,488               HHI   10000

BRAZORIA, TX
          PIPELINE              DELIVERIES           MARKET SHARE

 Florida Gas Transmiss              3,887               1.0000
          TOTALS                    3,887               HHI   10000

BRIDGEPORT-STAMF.-NORW.-DANB.,CT
          PIPELINE              DELIVERIES           MARKET SHARE

 Tenneco Inc.                  24,224,310               1.0000
          TOTALS               24,224,310               HHI   10000

BRYAN-COLLEGE STATION, TX
          PIPELINE              DELIVERIES           MARKET SHARE

 Enserch Corp.                  2,898,212               1.0000
          TOTALS                2,898,212               HHI   10000

BUFFALO, NY
          PIPELINE              DELIVERIES           MARKET SHARE

*National Fuel Gas Co.         38,277,357               0.6061
 Tenneco Inc.                  24,872,446               0.3939
          TOTALS               63,149,803               HHI     5225
                                               PCT. OF
DETAIL OF SUBSIDIARIES        DELIVERIES        PARENT DEL.  PARENT

National Fuel Gas Dist         38,211,159       99.83%  National Fuel Gas Co
National Fuel Gas Supp             66,198        0.17%  National Fuel Gas Co

CANTON, OH
          PIPELINE              DELIVERIES           MARKET SHARE

 Tenneco Inc.                   9,242,429               1.0000
          TOTALS                9,242,429               HHI   10000
```

CASPER, WY

PIPELINE	DELIVERIES	MARKET SHARE
KN Energy Inc.	830,863	0.4529
Montana-Dakota Utilit	1,003,532	0.5471
TOTALS	1,834,395	HHI 5044

CEDAR RAPIDS, IA

PIPELINE	DELIVERIES	MARKET SHARE
Northern Natural Gas	361,645	1.0000
TOTALS	361,645	HHI 10000

CHAMPAIGN-URBANA-RANTOUL, IL

PIPELINE	DELIVERIES	MARKET SHARE
*Panhandle Eastern Cor	1,372,688	1.0000
TOTALS	1,372,688	HHI 10000

DETAIL OF SUBSIDIARIES	DELIVERIES	PCT. OF PARENT DEL.	PARENT
Panhandle Eastern Pipe	926,356	67.48%	Panhandle Eastern Co
Trunkline Gas Co.	446,332	32.52%	Panhandle Eastern Co

CHARLESTON, SC

PIPELINE	DELIVERIES	MARKET SHARE
Transcontinental Gas	5,824,332	1.0000
TOTALS	5,824,332	HHI 10000

CHARLESTON, WV

PIPELINE	DELIVERIES	MARKET SHARE
Consolidated Gas Supp	6,115	0.0005
Tenneco Inc.	11,598,796	0.9995
TOTALS	11,604,911	HHI 9989

CHARLOTTE-GASTONIA-ROCK HILL (NC-SC)

PIPELINE	DELIVERIES	MARKET SHARE
Transcontinental Gas	995,854	1.0000
TOTALS	995,854	HHI 10000

CHARLOTTESVILLE, VA

PIPELINE	DELIVERIES	MARKET SHARE
Columbia Gas Transmis	33,543,980	1.0000
TOTALS	33,543,980	HHI 10000

CHATTANOOGA (TN-GA)

PIPELINE	DELIVERIES	MARKET SHARE
Southern Natural Gas	4,852,925	0.2875
East Tennessee Natura	12,024,548	0.7125
TOTALS	16,877,473	HHI 5903

CHEYENNE, WY

PIPELINE	DELIVERIES	MARKET SHARE
KN Energy Inc.	830,863	0.1180
Colorado Interstate G	6,211,557	0.8820
TOTALS	7,042,420	HHI 7919

CHICAGO, IL

PIPELINE	DELIVERIES	MARKET SHARE
Natural Gas Pipeline	137,184,696	1.0000
TOTALS	137,184,696	HHI 10000

CINCINNATI (OH-KY-IN)

PIPELINE	DELIVERIES	MARKET SHARE
Columbia Gas Transmis	56,483,176	0.1936
Panhandle Eastern Pip	22,489	0.0001
Texas Gas Transmissio	235,252,312	0.8063
TOTALS	291,757,977	HHI 6876

CLARKSVILLE-HOPKINSVILLE (TN-KY)

PIPELINE	DELIVERIES	MARKET SHARE
Tenneco Inc.	2,698,346	1.0000
TOTALS	2,698,346	HHI 10000

COLORADO SPRINGS, CO

PIPELINE	DELIVERIES	MARKET SHARE
Colorado Interstate G	19,311,310	1.0000
TOTALS	19,311,310	HHI 10000

COLUMBIA, MO

PIPELINE	DELIVERIES	MARKET SHARE
Panhandle Eastern Pip	11,173,043	1.0000
TOTALS	11,173,043	HHI 10000

COLUMBIA, SC

PIPELINE	DELIVERIES	MARKET SHARE
Southern Natural Gas	59,225,532	1.0000
TOTALS	59,225,532	HHI 10000

COLUMBUS, (GA-AL)

PIPELINE	DELIVERIES	MARKET SHARE
Southern Natural Gas	10,156,972	1.0000
TOTALS	10,156,972	HHI 10000

COLUMBUS, OH

PIPELINE	DELIVERIES	MARKET SHARE
Columbia Gas Transmis	1,874,403	0.5684
Tenneco Inc.	1,423,361	0.4316
TOTALS	3,297,764	HHI 5094

CORPUS CHRISTI, TX

PIPELINE	DELIVERIES	MARKET SHARE
Enserch Corp.	684,903	0.3647
Florida Gas Transmiss	62,921	0.0335
United Gas Pipeline C	697,841	0.3716
Valley Gas Transmissi	432,441	0.2303
TOTALS	1,878,106	HHI 3252

DALLAS, TX

PIPELINE	DELIVERIES	MARKET SHARE
Enserch Corp.	11,188,033	1.0000
TOTALS	11,188,033	HHI 10000

DANVILLE, VA

PIPELINE	DELIVERIES	MARKET SHARE
Transcontinental Gas	4,663,292	1.0000
TOTALS	4,663,292	HHI 10000

DAVENPORT-ROCK ISLAND-MOLINE (IA-IL)

PIPELINE	DELIVERIES	MARKET SHARE
ANR Pipeline Co.	1,524,312	0.0451
Natural Gas Pipeline	32,254,713	0.9549
TOTALS	33,779,025	HHI 9138

DAYTON-SPRINGFIELD, OH

PIPELINE	DELIVERIES	MARKET SHARE
Columbia Gas Transmis	44,446,893	1.0000
TOTALS	44,446,893	HHI 10000

DAYTONA BEACH, FL

PIPELINE	DELIVERIES	MARKET SHARE
Florida Gas Transmiss	2,431,877	1.0000
TOTALS	2,431,877	HHI 10000

DECATUR, IL

PIPELINE	DELIVERIES	MARKET SHARE
Natural Gas Pipeline	7,512,750	1.0000
TOTALS	7,512,750	HHI 10000

DENVER, CO

PIPELINE	DELIVERIES	MARKET SHARE
Panhandle Eastern Pip	17,857	0.0002
Colorado Interstate G	100,788,569	0.9998
TOTALS	100,806,426	HHI 9996

DES MOINES, IA

PIPELINE	DELIVERIES	MARKET SHARE
Natural Gas Pipeline	3,466,792	0.1173
Northern Natural Gas	26,088,128	0.8827
TOTALS	29,554,920	HHI 7929

DETROIT , MI

PIPELINE	DELIVERIES	MARKET SHARE
Great Lakes Gas Trans	11,279,495	0.2416
Panhandle Eastern Pip	35,412,036	0.7584
TOTALS	46,691,531	HHI 6336

DUBUQUE, IA

PIPELINE	DELIVERIES	MARKET SHARE
Northern Natural Gas	86,143	1.0000
TOTALS	86,143	HHI 10000

DULUTH (MN-WI)

PIPELINE	DELIVERIES	MARKET SHARE
Northern Natural Gas	12,868,473	1.0000
TOTALS	12,868,473	HHI 10000

EAU CLAIRE, WI

PIPELINE	DELIVERIES	MARKET SHARE
Midwestern Gas Transm	2,711,309	0.8584
Northern Natural Gas	447,069	0.1416
TOTALS	3,158,378	HHI 7570

EL PASO, TX

PIPELINE	DELIVERIES	MARKET SHARE
El Paso Natural Gas C	11,929,439	0.9710
Western Gas Interstat	356,229	0.0290
TOTALS	12,285,668	HHI 9437

ELKHART-GOSHEN, IN

PIPELINE	DELIVERIES	MARKET SHARE
Trunkline Gas Co.	129,087,473	1.0000
TOTALS	129,087,473	HHI 10000

ENID, OK

PIPELINE	DELIVERIES	MARKET SHARE
*Oklahoma Natural Gas	44,132,957	1.0000
TOTALS	44,132,957	HHI 10000

DETAIL OF SUBSIDIARIES	DELIVERIES	PCT. OF PARENT DEL.	PARENT
Ringwood Gathering Co.	6,783,632	15.37%	Oklahoma Natural Gas

ERIE, PA

PIPELINE	DELIVERIES	MARKET SHARE
National Fuel Gas Sup	18,096,471	1.0000
TOTALS	18,096,471	HHI 10000

EVANSVILLE (IN-KY)

PIPELINE	DELIVERIES	MARKET SHARE
Texas Eastern Transmi	51,155	0.0011
Texas Gas Transmissio	44,754,225	0.9989
TOTALS	44,805,380	HHI 9977

FARGO-MOORHEAD (ND-MN)

PIPELINE	DELIVERIES	MARKET SHARE
Midwestern Gas Transm	7,194,001	1.0000
TOTALS	7,194,001	HHI 10000

FLORENCE, AL

PIPELINE	DELIVERIES	MARKET SHARE
Alabama-Tennessee Nat	10,310,364	0.3200
Tenneco Inc.	16,823,517	0.5221
Texas Eastern Transmi	5,087,408	0.1579
TOTALS	32,221,289	HHI 3999

FORT LAUDERDALE-HOLLYWOOD-POMPANO BEACH, FL

PIPELINE	DELIVERIES	MARKET SHARE
Florida Gas Transmiss	284,540	1.0000
TOTALS	284,540	HHI 10000

FORT PIERCE, FL

PIPELINE	DELIVERIES	MARKET SHARE
Florida Gas Transmiss	3,529,584	1.0000
TOTALS	3,529,584	HHI 10000

FORT SMITH (AR-OK)

PIPELINE	DELIVERIES	MARKET SHARE
Arkansas Oklahoma Gas	12,014,475	0.9804
Arkla Inc.	240,204	0.0196
TOTALS	12,254,679	HHI 9616

FORT WAYNE, IN

PIPELINE	DELIVERIES	MARKET SHARE
Panhandle Eastern Pip	24,299,148	1.0000
TOTALS	24,299,148	HHI 10000

FORT WORTH-ARLINGTON, TX

PIPELINE	DELIVERIES	MARKET SHARE
Enserch Corp.	3,427,286	1.0000
TOTALS	3,427,286	HHI 10000

GADSEN, AL

PIPELINE	DELIVERIES	MARKET SHARE
Southern Natural Gas	10,413,562	1.0000
TOTALS	10,413,562	HHI 10000

```
GAINESVILLE, FL
        PIPELINE              DELIVERIES          MARKET SHARE

  Florida Gas Transmiss     11,758,519           1.0000
             TOTALS         11,758,519              HHI   10000

GALVESTON-TEXAS CITY, TX
        PIPELINE              DELIVERIES          MARKET SHARE

  Enserch Corp.              2,663,043            1.0000
             TOTALS          2,663,043               HHI   10000

GARY-HAMMOND, IN
        PIPELINE              DELIVERIES          MARKET SHARE

  Texas Gas Transmissio        386,723           1.0000
             TOTALS            386,723               HHI   10000

GRAND FORKS, ND
        PIPELINE              DELIVERIES          MARKET SHARE

  Midwestern Gas Transm        424,132           1.0000
             TOTALS            424,132               HHI   10000

GREELEY, CO
        PIPELINE              DELIVERIES          MARKET SHARE

  Colorado Interstate G     32,511,047           1.0000
             TOTALS         32,511,047               HHI   10000

GREENSBORO-WINSTON-SALEM-HIGH POINT, NC
        PIPELINE              DELIVERIES          MARKET SHARE

  Transcontinental Gas       4,682,379           1.0000
             TOTALS          4,682,379               HHI   10000

GREENVILLE-SPARTANBURG, SC
        PIPELINE              DELIVERIES          MARKET SHARE

  Transcontinental Gas       1,527,845           1.0000
             TOTALS          1,527,845               HHI   10000

HAMILTON-MIDDLETOWN, OH
        PIPELINE              DELIVERIES          MARKET SHARE

  Texas Eastern Transmi      8,217,236           0.4873
  Texas Gas Transmissio      8,643,996           0.5127
             TOTALS         16,861,232               HHI    5003

HARTFORD-N.BRIT.-MIDDLE.-BRIS.,CT
        PIPELINE              DELIVERIES          MARKET SHARE

  Tenneco Inc.                 937,196           0.0548
  Algonquin Gas Transmi     16,172,308           0.9452
             TOTALS         17,109,504               HHI    8964
```

HOUMA—THIBODAUX, LA

PIPELINE	DELIVERIES	MARKET SHARE
United Gas Pipeline C	1,914,587	0.9615
Texas Gas Transmissio	76,569	0.0385
TOTALS	1,991,156	HHI 9260

HOUSTON, TX

PIPELINE	DELIVERIES	MARKET SHARE
Enserch Corp.	5,601,679	0.1485
Tenneco Inc.	48,469	0.0013
Natural Gas Pipeline	32,078,508	0.8502
TOTALS	37,728,656	HHI 7450

HUNTINGTON—ASHLAND (WV—KY—OH)

PIPELINE	DELIVERIES	MARKET SHARE
*Columbia Gas System,	6,608,013	0.0982
Tenneco Inc.	60,673,684	0.9018
TOTALS	67,281,697	HHI 8229

DETAIL OF SUBSIDIARIES	DELIVERIES	PCT. OF PARENT DEL.	PARENT
Columbia Gas Transmiss	1,544	0.02%	Columbia Gas System,
Inland Gas Co. Inc.	6,606,469	99.98%	Columbia Gas System,

HUNTSVILLE, AL

PIPELINE	DELIVERIES	MARKET SHARE
Alabama-Tennessee Nat	5,256,734	1.0000
TOTALS	5,256,734	HHI 10000

INDIANAPOLIS, IN

PIPELINE	DELIVERIES	MARKET SHARE
Panhandle Eastern Pip	80,728,499	1.0000
TOTALS	80,728,499	HHI 10000

JACKSON, MS

PIPELINE	DELIVERIES	MARKET SHARE
Texas Eastern Transmi	99,115	0.0043
United Gas Pipeline C	23,078,529	0.9957
TOTALS	23,177,644	HHI 9915

JACKSON, TN

PIPELINE	DELIVERIES	MARKET SHARE
Texas Gas Transmissio	6,081,398	1.0000
TOTALS	6,081,398	HHI 10000

JACKSONVILLE, FL

PIPELINE	DELIVERIES	MARKET SHARE
Florida Gas Transmiss	14,067,369	1.0000
TOTALS	14,067,369	HHI 10000

JANESVILLE-BELOIT, WI

PIPELINE	DELIVERIES	MARKET SHARE
ANR Pipeline Co.	21,465,218	0.4984
Northern Natural Gas	21,606,914	0.5016
TOTALS	43,072,132	HHI 5000

JOHNSON CITY-KINGSPORT-BRISTOL (TN-VA)

PIPELINE	DELIVERIES	MARKET SHARE
East Tennessee Natura	10,483,766	1.0000
TOTALS	10,483,766	HHI 10000

JOLIET, IL

PIPELINE	DELIVERIES	MARKET SHARE
Natural Gas Pipeline	476,885	1.0000
TOTALS	476,885	HHI 10000

JOPLIN, MO

PIPELINE	DELIVERIES	MARKET SHARE
Northwest Central Pip	12,405,945	1.0000
TOTALS	12,405,945	HHI 10000

KANSAS CITY, MO

PIPELINE	DELIVERIES	MARKET SHARE
KN Energy Inc.	3,780,136	0.0233
Northwest Central Pip	147,711,399	0.9107
Panhandle Eastern Pip	1,609,924	0.0099
Union Gas System Inc.	8,969,863	0.0553
Northern Natural Gas	119,955	0.0007
TOTALS	162,191,277	HHI 8331

KILLEEN-TEMPLE, TX

PIPELINE	DELIVERIES	MARKET SHARE
Enserch Corp.	1,552,806	1.0000
TOTALS	1,552,806	HHI 10000

KNOXVILLE, TN

PIPELINE	DELIVERIES	MARKET SHARE
East Tennessee Natura	18,875,162	1.0000
TOTALS	18,875,162	HHI 10000

KOKOMO, IN

PIPELINE	DELIVERIES	MARKET SHARE
Panhandle Eastern Pip	8,011,562	1.0000
TOTALS	8,011,562	HHI 10000

LA CROSSE, WI

PIPELINE	DELIVERIES	MARKET SHARE
Northern Natural Gas	4,034,872	1.0000
TOTALS	4,034,872	HHI 10000

LAFAYETTE, LA

PIPELINE	DELIVERIES	MARKET SHARE
Southern Natural Gas	16,167	0.0030
United Gas Pipeline C	5,323,594	0.9970
TOTALS	5,339,761	HHI 9940

LAKE CHARLES, LA

PIPELINE	DELIVERIES	MARKET SHARE
Trunkline Lng Co.	92,379,933	0.7625
Texas Eastern Transmi	20,810	0.0002
Crab Run Gas Co.	47,119	0.0004
West Lake Arthur Corp	16,851,763	0.1391
United Gas Pipeline C	11,855,070	0.0979
TOTALS	121,154,695	HHI 6103

LAKELAND—WINTER HAVEN, FL

PIPELINE	DELIVERIES	MARKET SHARE
Florida Gas Transmiss	17,595,821	1.0000
TOTALS	17,595,821	HHI 10000

LAREDO, TX

PIPELINE	DELIVERIES	MARKET SHARE
Enserch Corp.	355,281	1.0000
TOTALS	355,281	HHI 10000

LAS CRUCES, NM

PIPELINE	DELIVERIES	MARKET SHARE
El Paso Natural Gas C	5,265,253	0.9100
Western Gas Interstat	520,477	0.0900
TOTALS	5,785,730	HHI 8363

LAS VEGAS, NV

PIPELINE	DELIVERIES	MARKET SHARE
Southwest Gas Corp.	11,071,845	1.0000
TOTALS	11,071,845	HHI 10000

LAWRENCE, KS

PIPELINE	DELIVERIES	MARKET SHARE
Northwest Central Pip	9,682,425	1.0000
TOTALS	9,682,425	HHI 10000

LAWTON, OK

PIPELINE	DELIVERIES	MARKET SHARE
Arkla Inc.	17,340,357	1.0000
TOTALS	17,340,357	HHI 10000

```
LEXINGTON-FAYETTE, KY
          PIPELINE          DELIVERIES        MARKET SHARE

*Columbia Gas System,        471,073            0.4115
 Tenneco Inc.                673,788            0.5885
          TOTALS           1,144,861              HHI    5157
                                         PCT. OF
 DETAIL OF SUBSIDIARIES     DELIVERIES   PARENT DEL.   PARENT

Columbia Gas Transmiss       170,819     36.26%  Columbia Gas System,
Inland Gas Co. Inc.          300,254     63.74%  Columbia Gas System,

LINCOLN, NE
          PIPELINE          DELIVERIES        MARKET SHARE

Northern Natural Gas       13,870,462           1.0000
          TOTALS           13,870,462             HHI   10000

LITTLE ROCK-N. LITTLE ROCK, AR
          PIPELINE          DELIVERIES        MARKET SHARE

Arkla Inc.                 82,336,414           0.9957
Texas Eastern Transmi         356,191           0.0043
          TOTALS           82,692,605             HHI   9914

LONGVIEW-MARSHALL, TX
          PIPELINE          DELIVERIES        MARKET SHARE

Arkla Inc.                        807           0.0000
Enserch Corp.               2,936,332           0.0690
KN Energy Inc.                  4,893           0.0001
United Gas Pipeline C       39,603,852          0.9309
          TOTALS           42,545,884             HHI   8712

LOUISVILLE (KY-IN)
          PIPELINE          DELIVERIES        MARKET SHARE

Ohio River Pipeline C       7,132,320           0.1082
Texas Gas Transmissio      58,784,815           0.8918
          TOTALS           65,917,135             HHI   8070

MACON-WARNER ROBINS, GA
          PIPELINE          DELIVERIES        MARKET SHARE

Southern Natural Gas       21,629,177           1.0000
          TOTALS           21,629,177             HHI   10000

MADISON, WI
          PIPELINE          DELIVERIES        MARKET SHARE

ANR Pipeline Co.           16,805,898           0.9939
Northern Natural Gas          103,779           0.0061
          TOTALS           16,909,677             HHI   9878

MANCHESTER-NASHUA, NH
          PIPELINE          DELIVERIES        MARKET SHARE

Tenneco Inc.                5,938,883           1.0000
          TOTALS            5,938,883             HHI   10000
```

MANSFIELD, OH

PIPELINE	DELIVERIES	MARKET SHARE
Texas Gas Transmissio	115,848	1.0000
TOTALS	115,848	HHI 10000

MCALLEN-EDINBURG-MISSION, TX

PIPELINE	DELIVERIES	MARKET SHARE
United Gas Pipeline C	88,025	0.6426
Valley Gas Transmissi	48,967	0.3574
TOTALS	136,992	HHI 5406

MEDFORD, OR

PIPELINE	DELIVERIES	MARKET SHARE
Northwest Pipeline Co	5,567,637	1.0000
TOTALS	5,567,637	HHI 10000

MELBOURNE-TITUSVILLE-PALM BAY, FL

PIPELINE	DELIVERIES	MARKET SHARE
Florida Gas Transmiss	1,605,367	1.0000
TOTALS	1,605,367	HHI 10000

MEMPHIS (TN-AR-MS)

PIPELINE	DELIVERIES	MARKET SHARE
Trunkline Gas Co.	132,376	0.0019
Texas Gas Transmissio	68,536,110	0.9981
TOTALS	68,668,486	HHI 9962

MIAMI-HIALEAH, FL

PIPELINE	DELIVERIES	MARKET SHARE
Florida Gas Transmiss	14,990,044	1.0000
TOTALS	14,990,044	HHI 10000

MIDDLESEX-SOMERSET-HUNTERDON, NJ

PIPELINE	DELIVERIES	MARKET SHARE
Equitable Gas Co.	4,586,241	0.0501
Texas Eastern Transmi	87,002,719	0.9499
TOTALS	91,588,960	HHI 9049

MILWAUKEE, WI

PIPELINE	DELIVERIES	MARKET SHARE
ANR Pipeline Co.	96,850,734	1.0000
TOTALS	96,850,734	HHI 10000

MINNEAPOLIS-ST. PAUL (MN-WI)

PIPELINE	DELIVERIES	MARKET SHARE
Midwestern Gas Transm	989,318	0.0067
Northern Natural Gas	146,998,175	0.9933
TOTALS	147,987,493	HHI 9867

MOBILE, AL

PIPELINE	DELIVERIES	MARKET SHARE
United Gas Pipeline C	21,067,052	1.0000
TOTALS	21,067,052	HHI 10000

MONROE, LA

PIPELINE	DELIVERIES	MARKET SHARE
Arkla Inc.	3,141,314	0.0142
United Gas Pipeline C	217,930,850	0.9855
Texas Gas Transmissio	68,592	0.0003
TOTALS	221,140,756	HHI 9714

MONTGOMERY, AL

PIPELINE	DELIVERIES	MARKET SHARE
Southern Natural Gas	15,990,695	1.0000
TOTALS	15,990,695	HHI 10000

MUNCIE, IN

PIPELINE	DELIVERIES	MARKET SHARE
ANR Pipeline Co.	104,392	1.0000
TOTALS	104,392	HHI 10000

NASHVILLE, TN

PIPELINE	DELIVERIES	MARKET SHARE
*Tenneco Inc.	262,292,995	0.9979
Texas Gas Transmissio	548,591	0.0021
TOTALS	262,841,586	HHI 9958

DETAIL OF SUBSIDIARIES	DELIVERIES	PCT. OF PARENT DEL.	PARENT
East Tennessee Natural	1,108,653	0.42%	Tenneco Inc.

NASSAU-SUFFOLK, NY

PIPELINE	DELIVERIES	MARKET SHARE
Transcontinental Gas	54,408,183	1.0000
TOTALS	54,408,183	HHI 10000

N.BEDFORD-FALL R.-ATTLEBORO, MA

PIPELINE	DELIVERIES	MARKET SHARE
Algonquin Gas Transmi	18,057,330	1.0000
TOTALS	18,057,330	HHI 10000

N.HAVEN-WATERBURY-MER., CT

PIPELINE	DELIVERIES	MARKET SHARE
Tenneco Inc.	1,392,607	0.0528
Algonquin Gas Transmi	24,960,491	0.9472
TOTALS	26,353,098	HHI 8999

N. LONDON-NORWICH, CT
PIPELINE	DELIVERIES	MARKET SHARE
Algonquin Gas Transmi	1,471,119	1.0000
TOTALS	1,471,119	HHI 10000

NEW ORLEANS, LA
PIPELINE	DELIVERIES	MARKET SHARE
Tenneco Inc.	37,736	0.0008
United Gas Pipeline C	45,839,415	0.9992
TOTALS	45,877,151	HHI 9984

NEW YORK, NY
PIPELINE	DELIVERIES	MARKET SHARE
Equitable Gas Co.	2,032	0.0000
Tenneco Inc.	48,532,520	0.1642
*Texas Eastern Corp.	78,961,671	0.2672
Transcontinental Gas	168,032,027	0.5686
TOTALS	295,528,250	HHI 4216

DETAIL OF SUBSIDIARIES	DELIVERIES	PCT. OF PARENT DEL.	PARENT
Algonquin Gas Transmis	5,017,023	6.35%	Texas Eastern Corp.
Texas Eastern Transmis	73,944,648	93.65%	Texas Eastern Corp.

NEWARK, NJ
PIPELINE	DELIVERIES	MARKET SHARE
Tenneco Inc.	223,471	0.0017
*Texas Eastern Corp.	134,970,903	0.9983
TOTALS	135,194,374	HHI 9967

DETAIL OF SUBSIDIARIES	DELIVERIES	PCT. OF PARENT DEL.	PARENT
Algonquin Gas Transmis	1,610,845	1.19%	Texas Eastern Corp.
Texas Eastern Transmis	133,360,058	98.81%	Texas Eastern Corp.

NIAGARA FALLS, NY
PIPELINE	DELIVERIES	MARKET SHARE
National Fuel Gas Dis	38,211,159	0.7769
Tenneco Inc.	10,974,292	0.2231
TOTALS	49,185,451	HHI 6533

OCALA, FL
PIPELINE	DELIVERIES	MARKET SHARE
Florida Gas Transmiss	853,864	1.0000
TOTALS	853,864	HHI 10000

ODESSA, TX
PIPELINE	DELIVERIES	MARKET SHARE
El Paso Natural Gas C	117,632	0.0093
West Texas Gathering	12,468,916	0.9907
TOTALS	12,586,548	HHI 9815

```
OKLAHOMA CITY, OK
         PIPELINE            DELIVERIES        MARKET SHARE

Northwest Central Pip        344,892           0.0506
Oklahoma Natural Gas       6,471,938           0.9494
         TOTALS            6,816,830              HHI    9039

OMAHA (NE-IA)
         PIPELINE            DELIVERIES        MARKET SHARE

Northern Natural Gas      37,483,024           1.0000
         TOTALS           37,483,024              HHI   10000

ORANGE COUNTY, NY
         PIPELINE            DELIVERIES        MARKET SHARE

Columbia Gas Transmis      1,504,321           1.0000
         TOTALS            1,504,321              HHI   10000

ORLANDO, FL
         PIPELINE            DELIVERIES        MARKET SHARE

Florida Gas Transmiss     26,201,254           1.0000
         TOTALS           26,201,254              HHI   10000

PANAMA CITY, FL
         PIPELINE            DELIVERIES        MARKET SHARE

Florida Gas Transmiss      3,525,464           1.0000
         TOTALS            3,525,464              HHI   10000

PARKERSBURG-MARIETTA (WV-OH)
         PIPELINE            DELIVERIES        MARKET SHARE

Columbia Gas Transmis      1,995,852           0.3628
Gas Transport Inc.         3,505,940           0.6372
         TOTALS            5,501,792              HHI    5377

PASCAGOULA, MS
         PIPELINE            DELIVERIES        MARKET SHARE

United Gas Pipeline C       6,555,557           1.0000
         TOTALS             6,555,557              HHI   10000

PENSACOLA, FL
         PIPELINE            DELIVERIES        MARKET SHARE

Florida Gas Transmiss         73,539           0.0051
United Gas Pipeline C      14,400,234           0.9949
         TOTALS            14,473,773              HHI    9899

PEORIA, IL
         PIPELINE            DELIVERIES        MARKET SHARE

Panhandle Eastern Pip     27,979,755           1.0000
         TOTALS           27,979,755              HHI   10000
```

PHILADELPHIA (PA-NJ)

PIPELINE	DELIVERIES	MARKET SHARE	
Texas Eastern Transmi	70,356,790	0.4301	
Transcontinental Gas	93,207,138	0.5699	
TOTALS	163,563,928	HHI	5098

PHOENIX, AZ

PIPELINE	DELIVERIES	MARKET SHARE	
El Paso Natural Gas C	39,593,479	1.0000	
TOTALS	39,593,479	HHI	10000

PINE BLUFF, AR

PIPELINE	DELIVERIES	MARKET SHARE	
Arkla Inc.	12,071,312	0.9951	
Mississippi River Tra	59,204	0.0049	
TOTALS	12,130,516	HHI	9903

PITTSBURG, PA

PIPELINE	DELIVERIES	MARKET SHARE	
Columbia Gas Transmis	154,482	0.0012	
Consolidated Gas Supp	8,492,981	0.0651	
Equitable Gas Co.	55,811,161	0.4279	
Tenneco Inc.	22,627,333	0.1735	
Texas Eastern Transmi	28,817,140	0.2209	
Carnegie Natural Gas	14,523,072	0.1114	
TOTALS	130,426,169	HHI	2787

PITTSFIELD, MA

PIPELINE	DELIVERIES	MARKET SHARE	
Tenneco Inc.	4,763,279	0.3441	
Algonquin Gas Transmi	9,078,959	0.6559	
TOTALS	13,842,238	HHI	5486

PORTSMOUTH-DOVER-ROCH., NH

PIPELINE	DELIVERIES	MARKET SHARE	
Granite State Gas Tra	4,896,301	1.0000	
TOTALS	4,896,301	HHI	10000

POUGHKEEPSIE, NY

PIPELINE	DELIVERIES	MARKET SHARE	
Tenneco Inc.	6,688,316	1.0000	
TOTALS	6,688,316	HHI	10000

PROV.-PAWTUCKET-WOONSOCKET, RI

PIPELINE	DELIVERIES	MARKET SHARE	
Tenneco Inc.	4,929,551	0.1950	
Algonquin Gas Transmi	20,355,474	0.8050	
TOTALS	25,285,025	HHI	6861

PUEBLO, CO

PIPELINE	DELIVERIES	MARKET SHARE
Colorado Interstate G	6,585,794	1.0000
TOTALS	6,585,794	HHI 10000

RAPID CITY, SD

PIPELINE	DELIVERIES	MARKET SHARE
Montana-Dakota Utilit	204,129	1.0000
TOTALS	204,129	HHI 10000

READING, PA

PIPELINE	DELIVERIES	MARKET SHARE
Consolidated Gas Supp	251,475	1.0000
TOTALS	251,475	HHI 10000

RENO, NV

PIPELINE	DELIVERIES	MARKET SHARE
Southwest Gas Corp.	6,749,761	1.0000
TOTALS	6,749,761	HHI 10000

RICHLAND-KENNEWICK-PASCO, WA

PIPELINE	DELIVERIES	MARKET SHARE
Northwest Pipeline Co	1,690,327	1.0000
TOTALS	1,690,327	HHI 10000

RIVERSIDE-SAN BERNADINO, CA

PIPELINE	DELIVERIES	MARKET SHARE
Southwest Gas Corp.	4,015,475	0.0144
Transwestern Pipeline	238,939,057	0.8591
Pacific Interstate Tr	35,164,988	0.1264
TOTALS	278,119,520	HHI 7543

ROANOKE, VA

PIPELINE	DELIVERIES	MARKET SHARE
Columbia Gas Transmis	3,211,158	0.4346
East Tennessee Natura	4,178,055	0.5654
TOTALS	7,389,213	HHI 5086

ROCHESTER, NY

PIPELINE	DELIVERIES	MARKET SHARE
Consolidated Gas Supp	46,770,132	1.0000
National Fuel Gas Dis	1,419	0.0000
TOTALS	46,771,551	HHI 9999

SACRAMENTO, CA

PIPELINE	DELIVERIES	MARKET SHARE
Southwest Gas Corp.	721,455	1.0000
TOTALS	721,455	HHI 10000

ST. CLOUD, MN

PIPELINE	DELIVERIES	MARKET SHARE
Northern Natural Gas	5,936,448	1.0000
TOTALS	5,936,448	HHI 10000

ST. JOSEPH, MO

PIPELINE	DELIVERIES	MARKET SHARE
Northwest Central Pip	6,566,254	1.0000
TOTALS	6,566,254	HHI 10000

ST. LOUIS (MO-IL)

PIPELINE	DELIVERIES	MARKET SHARE
Mississippi River Tra	130,731,721	0.7092
Natural Gas Pipeline	53,599,857	0.2908
TOTALS	184,331,578	HHI 5875

SALT LAKE CITY-OGDEN, UT

PIPELINE	DELIVERIES	MARKET SHARE
Mountain Fuel Supply	102,438,066	1.0000
TOTALS	102,438,066	HHI 10000

SAN ANGELO, TX

PIPELINE	DELIVERIES	MARKET SHARE
Enserch Corp.	5,647,040	1.0000
TOTALS	5,647,040	HHI 10000

SANTA BARBARA-SANTA MARIA-LOMPOC, CA

PIPELINE	DELIVERIES	MARKET SHARE
*Pacific Lighting Corp	257,000	1.0000
TOTALS	257,000	HHI 10000

DETAIL OF SUBSIDIARIES	DELIVERIES	PCT. OF PARENT DEL.	PARENT
Pacific Interstate Off	225,000	87.55%	Pacific Lighting Cor
Pacific Offshore Pipel	32,000	12.45%	Pacific Lighting Cor

SARASOTA, FL

PIPELINE	DELIVERIES	MARKET SHARE
Florida Gas Transmiss	755,298	1.0000
TOTALS	755,298	HHI 10000

SAVANNAH, GA

PIPELINE	DELIVERIES	MARKET SHARE
Southern Natural Gas	19,141,422	1.0000
TOTALS	19,141,422	HHI 10000

SCRANTON-WILKES-BARRE, PA

PIPELINE	DELIVERIES	MARKET SHARE
Transcontinental Gas	690,380	1.0000
TOTALS	690,380	HHI 10000

SEATTLE, WA
```
        PIPELINE          DELIVERIES        MARKET SHARE

Northwest Pipeline Co       227,689            1.0000
        TOTALS              227,689               HHI   10000
```

SHARON, PA
```
        PIPELINE          DELIVERIES        MARKET SHARE

*National Fuel Gas Co.  115,364,429            1.0000
        TOTALS          115,364,429               HHI   10000
                                           PCT. OF
DETAIL OF SUBSIDIARIES    DELIVERIES    PARENT DEL.   PARENT

National Fuel Gas Dist   38,211,159      33.12%   National Fuel Gas Co
National Fuel Gas Dist   38,211,159      33.12%   National Fuel Gas Co
National Fuel Gas Supp   38,942,111      33.76%   National Fuel Gas Co
```

SHERMAN-DENISON, TX
```
        PIPELINE          DELIVERIES        MARKET SHARE

Enserch Corp.               150,172            1.0000
        TOTALS              150,172               HHI   10000
```

SHREVEPORT, LA
```
        PIPELINE          DELIVERIES        MARKET SHARE

Arkla Inc.               23,372,322            0.7675
United Gas Pipeline C     7,079,269            0.2325
        TOTALS           30,451,591               HHI   6431
```

SIOUX CITY (IA-NE)
```
        PIPELINE          DELIVERIES        MARKET SHARE

Northern Natural Gas      9,823,222            1.0000
        TOTALS            9,823,222               HHI   10000
```

SIOUX FALLS, SD
```
        PIPELINE          DELIVERIES        MARKET SHARE

Northern Natural Gas      7,385,285            1.0000
        TOTALS            7,385,285               HHI   10000
```

SPRINGFIELD, IL
```
        PIPELINE          DELIVERIES        MARKET SHARE

Panhandle Eastern Pip    14,139,684            1.0000
        TOTALS           14,139,684               HHI   10000
```

SPRINGFIELD, MO
```
        PIPELINE          DELIVERIES        MARKET SHARE

Northwest Central Pip    12,161,489            1.0000
        TOTALS           12,161,489               HHI   10000
```

SPRINGFIELD, MA

PIPELINE	DELIVERIES	MARKET SHARE
Tenneco Inc.	7,726,781	1.0000
TOTALS	7,726,781	HHI 10000

TALLAHASSEE, FL

PIPELINE	DELIVERIES	MARKET SHARE
South Georgia Nautura	2,345,862	0.1785
Florida Gas Transmiss	10,793,249	0.8215
TOTALS	13,139,111	HHI 7067

TAMPA-ST.PETERSBURG-CLEARWATER, FL

PIPELINE	DELIVERIES	MARKET SHARE
Florida Gas Transmiss	15,593,375	1.0000
TOTALS	15,593,375	HHI 10000

TERRE HAUTE, IN

PIPELINE	DELIVERIES	MARKET SHARE
Texas Gas Transmissio	11,404,890	1.0000
TOTALS	11,404,890	HHI 10000

TEXARKANA, (TX-AR)

PIPELINE	DELIVERIES	MARKET SHARE
Arkla Inc.	8,472,989	1.0000
TOTALS	8,472,989	HHI 10000

TOLEDO, OH

PIPELINE	DELIVERIES	MARKET SHARE
ANR Pipeline Co.	339,001	0.0059
Columbia Gas Transmis	1,775,675	0.0308
Panhandle Eastern Pip	55,518,784	0.9633
TOTALS	57,633,460	HHI 9289

TOPEKA, KS

PIPELINE	DELIVERIES	MARKET SHARE
Northwest Central Pip	9,435,171	1.0000
TOTALS	9,435,171	HHI 10000

TUCSON, AZ

PIPELINE	DELIVERIES	MARKET SHARE
El Paso Natural Gas C	21,955,892	0.8841
Southwest Gas Corp.	2,877,799	0.1159
TOTALS	24,833,691	HHI 7951

TULSA, OK

PIPELINE	DELIVERIES	MARKET SHARE
Northwest Central Pip	4,942,254	0.1698
Union Gas System Inc.	294,030	0.0101
Oklahoma Natural Gas	23,867,984	0.8201
TOTALS	29,104,268	HHI 7015

TUSCALOOSA, AL

PIPELINE	DELIVERIES	MARKET SHARE
Southern Natural Gas	1,833,762	1.0000
TOTALS	1,833,762	HHI 10000

TYLER, TX

PIPELINE	DELIVERIES	MARKET SHARE
Enserch Corp.	180,360	0.6058
United Gas Pipeline C	117,384	0.3942
TOTALS	297,744	HHI 5224

VANCOUVER, WA

PIPELINE	DELIVERIES	MARKET SHARE
Northwest Pipeline Co	7,620,274	1.0000
TOTALS	7,620,274	HHI 10000

VICTORIA, TX

PIPELINE	DELIVERIES	MARKET SHARE
Enserch Corp.	560,698	0.6615
United Gas Pipeline C	286,870	0.3385
TOTALS	847,568	HHI 5522

WACO, TX

PIPELINE	DELIVERIES	MARKET SHARE
Enserch Corp.	24,939,196	1.0000
TOTALS	24,939,196	HHI 10000

WASHINGTON (DC-MD-VA)

PIPELINE	DELIVERIES	MARKET SHARE
Columbia Gas Transmis	57,145,701	0.2775
Transcontinental Gas	42,319,431	0.2055
Washington Gas Light	106,431,988	0.5169
TOTALS	205,897,120	HHI 3865

WATERLOO-CEDAR FALLS, IA

PIPELINE	DELIVERIES	MARKET SHARE
Northern Natural Gas	8,757,271	1.0000
TOTALS	8,757,271	HHI 10000

WAUSAU, WI

PIPELINE	DELIVERIES	MARKET SHARE
ANR Pipeline Co.	13,326,593	1.0000
TOTALS	13,326,593	HHI 10000

WEST PALM BEACH-BOCA RATON-DELRAY BEACH, FL

PIPELINE	DELIVERIES	MARKET SHARE
Florida Gas Transmiss	5,848,108	1.0000
TOTALS	5,848,108	HHI 10000

WHEELING (WV-OH)
PIPELINE	DELIVERIES	MARKET SHARE	
Columbia Gas Transmis	36,598	1.0000	
TOTALS	36,598	HHI	10000

WICHITA, KS
PIPELINE	DELIVERIES	MARKET SHARE	
Arkla Inc.	5,685,790	0.1575	
Northwest Central Pip	21,543,745	0.5969	
Natural Gas Pipeline	47,428	0.0013	
Northern Natural Gas	8,818,310	0.2443	
TOTALS	36,095,273	HHI	4407

WILLIAMSPORT, PA
PIPELINE	DELIVERIES	MARKET SHARE	
Transcontinental Gas	17,340,575.	1.0000	
TOTALS	17,340,575	HHI	10000

WILMINGTON (DE-NJ-MD)
PIPELINE	DELIVERIES	MARKET SHARE	
Transcontinental Gas	263,620	0.0420	
Eastern Shore Natural	6,006,879	0.9580	
TOTALS	6,270,499	HHI	9195

WORCH.-FITCHBURG-LEOMINSTER,MA
PIPELINE	DELIVERIES	MARKET SHARE	
Tenneco Inc.	7,039,890	0.2559	
Algonquin Gas Transmi	20,471,995	0.7441	
TOTALS	27,511,885	HHI	6192

Appendix C

THE SIZE OF THE POTENTIAL ENTRANT

THE LINEAR DEMAND CASE

If a competitive market becomes monopolized by a colluding group of current suppliers who face a linear demand curve and constant costs,[1] a 5 percent increase in price[2] will maximize profits if the residual demand elasticity of the group is 10.[3] Further, the profit-maximizing level of output is 50 percent of the competitive output supplied by the colluding group. Our reasoning is as follows:

Starting from the initial competitive level of output (Q_1) where the constant-cost market supply curve (S) intersects the residual demand curve (D), the colluding group will increase profits by reducing output as long as marginal revenue (MR) remains below constant marginal costs (MC). Profits are maximized at point M, where MR = MC. See Figure C.1.

At any price (P_1), the corresponding point on the marginal revenue curve (M) will determine a level of output (Q_2) that is one-half the quantity demanded (Q_1) at that price.[4] Facing a demand elasticity (E) of 10, the colluding group will maximize profits by increasing P_1 by 5 percent. That is, if

$$E = \frac{\text{percentage change in quantity}}{\text{percentage change in price}} = \frac{dQ/Q}{dP/P},$$

substituting E = 10 and dQ/Q = 50 and solving for dP/P yields dP/P = 5.[5] Thus, if a group of firms who initially supplied the competitive output formed a cartel and raised price 5 percent above the competitive level, the profit-maximizing cartel output would not exceed 50 percent of the competitive output.

Figure C.1

Residual Demand Analysis

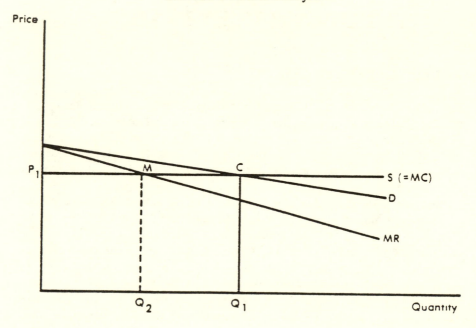

Thus, if a nearby supplier, or group of nearby suppliers, who is excluded from the cartel can expand output by more than 50 percent of the output sold at the competitive price, the colluding group would be left with less than 50 percent of the competitive output. This would imply $E > 10$ for the colluding group and therefore that a 5 percent price increase is not profit maximizing.[6] The cartel could increase profits by setting a price less than 5 percent over cost. In this case, however, the 5 percent price increase is *transitory*, which indicates that the colluding group does not possess substantial market power.

If a pipeline is currently supplying the competitive market, its ability to gain admission into the colluding group will depend on the percentage of the monopolized market supplied by the colluding group. If the colluding group supplies *over 33.3 percent* of the monopolized market, no additional current suppliers will be admitted into the colluding group.

The intuition is the following. Since we know that the newly formed cartel will supply only 50 percent of the output it supplied when it behaved competitively, a cartel that sets a monopoly price and reduces its supply to 34 percent of the total competitive output must have supplied 68 percent of the competitive output (or double its collusive output). Hence, the remainder of the competitive output is only 32 percent ($= 100 - 68$), which is insufficient to offset the output reduction of the cartel. Thus, if one current supplier provides 68 percent of the competitive output, it will be a dominant firm in the short run and all other current suppliers are fringe suppliers. The fringe suppliers are too small to prevent the dominant firm from setting a price 5 percent over cost.

On the other hand, if the colluding group supplied 66.6 percent of the competitive output, another current supplier, or group of current suppliers, who supplied the remaining 33.3 percent of the competitive market would be able to undercut the cartel price and therefore would be expected to gain admission into the cartel.[7] Using the same reasoning, in our simple model, the *maximum* number of *equal-sized* firms in the cartel will vary with the percentages of the monopolized market[8] supplied by the colluding group as shown in Table C.1.

Thus, only one additional current supplier is likely to gain admission into the colluding group even if that group supplies only 50.1 percent of the competitive output. In this case, the addition of one supplier in the monopolized market would mean that there are two colluding firms with individual market shares of at least $25.05 = (50.1)(1/2)$. The colluding group could expand to three members when the percentage of the competitive output initially supplied by the dominant firm falls to the 40.1 to 50.0 percent range.

Table C.1

Maximum Size of the Colluding Group

% Competitive Output	% Monopolized Output	Number of Firms
100.0	50.0	1
66.6	33.3	2
50.0	25.0	3
40.0	20.0	4
33.3	16.6	5

THE CONSTANT ELASTICITY DEMAND CASE

If the residual demand curve of the colluding group is of constant elasticity rather than linear, the excluded nearby firm must be able to supply at least 65 percent of the competitive output to prevent the cartel from setting a price 5 percent above cost.

Assuming profit-maximizing behavior, the Lerner Index (L) can be expressed in terms of the elasticity of the firm's residual demand.[9] That is,

$$L = (P - MC)/P = 1/E.$$

If a price 5 percent above cost is to be profitable, E must be less than or equal to 21. That is, if $P = [(1.05)(MC)]$ is to be profit maximizing, then the Lerner Index becomes

$$(1.05MC - MC)/1.05MC = 1/E; \text{ and } E = 21.$$

For a constant elasticity residual demand curve with an elasticity of 21,[10] the quantity demanded from the colluding group at a price 5 percent above cost will be 35 percent of the quantity demanded at a competitive price. The intuition is as follows:

Assume that the form of the demand function is

$$(1) \quad Q_1 = AP_1^{-21}$$

where

$\quad\quad$ Q = quantity demanded,

$$A = \text{a constant, and}$$
$$P = \text{price.}$$

If price is increased by a proportionality factor of 1.05,

$$(2) \quad Q_2 = A[(1.05)P_1]^{-21}$$

and the demand function suggests that the quantity demanded must decrease by a proportionality factor equal to

$$(3) \quad Q_2/Q_1 = (A/A)(1.05P_1/P_1)^{-21} = (1.05)^{-21} = 1/(2.786) = .36.$$

For expositional purposes, we use .35.

Thus, if a group of firms who initially supplied the competitive output formed a cartel and set a price 5 percent above the competitive level (Q_1), the cartel output (Q_2) would be 35 percent of the competitive output (Q_1). Thus, if a nearby pipeline can expand output in the new market by at least 65 percent, the nearby pipeline is a potential entrant and must be included in the cartel.

The constant elasticity case is therefore more restrictive in the sense that it requires a noncolluding firm to be larger in size (65 percent versus 50 percent) to pose a competitive threat to the cartel if denied membership. Except in the long run, the larger size requirement tends to reduce the number of potential entrants, thereby limiting the size of the colluding group, and therefore it tends to increase the ability of the cartel to set a monopoly price and earn supracompetitive profits.

In Chapter 5, "The Intermediate Run", the number of competitive markets is estimated using both demand elasticity assumptions. Since divertible gas is limited in the intermediate run, the larger size requirement implicit in the constant elasticity case is expected to reduce the number of potential entrants and, in turn, reduce the number of competitive markets.

NOTES

1. The following analysis applies to entry into the colluding group of current suppliers. In addition, when the colluding group initially controls total market output (e.g., in the short run), potential entry into the market may result in entry into the colluding group. That is, if a potential entrant can prevent the colluding group of current suppliers from maximizing profit subject to a 5 percent increase in price, it will gain admission into the colluding group in the longer run.

2. Five to ten percent is considered a "small but significant and nontransitory increase in price." See the discussion in Chapter 3 at p. 31, *supra*.

3. Although the colluding group *could* raise price by 5 percent over cost and earn a positive profit as long as the demand elasticity is less than 20, the resulting profit will be a maximum only at that output which corresponds to an elasticity of 10. Given all the possible combinations of a 5 percent price increase and demand elasticities between 0 and 20, we therefore assume the elasticity (and output) implicit in the most profitable 5 percent increase over cost. This is the price that the cartel *would* charge to maximize profits. For a further discussion of these two pricing policies (i.e, positive-profit versus maximum-profit pricing) and their associated market definitions, see Johnson (1986), pp. 1-10.

Although empirical studies estimate the market demand elasticity at 1.0 or less, we use the theoretical elasticity coefficient of 10 for two reasons. First, the empirical studies estimate the elasticity of the *market* demand curve rather than the *residual* demand curve facing the colluding group. It is the residual demand curve that is necessary to determine antitrust markets. (See Chapter 3.) Rather than debate the circumstances under which the market demand curve is a good approximation of the residual demand curve, we use the more elastic measure. Second, a higher elasticity estimate implies a smaller price increase or a larger output reduction by the colluding group, which, in turn, makes entry into the market less attractive. Thus, any bias in our elasticity assumption tends to reduce the number of potential entrants and to increase the HHI. As a result, our analysis may underestimate the number of markets that are competitive.

4. For an explanation of the derivation of the marginal revenue curve, see Ferguson (1972), pp. 114-16.

5. Alternatively, given $E = 10$, a profit-maximizing $dP/P = 5$ implies $dQ/Q = 50$.

6. Given $E = 10 + k$ and $dQ/Q = 50$ (where $k > 0$ indicates the increment in E due to a noncolluding rival), the profit-maximizing $dP/P = 50/(10 + k) < 5$. Diagrammatically, potential entry causes the initial (short-run) residual demand curve (based on current suppliers) to become flatter or more elastic (in the longer run) at the competitive price and competitive output of the cartel. The existence of nearby suppliers large enough to supply 50 percent of the competitive output implies that sales of the colluding group of current suppliers fall to zero at a price 5 percent over cost.

7. Although current suppliers with less than a 33.3 percent share may be able to expand sales by renegotiating contracts and diverting gas from lower-valued to higher-valued customers, such an expansion is unlikely to occur in the immediate period, or short run. Furthermore, since pipelines are designed to operate at full capacity during peak demand periods, excess capacity does not provide a means to expand contract demand service. Thus, the ability to expand service is severely limited in the short run. However, these same current suppliers may represent potential entrants in the intermediate run and do represent potential entrants in the long run.

8. The percentages of output in column 2 of Table C.1 represent the quantity supplied by the cartel (at the monopoly price) expressed as a percentage of the total competitive market output. For example, to say that the cartel supplies 33.3 percent in the monopolized market means that the cartel's output is equivalent to 33.3 percent of the competitive output of all suppliers--not 33.3 percent of the monopolized market. Hence, column 2 of Table C.1 does not show the market share of the cartel.

9. See Landes and Posner (1981), Appendix.

10. The elasticity of 21 in the constant demand elasticity case is consistent with the elasticity of 10 in the linear case. Since the elasticity increases along the linear demand curve as the price increases, it can be shown that $E = 10$ is associated with the initial competitive equilibrium (i.e., $P = MC = MR$) whereas $E = 21$ corresponds to the collusive equilibrium (i.e., $P = 1.05MC > MR$).

Appendix D

U.S. CENSUS REGIONS

Region/State	Region/State

1. New England

    Maine (ME)
    New Hampshire (NH)
    Vermont (VT)
    Massachusetts (MA)
    Rhode Island (RI)
    Connecticut (CT)

2. Mid-Atlantic

    New York (NY)
    New Jersey (NJ)
    Pennsylvania (PA)

3. East North Central

    Ohio (OH)
    Indiana (IN)
    Illinois (IL)
    Michigan (MI)

Wisconsin (WI)

4. West North Central

    Minnesota (MN)
    Iowa (IA)
    Missouri (MO)
    North Dakota (ND)
    South Dakota (SD)
    Nebraska (NE)
    Kansas (KS)

5. South Atlantic

    Delaware (DE)
    Maryland (MD)
    District of Columbia (DC)
    Virginia (VA)
    West Virginia (WV)

U.S. Census Regions

Region/State	Region/State

South Atlantic *(continued)*

   North Carolina (NC)
   South Carolina (SC
   Georgia (GA)
   Florida (FL)

6. East South Central

   Kentucky (KY)
   Tennessee (TN)
   Alabama (AL)
   Mississippi (MS)

7. West South Central

   Arkansas (AR)
   Louisiana (LA)
   Oklahoma (OK)
   Texas (TX)

8. Mountain

   Montana (MT)
   Idaho (ID)
   Wyoming (WY)
   Colorado (CO)
   New Mexico (NM)
   Arizona (AZ)
   Utah (UT)
   Nevada (NV)

9. Pacific

   Washington (WA)
   Oregon (OR)
   California (CA)

Source: U.S. Department of Commerce, Bureau of the Census, *Statistical Abstract of the United States: 1982-83*, 103rd Edition, Figure 1.

Appendix E

NEARBY SUPPLIERS
BY TYPE AND BY MARKET

For each market in our sample, Appendix E identifies each of the three types of nearby suppliers with the prefix PT, NPT, or NDL where

PT   =   pass-through pipeline,
NPT =   nearby pass-through pipeline, and
NDL =   nearby delivery pipeline.

Current suppliers are listed without a prefix. For a further explanation of this appendix refer to Chapter 4, subsection "Limitations of the Short-Run Analysis."

ABILENE, TX

(0)   Enserch Corp.
(0) PT-Western Gas Interstate Co.
(100)NDL*El Paso Natural Gas Co.
(100)NDL-Energas Co.
(100)NDL*United Energy Resources Inc.
(100)NDL*Pioneer Corp.
(100)NDL*Houston Natural Gas Corp.
(100)NPT-Producers Gas Co.
(100)NPT-Red River Gas Pipeline Corp.
(100)NPT-Southwestern Gas Pipeline Inc.
(100)NPT-Texas Gas Transmission Co.
(100)NPT-Texacol Gas Services, Inc.
(100)NPT-Northern Natural Gas Co.
(140)NDL-Natural Gas Pipeline Co. of America
(140)NPT-Winnie Pipeline Co.

DETAIL OF SUBSIDIARIES	PARENT
United Gas Pipeline Co.	United Energy Resources
Palo Duro Pipeline Co.	United Energy Resources
Valley Gas Transmission, Inc.	Houston Natural Gas Corp.
Odessa Natural Gas Corp.	El Paso Natural Gas Co.
Intratex Gas Co.	Houston Natural Gas Corp.
West Texas Gathering Co.	Pioneer Corp.
Oasis Pipeline Co.	Houston Natural Gas Corp.

ALBANY, GA

(0)   *Southern Natural Gas Co.
(100)NDL-Transcontinental Gas Pipeline Corp.
(100)NDL-Florida Gas Transmission Co.
(100)NPT-United Cities Gas Co.
(100)NPT-Southeast Alabama Gas District, The
(140)NPT*South Carolina Electric & Gas Co.

DETAIL OF SUBSIDIARIES	PARENT
South Georgia Nautural Gas Co.	Southern Natural Gas Co.
Carolina Pipeline Co.	South Carolina Electric

ALBANY-SCHENECTADY-TROY, NY

```
(  0)    Consolidated Gas Supply Corp.
(  0) PT-Central Hudson Gas & Electric Corp.
(  0) PT-Niagara Mohawk Power Corp.
(100)NDL-Columbia Gas Transmission Corp.
(100)NDL-Equitable Gas Co.
(100)NDL-National Fuel Gas Distribution Corp.
(100)NDL*Tenneco Inc.
(100)NDL*Texas Eastern Corp.
(100)NDL-Transcontinental Gas Pipeline Corp.
(100)NDL-Distrigas of Massachusetts Corp.
(100)NDL-North Penn Gas Co.
(100)NPT-Rochester Gas & Electric Corp.
(120)NPT-South Jersey Gas Co.
```

```
 DETAIL OF SUBSIDIARIES              PARENT

Granite State Gas Transmission, Inc  Tenneco Inc.
Algonquin Gas Transmission Co.       Texas Eastern Corp.
Texas Eastern Transmission Corp.     Texas Eastern Corp.
Northern Utilities, Inc., - ME       Tenneco Inc.
```

ALEXANDRIA, LA

```
(  0)    Arkla Inc.
(  0)   *Panhandle Eastern Corp.
(  0)   *Tenneco Inc.
(  0)   *United Energy Resources Inc.
(  0) PT-Columbia Gulf Transmission Co.
(100)NDL-Enserch Corp.
(100)NDL-KN Energy Inc.
(100)NDL-Southern Natural Gas Co.
(100)NDL-Texas Eastern Transmission Corp.
(100)NDL-Transcontinental Gas Pipeline Corp.
(100)NDL-Crab Run Gas Co.
(100)NDL-West Lake Arthur Corp.
(100)NDL-Shell Oil Co.
(100)NDL-Louisiana Resources Co.
(100)NDL-Mississippi Valley Gas Co.
(100)NDL-Mid-Louisiana Gas Co.
(100)NDL-Monterey Pipeline Co.
(100)NDL-Natural Gas Pipeline Co. of America
(100)NDL-Texas Gas Pipeline Co.
(100)NDL*Houston Natural Gas Corp.
(100)NDL-Texas Gas Transmission Co.
(100)NDL-Northern Natural Gas Co.
(100)NPT-Seagull Pipeline Corp.
(100)NPT-Delhi Gas Pipeline Corp.
(100)NPT-Louisiana State Gas Corp.
(100)NPT-Sabine Pipeline Co.
(120)NPT-Florida Gas Transmission Co.
(140)NDL-Mississippi River Transmission Corp.
(140)NPT-Esperanza Transmission Co.
```

DETAIL OF SUBSIDIARIES	PARENT
Trunkline Gas Co.	Panhandle Eastern Corp.
Louisiana Intrastate Gas Corp.	Tenneco Inc.
United Gas Pipeline Co.	United Energy Resources
Trunkline Lng Co.	Panhandle Eastern Corp.
Channel Industries Gas Co.	Tenneco Inc.
United Texas Transmission Co.	United Energy Resources
Valley Gas Transmission, Inc.	Houston Natural Gas Corp.
Houston Pipeline Co.	Houston Natural Gas Corp.

ALLENTOWN-BETHLEHEM (PA-NJ)

```
(  0)    Columbia Gas Transmission Corp.
(  0)    Transcontinental Gas Pipeline Corp.
(  0)    North Penn Gas Co.
(100)NDL-Consolidated Gas Supply Corp.
(100)NDL-Equitable Gas Co.
(100)NDL-Tenneco Inc.
(100)NDL*Texas Eastern Corp.
(100)NDL*Washington Gas Light Co.
(100)NDL-Eastern Shore Natural Gas Co.
(100)NPT-Central Hudson Gas & Electric Corp.
(100)NPT-Niagara Mohawk Power Corp.
(100)NPT-South Jersey Gas Co.
(140)NDL*National Fuel Gas Co.
(140)NPT-Rochester Gas & Electric Corp.
```

```
 DETAIL OF SUBSIDIARIES                  PARENT

Algonquin Gas Transmission Co.       Texas Eastern Corp.
Texas Eastern Transmission Corp.     Texas Eastern Corp.
Frederick Gas Co.                    Washington Gas Light Co.
National Fuel Gas Distribution Corp  National Fuel Gas Co.
National Fuel Gas Supply Corp.       National Fuel Gas Co.
```

AMARILLO, TX

```
(  0)    Energas Co.
(  0)    Western Gas Interstate Co.
(  0)    Colorado Interstate Gas Co.
(  0) PT-Pioneer Corp.
(100)NDL-El Paso Natural Gas Co.
(100)NDL-Mississippi River Transmission Corp.
(100)NDL-Northwest Central Pipeline Corp.
(100)NDL-Panhandle Eastern Pipeline Co.
(100)NDL-Transwestern Pipeline Co.
(100)NDL-Delhi Gas Pipeline Corp.
(100)NDL-Natural Gas Pipeline Co. of America
(100)NDL-Northern Natural Gas Co.
(100)NPT-Red River Gas Pipeline Corp.
(120)NDL-Arkla Inc.
(120)NDL-Enserch Corp.
(120)NDL-Mountain Fuel Supply Co.
(120)NDL-Producers Gas Co.
(120)NDL-Oklahoma Natural Gas Co. (Oneok Inc.)
```

ANDERSON, IN

```
(  0)  *Panhandle Eastern Corp.
(100)NDL*ANR Pipeline Co.
(100)NDL*Columbia Gas System, Inc.
(100)NDL*Tenneco Inc.
(100)NDL-Texas Eastern Transmission Corp.
(100)NDL-Ohio River Pipeline Corp.
(100)NDL-Texas Gas Transmission Co.
(100)NPT*Consolidated Natural Gas Corp.
(100)NPT-Cincinnati Gas & Electric Co.
(100)NPT-Louisville Gas & Electric Co.
(100)NPT-Northern Illinois Gas Co.
(100)NPT-Northern Indiana Public Service Co.
(100)NPT-Western Kentucky Gas Co.
(120)NDL-Michigan Consolidated Gas Co.
(120)NDL-Natural Gas Pipeline Co. of America
(120)NPT-Central Illinois Light Co.
(120)NPT-Illinois Power Co.
(140)NPT-Michigan Gas Storage Co.
```

DETAIL OF SUBSIDIARIES	PARENT
Panhandle Eastern Pipeline Co.	Panhandle Eastern Corp.
Columbia Gas Transmission Corp.	Columbia Gas System, Inc.
Trunkline Gas Co.	Panhandle Eastern Corp.
Midwestern Gas Transmission Co.	Tenneco Inc.
Ohio Valley Gas Corp.	Columbia Gas System, Inc.
East Ohio Gas Co.	Consolidated Natural Gas
Inland Gas Co. Inc.	Columbia Gas System, Inc.
Consolidated Gas Supply Corp.	Consolidated Natural Gas
Great Lakes Gas Transmission Co.	ANR Pipeline Co.

ANDERSON, SC

```
(  0)    *Transcontinental Gas Pipeline Corp.
(  0) PT*South Carolina Electric & Gas Co.
(100)NDL-Southern Natural Gas Co.
(100)NDL*Tenneco Inc.
(100)NPT-United Cities Gas Co.
```

DETAIL OF SUBSIDIARIES	PARENT
Carolina Pipeline Co.	South Carolina Electric
East Tennessee Natural Gas Co.	Tenneco Inc.
North Carolina Natural Gas Corp.	Tenneco Inc.
Public Service Co. of N.C., Inc.	Transcontinental Gas

ANNISTON, AL

    (0)   *Southern Natural Gas Co.
    (100)NDL-Alabama-Tennessee Natural Gas Co.
    (100)NDL*Tenneco Inc.
    (100)NDL-Texas Eastern Transmission Corp.
    (100)NDL-Transcontinental Gas Pipeline Corp.
    (100)NDL-United Gas Pipeline Co.
    (100)NPT-United Cities Gas Co.
    (100)NPT-Carolina Pipeline Co.
    (100)NPT-Southeast Alabama Gas District, The
    (120)NDL-Texas Gas Transmission Co.
    (120)NPT-Columbia Gulf Transmission Co.
    (140)NDL-Mississippi Valley Gas Co.

DETAIL OF SUBSIDIARIES	PARENT
South Georgia Nautural Gas Co.	Southern Natural Gas Co.
East Tennessee Natural Gas Co.	Tenneco Inc.
Tennessee Natural Gas Lines, Inc.	Tenneco Inc.

ATHENS, GA

    (0)   *Transcontinental Gas Pipeline Corp.
    (100)NDL*Southern Natural Gas Co.
    (100)NDL*Tenneco Inc.
    (100)NPT-United Cities Gas Co.
    (100)NPT*South Carolina Electric & Gas Co.
    (120)NPT-Southeast Alabama Gas District, The
    (140)NDL-United Gas Pipeline Co.

DETAIL OF SUBSIDIARIES	PARENT
East Tennessee Natural Gas Co.	Tenneco Inc.
North Carolina Natural Gas Corp.	Tenneco Inc.
Public Service Co. of N.C., Inc.	Transcontinental Gas
Carolina Pipeline Co.	South Carolina Electric
South Georgia Nautural Gas Co.	Southern Natural Gas Co.

ATLANTA, GA

```
(  0)    *Southern Natural Gas Co.
(  0)    *Transcontinental Gas Pipeline Corp.
(100)NDL-Alabama-Tennessee Natural Gas Co.
(100)NDL*Tenneco Inc.
(100)NDL-United Gas Pipeline Co.
(100)NPT-United Cities Gas Co.
(100)NPT*South Carolina Electric & Gas Co.
(100)NPT-Southeast Alabama Gas District, The
(140)NDL-Texas Eastern Transmission Corp.
(140)NDL-Texas Gas Transmission Co.
(140)NPT-Columbia Gulf Transmission Co.
```

```
   DETAIL OF SUBSIDIARIES                 PARENT

South Georgia Nautural Gas Co.       Southern Natural Gas Co.
East Tennessee Natural Gas Co.       Tenneco Inc.
Public Service Co. of N.C., Inc.     Transcontinental Gas
Carolina Pipeline Co.                South Carolina Electric
North Carolina Natural Gas Corp.     Tenneco Inc.
Tennessee Natural Gas Lines, Inc.    Tenneco Inc.
```

AUGUSTA (GA-SC)

```
(  0)    *Southern Natural Gas Co.
(  0) PT*South Carolina Electric & Gas Co.
(100)NDL*Transcontinental Gas Pipeline Corp.
(100)NPT-North Carolina Natural Gas Corp.
(100)NPT-United Cities Gas Co.
(140)NPT-Southeast Alabama Gas District, The
```

```
   DETAIL OF SUBSIDIARIES                 PARENT

Carolina Pipeline Co.                South Carolina Electric
Public Service Co. of N.C., Inc.     Transcontinental Gas
South Georgia Nautural Gas Co.       Southern Natural Gas Co.
```

AUSTIN, TX

```
(  0)    Enserch Corp.
(  0)    *United Energy Resources Inc.
(  0)    *Houston Natural Gas Corp.
(  0) PT-Producers Gas Co.
(  0) PT-Winnie Pipeline Co.
(  0) PT-Texas Gas Transmission Co.
(  0) PT-Northern Natural Gas Co.
(100)NDL*Tenneco Inc.
(100)NDL-Valero Interstate Transmission Co.
(100)NDL-Natural Gas Pipeline Co. of America
(100)NDL-Texacol Gas Services, Inc.
(100)NPT-Arkla Inc.
(100)NPT*El Paso Natural Gas Co.
(100)NPT-Trunkline Gas Co.
(100)NPT-Intrastate Gathering Corp.
(100)NPT-Southern Natural Gas Co.
(100)NPT-Texas Eastern Transmission Corp.
(100)NPT-Seagull Pipeline Corp.
(100)NPT-Delhi Gas Pipeline Corp.
(100)NPT-Southwestern Gas Pipeline Inc.
(120)NDL-Florida Gas Transmission Co.
(120)NPT-Transcontinental Gas Pipeline Corp.
(120)NPT-Esperanza Transmission Co.
(140)NPT-Western Gas Interstate Co.
```

DETAIL OF SUBSIDIARIES	PARENT
United Gas Pipeline Co.	United Energy Resources
Intratex Gas Co.	Houston Natural Gas Corp.
Oasis Pipeline Co.	Houston Natural Gas Corp.
Channel Industries Gas Co.	Tenneco Inc.
United Texas Transmission Co.	United Energy Resources
Houston Pipeline Co.	Houston Natural Gas Corp.
Valley Gas Transmission, Inc.	Houston Natural Gas Corp.
Odessa Natural Gas Corp.	El Paso Natural Gas Co.
Palo Duro Pipeline Co.	United Energy Resources

BALTIMORE, MD

```
(  0)   *Columbia Gas System, Inc.
(100)NDL*Consolidated Natural Gas Corp.
(100)NDL-Equitable Gas Co.
(100)NDL-Tenneco Inc.
(100)NDL*Texas Eastern Corp.
(100)NDL-Transcontinental Gas Pipeline Corp.
(100)NDL*Washington Gas Light Co.
(100)NDL-Eastern Shore Natural Gas Co.
(100)NDL-North Penn Gas Co.
(100)NPT-South Jersey Gas Co.
(120)NDL-Carnegie Natural Gas Co.
(140)NPT-Central Hudson Gas & Electric Corp.
```

DETAIL OF SUBSIDIARIES	PARENT
Columbia Gas Transmission Corp.	Columbia Gas System, Inc.
Frederick Gas Co.	Washington Gas Light Co.
Consolidated Gas Supply Corp.	Consolidated Natural Gas
Texas Eastern Transmission Corp.	Texas Eastern Corp.
Shenandoah Gas Co.	Washington Gas Light Co.
Commonwealth Gas Pipeline Corp.	Columbia Gas System, Inc.
Algonquin Gas Transmission Co.	Texas Eastern Corp.
East Ohio Gas Co.	Consolidated Natural Gas

BATON ROUGE, LA

```
(  0)    *Tenneco Inc.
(  0)     Mid-Louisiana Gas Co.
(  0)     Monterey Pipeline Co.
(  0)    *United Energy Resources Inc.
(  0)     Northern Natural Gas Co.
(100)NDL-Arkla Inc.
(100)NDL*Panhandle Eastern Corp.
(100)NDL-Southern Natural Gas Co.
(100)NDL-Texas Eastern Transmission Corp.
(100)NDL-Transcontinental Gas Pipeline Corp.
(100)NDL-Crab Run Gas Co.
(100)NDL-West Lake Arthur Corp.
(100)NDL-Shell Oil Co.
(100)NDL-Louisiana Resources Co.
(100)NDL-Mississippi Valley Gas Co.
(100)NDL-Delta Gas Inc.
(100)NDL-Natural Gas Pipeline Co. of America
(100)NDL-Texas Gas Transmission Co.
(100)NPT-Columbia Gulf Transmission Co.
(100)NPT-Florida Gas Transmission Co.
(100)NPT-Louisiana State Gas Corp.
(100)NPT-Sabine Pipeline Co.
(120)NDL*Houston Natural Gas Corp.
(140)NDL-Enserch Corp.
(140)NDL-Texas Gas Pipeline Co.
(140)NPT-Seagull Pipeline Corp.
```

```
  DETAIL OF SUBSIDIARIES                PARENT

Louisiana Intrastate Gas Corp.      Tenneco Inc.
United Gas Pipeline Co.             United Energy Resources
Trunkline Gas Co.                  Panhandle Eastern Corp.
Trunkline Lng Co.                  Panhandle Eastern Corp.
Valley Gas Transmission, Inc.      Houston Natural Gas Corp.
Channel Industries Gas Co.         Tenneco Inc.
United Texas Transmission Co.       United Energy Resources
Houston Pipeline Co.               Houston Natural Gas Corp.
```

BATTLE CREEK, MI

```
(  0)   *Panhandle Eastern Corp.
(  0)    Michigan Consolidated Gas Co.
(100)NDL*ANR Pipeline Co.
(100)NDL-Columbia Gas Transmission Corp.
(100)NDL-Texas Gas Transmission Co.
(100)NPT*Consolidated Natural Gas Corp.
(100)NPT-Michigan Gas Storage Co.
(100)NPT-Northern Illinois Gas Co.
(100)NPT-Northern Indiana Public Service Co.
(120)NDL-Natural Gas Pipeline Co. of America
(140)NDL*Tenneco Inc.
(140)NPT-Texas Eastern Transmission Corp.
(140)NPT-Transcontinental Gas Pipeline Corp.
(140)NPT-Cincinnati Gas & Electric Co.
```

DETAIL OF SUBSIDIARIES	PARENT
Panhandle Eastern Pipeline Co.	Panhandle Eastern Corp.
Great Lakes Gas Transmission Co.	ANR Pipeline Co.
Trunkline Gas Co.	Panhandle Eastern Corp.
East Ohio Gas Co.	Consolidated Natural Gas
Consolidated Gas Supply Corp.	Consolidated Natural Gas
Midwestern Gas Transmission Co.	Tenneco Inc.

BEAUMONT-PORT ARTHUR, TX

```
(  0)    Enserch Corp.
(  0)   *Tenneco Inc.
(  0)   *United Energy Resources Inc.
(  0)    Texas Gas Pipeline Co.
(  0)   *Houston Natural Gas Corp.
(  0) PT-Seagull Pipeline Corp.
(  0) PT-Sabine Pipeline Co.
(100)NDL-Arkla Inc.
(100)NDL*Panhandle Eastern Corp.
(100)NDL-Southern Natural Gas Co.
(100)NDL-Texas Eastern Transmission Corp.
(100)NDL-Crab Run Gas Co.
(100)NDL-West Lake Arthur Corp.
(100)NDL-Shell Oil Co.
(100)NDL-Louisiana Resources Co.
(100)NDL-Florida Gas Transmission Co.
(100)NDL-Mid-Louisiana Gas Co.
(100)NDL-Natural Gas Pipeline Co. of America
(100)NDL-Texas Gas Transmission Co.
(100)NDL-Northern Natural Gas Co.
(100)NPT-Columbia Gulf Transmission Co.
(100)NPT-Transcontinental Gas Pipeline Corp.
(100)NPT-Valero Interstate Transmission Co.
(100)NPT-Producers Gas Co.
(100)NPT-Delhi Gas Pipeline Corp.
(120)NDL-Monterey Pipeline Co.
(120)NPT-Esperanza Transmission Co.
(140)NDL-KN Energy Inc.
```

DETAIL OF SUBSIDIARIES   PARENT

Channel Industries Gas Co.	Tenneco Inc.
United Texas Transmission Co.	United Energy Resources
Valley Gas Transmission, Inc.	Houston Natural Gas Corp.
Houston Pipeline Co.	Houston Natural Gas Corp.
Trunkline Gas Co.	Panhandle Eastern Corp.
Trunkline Lng Co.	Panhandle Eastern Corp.
Louisiana Intrastate Gas Corp.	Tenneco Inc.
United Gas Pipeline Co.	United Energy Resources

BEAVER COUNTY, PA

```
(  0)    Columbia Gas Transmission Corp.
(  0)    Tenneco Inc.
(100)NDL*Consolidated Natural Gas Corp.
(100)NDL-Equitable Gas Co.
(100)NDL-Gas Transport Inc.
(100)NDL*National Fuel Gas Co.
(100)NDL-Texas Eastern Transmission Corp.
(100)NDL-Transcontinental Gas Pipeline Corp.
(100)NDL-Carnegie Natural Gas Co.
(100)NDL-North Penn Gas Co.
(100)NDL-Texas Gas Transmission Co.
(140)NDL-Shenandoah Gas Co.
```

DETAIL OF SUBSIDIARIES	PARENT
Consolidated Gas Supply Corp.	Consolidated Natural Gas
National Fuel Gas Distribution Corp	National Fuel Gas Co.
National Fuel Gas Supply Corp.	National Fuel Gas Co.
East Ohio Gas Co.	Consolidated Natural Gas
River Gas Co.	Consolidated Natural Gas

BENTON HARBOR, MI

```
(  0)    *ANR Pipeline Co.
(  0)    *Panhandle Eastern Corp.
(100)NDL-Columbia Gas Transmission Corp.
(100)NDL-Midwestern Gas Transmission Co.
(100)NDL-Michigan Consolidated Gas Co.
(100)NDL-Natural Gas Pipeline Co. of America
(100)NDL-Texas Gas Transmission Co.
(100)NPT-East Ohio Gas Co.
(100)NPT-Michigan Gas Storage Co.
(100)NPT-Northern Illinois Gas Co.
(100)NPT-Northern Indiana Public Service Co.
(120)NPT-Central Illinois Light Co.
(120)NPT-Illinois Power Co.
```

DETAIL OF SUBSIDIARIES	PARENT
Panhandle Eastern Pipeline Co.	Panhandle Eastern Corp.
Great Lakes Gas Transmission Co.	ANR Pipeline Co.
Trunkline Gas Co.	Panhandle Eastern Corp.
Wisconsin Natural Gas Co.	ANR Pipeline Co.

BERGEN-PASSAIC, NJ

```
(  0)    Tenneco Inc.
(100)NDL-Columbia Gas Transmission Corp.
(100)NDL-Consolidated Gas Supply Corp.
(100)NDL-Equitable Gas Co.
(100)NDL*Texas Eastern Corp.
(100)NDL-Transcontinental Gas Pipeline Corp.
(100)NDL-Eastern Shore Natural Gas Co.
(100)NDL-North Penn Gas Co.
(100)NPT-Central Hudson Gas & Electric Corp.
(100)NPT-Niagara Mohawk Power Corp.
(100)NPT-South Jersey Gas Co.
(140)NPT-Frederick Gas Co.
```

```
   DETAIL OF SUBSIDIARIES               PARENT

   Algonquin Gas Transmission Co.       Texas Eastern Corp.
   Texas Eastern Transmission Corp.     Texas Eastern Corp.
```

BILLINGS, MT

```
(  0)    Montana-Dakota Utilities Co.
(  0) PT-Montana Power Co.
(140)NDL-KN Energy Inc.
(140)NDL-Mountain Fuel Supply Co.
```

BILOXI-GULFPORT, MS

```
(  0)    *Tenneco Inc.
(  0)    United Gas Pipeline Co.
(100)NDL-Arkla Inc.
(100)NDL-Southern Natural Gas Co.
(100)NDL-Texas Eastern Transmission Corp.
(100)NDL-Transcontinental Gas Pipeline Corp.
(100)NDL-Shell Oil Co.
(100)NDL-Mississippi Valley Gas Co.
(100)NDL-Delta Gas Inc.
(100)NDL-Florida Gas Transmission Co.
(100)NDL-Mid-Louisiana Gas Co.
(100)NDL-Monterey Pipeline Co.
(100)NDL-Texas Gas Transmission Co.
(100)NDL-Northern Natural Gas Co.
(100)NPT-Columbia Gulf Transmission Co.
(100)NPT-Louisiana State Gas Corp.
(100)NPT-Okaloosa County Gas District
```

```
   DETAIL OF SUBSIDIARIES               PARENT

   Louisiana Intrastate Gas Corp.       Tenneco Inc.
```

BINGHAMTON, NY

```
( 0)    Columbia Gas Transmission Corp.
( 0)    Consolidated Gas Supply Corp.
(100)NDL-Equitable Gas Co.
(100)NDL*National Fuel Gas Co.
(100)NDL-Tenneco Inc.
(100)NDL*Texas Eastern Corp.
(100)NDL-Transcontinental Gas Pipeline Corp.
(100)NDL-North Penn Gas Co.
(100)NPT-Central Hudson Gas & Electric Corp.
(100)NPT-Niagara Mohawk Power Corp.
(100)NPT-Rochester Gas & Electric Corp.
(100)NPT-South Jersey Gas Co.
```

```
  DETAIL OF SUBSIDIARIES                 PARENT

National Fuel Gas Distribution Corp  National Fuel Gas Co.
National Fuel Gas Supply Corp.       National Fuel Gas Co.
Algonquin Gas Transmission Co.       Texas Eastern Corp.
Texas Eastern Transmission Corp.     Texas Eastern Corp.
```

BIRMINGHAM, AL

```
( 0)    *Southern Natural Gas Co.
(100)NDL-Alabama-Tennessee Natural Gas Co.
(100)NDL*Tenneco Inc.
(100)NDL-Texas Eastern Transmission Corp.
(100)NDL-Transcontinental Gas Pipeline Corp.
(100)NDL-Mississippi Valley Gas Co.
(100)NDL-United Gas Pipeline Co.
(100)NDL-Texas Gas Transmission Co.
(100)NPT-Columbia Gulf Transmission Co.
(100)NPT-United Cities Gas Co.
(100)NPT-Southeast Alabama Gas District, The
(120)NDL-Trunkline Gas Co.
(140)NPT*South Carolina Electric & Gas Co.
```

```
  DETAIL OF SUBSIDIARIES                 PARENT

South Georgia Nautural Gas Co.       Southern Natural Gas Co.
East Tennessee Natural Gas Co.       Tenneco Inc.
Tennessee Natural Gas Lines, Inc.    Tenneco Inc.
Carolina Pipeline Co.                South Carolina Electric
```

BISMARCK, ND

```
( 0)    Montana-Dakota Utilities Co.
(100)NDL*Internorth Inc.
(120)NDL-Midwestern Gas Transmission Co.
```

```
  DETAIL OF SUBSIDIARIES                 PARENT

Northern Border Pipeline Co.         Internorth Inc.
Northern Natural Gas Co.             Internorth Inc.
```

BOISE CITY, ID

```
( 0)    Northwest Pipeline Corp.
```

BOSTON-LAWR.-SALEM-LOW.-BROCK.,MA

```
(  0)    *Tenneco Inc.
(  0)    *Texas Eastern Corp.
(  0)     Distrigas of Massachusetts Corp.
(100)NDL-Consolidated Gas Supply Corp.
(100)NPT-Central Hudson Gas & Electric Corp.
(100)NPT-Niagara Mohawk Power Corp.
(120)NDL-ANR Pipeline Co.
(120)NDL-Columbia Gas Transmission Corp.
(120)NDL-Equitable Gas Co.
(120)NDL-Transcontinental Gas Pipeline Corp.
```

```
 DETAIL OF SUBSIDIARIES                  PARENT

Granite State Gas Transmission, Inc  Tenneco Inc.
Algonquin Gas Transmission Co.       Texas Eastern Corp.
Northern Utilities, Inc., - ME       Tenneco Inc.
Texas Eastern Transmission Corp.     Texas Eastern Corp.
```

BRADENTON, FL

```
(  0)    Florida Gas Transmission Co.
```

BRAZORIA, TX

```
(  0)     Florida Gas Transmission Co.
(  0)    *United Energy Resources Inc.
(  0) PT-Transcontinental Gas Pipeline Corp.
(100)NDL-Enserch Corp.
(100)NDL*Panhandle Eastern Corp.
(100)NDL*Tenneco Inc.
(100)NDL-Texas Eastern Transmission Corp.
(100)NDL-Crab Run Gas Co.
(100)NDL-West Lake Arthur Corp.
(100)NDL-Natural Gas Pipeline Co. of America
(100)NDL-Texas Gas Pipeline Co.
(100)NDL*Houston Natural Gas Corp.
(100)NPT-Arkla Inc.
(100)NPT-El Paso Natural Gas Co.
(100)NPT-Intrastate Gathering Corp.
(100)NPT-Southern Natural Gas Co.
(100)NPT-Valero Interstate Transmission Co.
(100)NPT-Shell Oil Co.
(100)NPT-Seagull Pipeline Corp.
(100)NPT-Producers Gas Co.
(100)NPT-Delhi Gas Pipeline Corp.
(100)NPT-Sabine Pipeline Co.
(120)NPT-Winnie Pipeline Co.
(120)NPT-Esperanza Transmission Co.
(120)NPT-Texas Gas Transmission Co.
(120)NPT-Northern Natural Gas Co.
(140)NPT-Texacol Gas Services, Inc.
```

DETAIL OF SUBSIDIARIES   PARENT

United Texas Transmission Co.	United Energy Resources
Trunkline Lng Co.	Panhandle Eastern Corp.
Channel Industries Gas Co.	Tenneco Inc.
United Gas Pipeline Co.	United Energy Resources
Valley Gas Transmission, Inc.	Houston Natural Gas Corp.
Houston Pipeline Co.	Houston Natural Gas Corp.
Trunkline Gas Co.	Panhandle Eastern Corp.
Intratex Gas Co.	Houston Natural Gas Corp.
Oasis Pipeline Co.	Houston Natural Gas Corp.

BRIDGEPORT-STAMF.-NORW.-DANB.,CT

```
(  0)  *Tenneco Inc.
(100)NDL-Columbia Gas Transmission Corp.
(100)NDL-Consolidated Gas Supply Corp.
(100)NDL-Equitable Gas Co.
(100)NDL*Texas Eastern Corp.
(100)NDL-Transcontinental Gas Pipeline Corp.
(100)NDL-Distrigas of Massachusetts Corp.
(100)NDL-North Penn Gas Co.
(100)NPT-Central Hudson Gas & Electric Corp.
(100)NPT-Niagara Mohawk Power Corp.
(100)NPT-South Jersey Gas Co.
(140)NDL-Eastern Shore Natural Gas Co.
```

```
 DETAIL OF SUBSIDIARIES              PARENT

Granite State Gas Transmission, Inc  Tenneco Inc.
Algonquin Gas Transmission Co.       Texas Eastern Corp.
Texas Eastern Transmission Corp.     Texas Eastern Corp.
Northern Utilities, Inc., - ME       Tenneco Inc.
```

BRYAN-COLLEGE STATION, TX

```
(  0)    Enserch Corp.
(  0) PT-Valero Interstate Transmission Co.
(  0) PT-Producers Gas Co.
(  0) PT-Delhi Gas Pipeline Corp.
(100)NDL-Arkla Inc.
(100)NDL*Panhandle Eastern Corp.
(100)NDL*Tenneco Inc.
(100)NDL-Texas Eastern Transmission Corp.
(100)NDL-Florida Gas Transmission Co.
(100)NDL-Natural Gas Pipeline Co. of America
(100)NDL*United Energy Resources Inc.
(100)NDL-Texas Gas Pipeline Co.
(100)NDL*Houston Natural Gas Corp.
(100)NPT-El Paso Natural Gas Co.
(100)NPT-Intrastate Gathering Corp.
(100)NPT-Southern Natural Gas Co.
(100)NPT-Transcontinental Gas Pipeline Corp.
(100)NPT-Seagull Pipeline Corp.
(100)NPT-Sabine Pipeline Co.
(100)NPT-Winnie Pipeline Co.
(100)NPT-Esperanza Transmission Co.
(100)NPT-Texas Gas Transmission Co.
(100)NPT-Texacol Gas Services, Inc.
(100)NPT-Northern Natural Gas Co.
(120)NDL-KN Energy Inc.
(120)NPT-Southwestern Gas Pipeline Inc.
(140)NDL-Crab Run Gas Co.
(140)NDL-West Lake Arthur Corp.
(140)NPT-Shell Oil Co.
```

DETAIL OF SUBSIDIARIES	PARENT
Channel Industries Gas Co.	Tenneco Inc.
United Gas Pipeline Co.	United Energy Resources
United Texas Transmission Co.	United Energy Resources
Valley Gas Transmission, Inc.	Houston Natural Gas Corp.
Houston Pipeline Co.	Houston Natural Gas Corp.
Trunkline Gas Co.	Panhandle Eastern Corp.
Intratex Gas Co.	Houston Natural Gas Corp.
Oasis Pipeline Co.	Houston Natural Gas Corp.
Trunkline Lng Co.	Panhandle Eastern Corp.

BUFFALO, NY

```
(  0)    *National Fuel Gas Co.
(  0)     Tenneco Inc.
(100)NDL-Columbia Gas Transmission Corp.
(100)NDL*Consolidated Natural Gas Corp.
(100)NDL-Equitable Gas Co.
(100)NDL-Transcontinental Gas Pipeline Corp.
(100)NDL-North Penn Gas Co.
(100)NPT-Niagara Mohawk Power Corp.
(100)NPT-Rochester Gas & Electric Corp.
(140)NDL-Texas Eastern Transmission Corp.
(140)NDL-Carnegie Natural Gas Co.
```

```
 DETAIL OF SUBSIDIARIES                 PARENT

National Fuel Gas Distribution Corp  National Fuel Gas Co.
National Fuel Gas Supply Corp.       National Fuel Gas Co.
Consolidated Gas Supply Corp.        Consolidated Natural Gas
East Ohio Gas Co.                    Consolidated Natural Gas
```

CANTON, OH

```
(  0)     Tenneco Inc.
(100)NDL*ANR Pipeline Co.
(100)NDL*Columbia Gas System, Inc.
(100)NDL*Consolidated Natural Gas Corp.
(100)NDL-Equitable Gas Co.
(100)NDL-Gas Transport Inc.
(100)NDL*National Fuel Gas Co.
(100)NDL-Panhandle Eastern Pipeline Co.
(100)NDL-Texas Eastern Transmission Corp.
(100)NDL-Carnegie Natural Gas Co.
(100)NDL-Texas Gas Transmission Co.
(100)NPT-Transcontinental Gas Pipeline Corp.
(120)NDL-Michigan Consolidated Gas Co.
(120)NDL-North Penn Gas Co.
(120)NPT-Michigan Gas Storage Co.
(120)NPT-Cincinnati Gas & Electric Co.
```

```
 DETAIL OF SUBSIDIARIES                 PARENT

East Ohio Gas Co.                    Consolidated Natural Gas
Columbia Gas Transmission Corp.      Columbia Gas System, Inc.
Consolidated Gas Supply Corp.        Consolidated Natural Gas
National Fuel Gas Distribution Corp  National Fuel Gas Co.
National Fuel Gas Supply Corp.       National Fuel Gas Co.
River Gas Co.                        Consolidated Natural Gas
Great Lakes Gas Transmission Co.     ANR Pipeline Co.
Inland Gas Co. Inc.                  Columbia Gas System, Inc.
Columbia Gulf Transmission Co.       Columbia Gas System, Inc.
```

CASPER, WY

```
(  0)    KN Energy Inc.
(  0)    Montana-Dakota Utilities Co.
(100)NDL-ANR Pipeline Co.
(100)NDL-Mountain Fuel Supply Co.
(100)NDL-Northwest Pipeline Corp.
(100)NDL-Panhandle Eastern Pipeline Co.
(100)NDL-Western Slope Gas Co.
(100)NDL-Colorado Interstate Gas Co.
(140)NPT-Montana Power Co.
```

CEDAR RAPIDS, IA

```
(  0)    *Internorth Inc.
(100)NDL*ANR Pipeline Co.
(100)NDL-Panhandle Eastern Pipeline Co.
(100)NDL-Natural Gas Pipeline Co. of America
(100)NPT-Central Illinois Light Co.
(100)NPT-Northern Illinois Gas Co.
(140)NPT-Central Illinois Public Service Co.
(140)NPT-Illinois Power Co.
(140)NPT-Northern Indiana Public Service Co.
```

DETAIL OF SUBSIDIARIES	PARENT
Northern Natural Gas Co.	Internorth Inc.
Northern Border Pipeline Co.	Internorth Inc.
Wisconsin Natural Gas Co.	ANR Pipeline Co.

CHAMPAIGN-URBANA-RANTOUL, IL

```
(  0)    *Panhandle Eastern Corp.
(  0) PT-Central Illinois Light Co.
(  0) PT-Illinois Power Co.
(  0) PT-Northern Illinois Gas Co.
(100)NDL-ANR Pipeline Co.
(100)NDL-Mississippi River Transmission Corp.
(100)NDL-Midwestern Gas Transmission Co.
(100)NDL-Natural Gas Pipeline Co. of America
(100)NDL-Texas Gas Transmission Co.
(100)NPT-United Cities Gas Co.
(100)NPT-Central Illinois Public Service Co.
(100)NPT-Northern Indiana Public Service Co.
(120)NDL-Texas Eastern Transmission Corp.
(140)NDL-Ohio River Pipeline Corp.
(140)NPT-Louisville Gas & Electric Co.
(140)NPT-Western Kentucky Gas Co.
```

DETAIL OF SUBSIDIARIES	PARENT
Panhandle Eastern Pipeline Co.	Panhandle Eastern Corp.
Trunkline Gas Co.	Panhandle Eastern Corp.

CHARLESTON, SC

```
(  0)   *Transcontinental Gas Pipeline Corp.
(  0) PT*South Carolina Electric & Gas Co.
(100)NDL-Southern Natural Gas Co.
(100)NPT-North Carolina Natural Gas Corp.
(140)NPT-United Cities Gas Co.
```

DETAIL OF SUBSIDIARIES   PARENT

```
Public Service Co. of N.C., Inc.      Transcontinental Gas
Carolina Pipeline Co.                 South Carolina Electric
```

CHARLESTON, WV

```
(  0)   *Consolidated Natural Gas Corp.
(  0)   *Tenneco Inc.
(100)NDL*Columbia Gas System, Inc.
(100)NDL*Equitable Gas Co.
(100)NDL-Gas Transport Inc.
(100)NDL-Texas Eastern Transmission Corp.
(100)NDL-Carnegie Natural Gas Co.
(100)NPT-United Cities Gas Co.
(100)NPT-Roanoke Gas Co.
(120)NDL-Panhandle Eastern Pipeline Co.
(120)NDL-Transcontinental Gas Pipeline Corp.
(120)NDL-Texas Gas Transmission Co.
(120)NPT-Cincinnati Gas & Electric Co.
(140)NPT-National Fuel Gas Supply Corp.
```

DETAIL OF SUBSIDIARIES   PARENT

```
Consolidated Gas Supply Corp.       Consolidated Natural Gas
Columbia Gulf Transmission Co.      Columbia Gas System, Inc.
Columbia Gas Transmission Corp.     Columbia Gas System, Inc.
Inland Gas Co. Inc.                 Columbia Gas System, Inc.
Kentucky-West Virginia Gas Co.      Equitable Gas Co.
East Tennessee Natural Gas Co.      Tenneco Inc.
East Ohio Gas Co.                   Consolidated Natural Gas
River Gas Co.                       Consolidated Natural Gas
Ohio Valley Gas Corp.              Columbia Gas System, Inc.
Commonwealth Gas Pipeline Corp.     Columbia Gas System, Inc.
```

CHARLOTTE-GASTONIA-ROCK HILL (NC-SC)

```
(  0)   *Transcontinental Gas Pipeline Corp.
(100)NDL-Columbia Gas Transmission Corp.
(100)NDL-Southern Natural Gas Co.
(100)NDL*Tenneco Inc.
(100)NPT-United Cities Gas Co.
(100)NPT-Roanoke Gas Co.
(100)NPT*South Carolina Electric & Gas Co.
(140)NDL-Consolidated Gas Supply Corp.
```

DETAIL OF SUBSIDIARIES	PARENT
North Carolina Natural Gas Corp.	Tenneco Inc.
Public Service Co. of N.C., Inc.	Transcontinental Gas
East Tennessee Natural Gas Co.	Tenneco Inc.
Carolina Pipeline Co.	South Carolina Electric

CHARLOTTESVILLE, VA

```
(  0)   *Columbia Gas System, Inc.
(100)NDL*Consolidated Natural Gas Corp.
(100)NDL*Tenneco Inc.
(100)NDL*Transcontinental Gas Pipeline Corp.
(100)NDL*Washington Gas Light Co.
(100)NPT-Roanoke Gas Co.
(120)NDL-Equitable Gas Co.
(120)NDL-Texas Eastern Transmission Corp.
(120)NDL-Carnegie Natural Gas Co.
```

DETAIL OF SUBSIDIARIES	PARENT
Columbia Gas Transmission Corp.	Columbia Gas System, Inc.
Commonwealth Gas Pipeline Corp.	Columbia Gas System, Inc.
Consolidated Gas Supply Corp.	Consolidated Natural Gas
East Tennessee Natural Gas Co.	Tenneco Inc.
Shenandoah Gas Co.	Washington Gas Light Co.
Public Service Co. of N.C., Inc.	Transcontinental Gas
Frederick Gas Co.	Washington Gas Light Co.
East Ohio Gas Co.	Consolidated Natural Gas
Columbia Gulf Transmission Co.	Columbia Gas System, Inc.
River Gas Co.	Consolidated Natural Gas

CHATTANOOGA (TN-GA)

```
(  0)    *Southern Natural Gas Co.
(  0)    *Tenneco Inc.
(100)NDL-Alabama-Tennessee Natural Gas Co.
(100)NDL*Columbia Gas System, Inc.
(100)NDL-Texas Eastern Transmission Corp.
(100)NDL*Transcontinental Gas Pipeline Corp.
(100)NDL-United Gas Pipeline Co.
(100)NDL-Texas Gas Transmission Co.
(100)NPT-United Cities Gas Co.
(120)NPT-Carolina Pipeline Co.
(120)NPT-Western Kentucky Gas Co.
(140)NPT-Southeast Alabama Gas District, The
```

DETAIL OF SUBSIDIARIES	PARENT
East Tennessee Natural Gas Co.	Tenneco Inc.
Columbia-Gulf Transmission Co.	Columbia Gas System, Inc.
Tennessee Natural Gas Lines, Inc.	Tenneco Inc.
Public Service Co. of N.C., Inc.	Transcontinental Gas
Columbia Gas Transmission Corp.	Columbia Gas System, Inc.
Midwestern Gas Transmission Co.	Tenneco Inc.
South Georgia Nautral Gas Co.	Southern Natural Gas Co.

CHEYENNE, WY

```
(  0)    KN Energy Inc.
(  0)    Colorado Interstate Gas Co.
(100)NDL-Montana-Dakota Utilities Co.
(100)NDL-Panhandle Eastern Pipeline Co.
(100)NDL-Western Slope Gas Co.
```

CHICAGO, IL

```
(  0)    Natural Gas Pipeline Co. of America
(  0) PT-Northern Illinois Gas Co.
(  0) PT-Northern Indiana Public Service Co.
(100)NDL*ANR Pipeline Co.
(100)NDL*Panhandle Eastern Corp.
(100)NDL-Midwestern Gas Transmission Co.
(100)NDL-Texas Gas Transmission Co.
(100)NDL*Internorth Inc.
(100)NPT-Central Illinois Light Co.
(100)NPT-Illinois Power Co.
(120)NDL-Michigan Consolidated Gas Co.
(120)NPT-Central Illinois Public Service Co.
```

DETAIL OF SUBSIDIARIES	PARENT
Panhandle Eastern Pipeline Co.	Panhandle Eastern Corp.
Trunkline Gas Co.	Panhandle Eastern Corp.
Northern Natural Gas Co.	Internorth Inc.
Wisconsin Natural Gas Co.	ANR Pipeline Co.
Northern Border Pipeline Co.	Internorth Inc.

CINCINNATI (OH-KY-IN)

```
(  0)     *Columbia Gas System, Inc.
(  0)      Panhandle Eastern Pipeline Co.
(  0)      Texas Gas Transmission Co.
(  0) PT-Cincinnati Gas & Electric Co.
(100)NDL-ANR Pipeline Co.
(100)NDL*Consolidated Natural Gas Corp.
(100)NDL-Kentucky-West Virginia Gas Co.
(100)NDL*Tenneco Inc.
(100)NDL-Texas Eastern Transmission Corp.
(100)NDL-Ohio River Pipeline Corp.
(100)NPT-Louisville Gas & Electric Co.
(100)NPT-Northern Indiana Public Service Co.
(100)NPT-Western Kentucky Gas Co.
(120)NDL-Gas Transport Inc.
(140)NDL-Carnegie Natural Gas Co.
(140)NPT-Transcontinental Gas Pipeline Corp.
```

DETAIL OF SUBSIDIARIES	PARENT
Columbia Gas Transmission Corp.	Columbia Gas System, Inc.
Ohio Valley Gas Corp.	Columbia Gas System, Inc.
Inland Gas Co. Inc.	Columbia Gas System, Inc.
Consolidated Gas Supply Corp.	Consolidated Natural Gas
Midwestern Gas Transmission Co.	Tenneco Inc.
Columbia Gulf Transmission Co.	Columbia Gas System, Inc.
East Ohio Gas Co.	Consolidated Natural Gas
River Gas Co.	Consolidated Natural Gas

CLARKSVILLE-HOPKINSVILLE (TN-KY)

```
(  0)     *Tenneco Inc.
(  0) PT-Western Kentucky Gas Co.
(100)NDL-Alabama-Tennessee Natural Gas Co.
(100)NDL-ANR Pipeline Co.
(100)NDL-Trunkline Gas Co.
(100)NDL-Southern Natural Gas Co.
(100)NDL-Texas Eastern Transmission Corp.
(100)NDL-Ohio River Pipeline Corp.
(100)NDL-Texas Gas Transmission Co.
(100)NPT-Columbia Gulf Transmission Co.
(100)NPT-United Cities Gas Co.
(100)NPT-Louisville Gas & Electric Co.
(120)NDL-Natural Gas Pipeline Co. of America
(120)NPT-Mississippi Valley Gas Co.
(140)NDL-Mississippi River Transmission Corp.
(140)NDL-Monterey Pipeline Co.
(140)NDL-United Gas Pipeline Co.
(140)NPT-Central Illinois Public Service Co.
(140)NPT-Illinois Power Co.
```

DETAIL OF SUBSIDIARIES	PARENT
East Tennessee Natural Gas Co.	Tenneco Inc.
Midwestern Gas Transmission Co.	Tenneco Inc.
Tennessee Natural Gas Lines, Inc.	Tenneco Inc.

COLORADO SPRINGS, CO

```
(  0)    Colorado Interstate Gas Co.
(100)NDL-KN Energy Inc.
(100)NDL-Panhandle Eastern Pipeline Co.
(100)NDL-Kansas Power & Light Co.
(100)NDL-Western Slope Gas Co.
(100)NDL-Northern Natural Gas Co.
(100)NPT-Rocky Mountain Natural Gas Co., Inc.
(140)NDL-Mountain Fuel Supply Co.
(140)NDL-Northwest Central Pipeline Corp.
```

COLUMBIA, MO

```
(  0)    Panhandle Eastern Pipeline Co.
(100)NDL-ANR Pipeline Co.
(100)NDL-KN Energy Inc.
(100)NDL-Mississippi River Transmission Corp.
(100)NDL*Northwest Energy Co.
(100)NDL-Union Gas System Inc.
(100)NDL-Natural Gas Pipeline Co. of America
(100)NDL-Northern Natural Gas Co.
(100)NPT-Central Illinois Public Service Co.
(100)NPT-Illinois Power Co.
(100)NPT-Missouri Public Service Co.
(120)NDL-Associated Natural Gas Co.
(120)NPT-Central Illinois Light Co.
```

DETAIL OF SUBSIDIARIES   PARENT

Northwest Central Pipeline Corp.   Northwest Energy Co.
Commercial Pipeline Corp.   Northwest Energy Co.

COLUMBIA, SC

```
(  0)    Southern Natural Gas Co.
(  0) PT*South Carolina Electric & Gas Co.
(100)NDL*Tenneco Inc.
(100)NDL*Transcontinental Gas Pipeline Corp.
(100)NPT-United Cities Gas Co.
```

DETAIL OF SUBSIDIARIES   PARENT

Carolina Pipeline Co.   South Carolina Electric
North Carolina Natural Gas Corp.   Tenneco Inc.
Public Service Co. of N.C., Inc.   Transcontinental Gas
East Tennessee Natural Gas Co.   Tenneco Inc.

COLUMBUS, (GA-AL)

```
(  0)   *Southern Natural Gas Co.
(  0) PT-United Cities Gas Co.
(  0) PT-Southeast Alabama Gas District, The
(100)NDL-Transcontinental Gas Pipeline Corp.
(100)NDL-Florida Gas Transmission Co.
(100)NPT-Okaloosa County Gas District
(120)NDL-United Gas Pipeline Co.
(140)NDL-East Tennessee Natural Gas Co.
(140)NPT*South Carolina Electric & Gas Co.
```

DETAIL OF SUBSIDIARIES   PARENT

```
South Georgia Nautural Gas Co.        Southern Natural Gas Co.
Carolina Pipeline Co.                 South Carolina Electric
```

COLUMBUS, OH

```
(  0)   *Columbia Gas System, Inc.
(  0)    Tenneco Inc.
(100)NDL*ANR Pipeline Co.
(100)NDL*Consolidated Natural Gas Corp.
(100)NDL*Equitable Gas Co.
(100)NDL-Gas Transport Inc.
(100)NDL*National Fuel Gas Co.
(100)NDL*Panhandle Eastern Corp.
(100)NDL-Texas Eastern Transmission Corp.
(100)NDL-Carnegie Natural Gas Co.
(100)NDL-Michigan Consolidated Gas Co.
(100)NDL-Texas Gas Transmission Co.
(100)NPT-Transcontinental Gas Pipeline Corp.
(100)NPT-Michigan Gas Storage Co.
(100)NPT-Cincinnati Gas & Electric Co.
(100)NPT-Northern Indiana Public Service Co.
(140)NDL-Ohio River Pipeline Corp.
(140)NPT-Louisville Gas & Electric Co.
(140)NPT-Western Kentucky Gas Co.
```

DETAIL OF SUBSIDIARIES   PARENT

```
Columbia Gas Transmission Corp.       Columbia Gas System, Inc.
Great Lakes Gas Transmission Co.      ANR Pipeline Co.
Inland Gas Co. Inc.                   Columbia Gas System, Inc.
Consolidated Gas Supply Corp.         Consolidated Natural Gas
National Fuel Gas Supply Corp.        National Fuel Gas Co.
Panhandle Eastern Pipeline Co.        Panhandle Eastern Corp.
Columbia Gulf Transmission Co.        Columbia Gas System, Inc.
Ohio Valley Gas Corp.                 Columbia Gas System, Inc.
East Ohio Gas Co.                     Consolidated Natural Gas
River Gas Co.                         Consolidated Natural Gas
Kentucky-West Virginia Gas Co.        Equitable Gas Co.
National Fuel Gas Distribution Corp   National Fuel Gas Co.
Trunkline Gas Co.                     Panhandle Eastern Corp.
```

CORPUS CHRISTI, TX

```
(   0)    Enserch Corp.
(   0)    *Tenneco Inc.
(   0)     Florida Gas Transmission Co.
(   0)    *United Energy Resources Inc.
(   0)    *Houston Natural Gas Corp.
(   0) PT-Trunkline Gas Co.
(   0) PT-Intrastate Gathering Corp.
(   0) PT-Seagull Pipeline Corp.
(   0) PT-Delhi Gas Pipeline Corp.
(   0) PT-Esperanza Transmission Co.
(100)NDL*Valero Interstate Transmission Co.
(100)NDL-Natural Gas Pipeline Co. of America
(100)NDL-Texacol Gas Services, Inc.
(100)NPT-El Paso Natural Gas Co.
(100)NPT-Southern Natural Gas Co.
(100)NPT-Transcontinental Gas Pipeline Corp.
(100)NPT-Winnie Pipeline Co.
(120)NPT-Texas Eastern Transmission Corp.
(120)NPT-Producers Gas Co.
(120)NPT-Texas Gas Transmission Co.
(120)NPT-Northern Natural Gas Co.
```

DETAIL OF SUBSIDIARIES	PARENT
Channel Industries Gas Co.	Tenneco Inc.
United Gas Pipeline Co.	United Energy Resources
Valley Gas Transmission, Inc.	Houston Natural Gas Corp.
Houston Pipeline Co.	Houston Natural Gas Corp.
Rio Grande Valley Gas Co.	Valero Interstate Trans
United Texas Transmission Co.	United Energy Resources
Intratex Gas Co.	Houston Natural Gas Corp.
Oasis Pipeline Co.	Houston Natural Gas Corp.

DALLAS, TX

```
(  0)    Enserch Corp.
(  0) PT-Texas Gas Transmission Co.
(  0) PT-Texacol Gas Services, Inc.
(100)NDL-Arkla Inc.
(100)NDL-KN Energy Inc.
(100)NDL-Northwest Central Pipeline Corp.
(100)NDL-Producers Gas Co.
(100)NDL-Delhi Gas Pipeline Corp.
(100)NDL-Natural Gas Pipeline Co. of America
(100)NDL*United Energy Resources Inc.
(100)NDL-Transok, Inc.
(100)NDL-Oklahoma Natural Gas Co. (Oneok Inc.)
(100)NDL*Houston Natural Gas Corp.
(100)NPT-Valero Interstate Transmission Co.
(100)NPT-Winnie Pipeline Co.
(100)NPT-Southwestern Gas Pipeline Inc.
(100)NPT-Esperanza Transmission Co.
(100)NPT-Northern Natural Gas Co.
(120)NDL-Mississippi River Transmission Corp.
(120)NDL*Tenneco Inc.
(120)NPT-Texas Eastern Transmission Corp.
```

DETAIL OF SUBSIDIARIES	PARENT
United Gas Pipeline Co.	United Energy Resources
Houston Pipeline Co.	Houston Natural Gas Corp.
Intratex Gas Co.	Houston Natural Gas Corp.
Oasis Pipeline Co.	Houston Natural Gas Corp.
Channel Industries Gas Co.	Tenneco Inc.
United Texas Transmission Co.	United Energy Resources
Louisiana Intrastate Gas Corp.	Tenneco Inc.

DANVILLE, VA

```
(  0)    *Transcontinental Gas Pipeline Corp.
(100)NDL*Columbia Gas System, Inc.
(100)NDL*Tenneco Inc.
(100)NPT-Roanoke Gas Co.
(120)NDL-Consolidated Gas Supply Corp.
(120)NPT-United Cities Gas Co.
(140)NDL*Washington Gas Light Co.
(140)NDL-Carnegie Natural Gas Co.
```

DETAIL OF SUBSIDIARIES	PARENT
Columbia Gas Transmission Corp.	Columbia Gas System, Inc.
East Tennessee Natural Gas Co.	Tenneco Inc.
Commonwealth Gas Pipeline Corp.	Columbia Gas System, Inc.
North Carolina Natural Gas Corp.	Tenneco Inc.
Public Service Co. of N.C., Inc.	Transcontinental Gas
Columbia Gulf Transmission Co.	Columbia Gas System, Inc.
Shenandoah Gas Co.	Washington Gas Light Co.

DAVENPORT-ROCK ISLAND-MOLINE (IA-IL)

```
(  0)   *ANR Pipeline Co.
(  0)    Natural Gas Pipeline Co. of America
(100)NDL*Panhandle Eastern Corp.
(100)NDL-Midwestern Gas Transmission Co.
(100)NDL*Internorth Inc.
(100)NPT-Central Illinois Light Co.
(100)NPT-Central Illinois Public Service Co.
(100)NPT-Illinois Power Co.
(100)NPT-Northern Illinois Gas Co.
(100)NPT-Northern Indiana Public Service Co.
(120)NDL-Texas Gas Transmission Co.
(140)NDL-Mississippi River Transmission Corp.
```

DETAIL OF SUBSIDIARIES	PARENT
Panhandle Eastern Pipeline Co.	Panhandle Eastern Corp.
Trunkline Gas Co.	Panhandle Eastern Corp.
Northern Natural Gas Co.	Internorth Inc.
Wisconsin Natural Gas Co.	ANR Pipeline Co.
Northern Border Pipeline Co.	Internorth Inc.

DAYTON-SPRINGFIELD, OH

```
(  0)   *Columbia Gas System, Inc.
(  0) PT-Cincinnati Gas & Electric Co.
(100)NDL*ANR Pipeline Co.
(100)NDL*Consolidated Natural Gas Corp.
(100)NDL-Gas Transport Inc.
(100)NDL*Panhandle Eastern Corp.
(100)NDL-Tenneco Inc.
(100)NDL-Texas Eastern Transmission Corp.
(100)NDL-Ohio River Pipeline Corp.
(100)NDL-Texas Gas Transmission Co.
(100)NPT-Transcontinental Gas Pipeline Corp.
(100)NPT-Louisville Gas & Electric Co.
(100)NPT-Northern Indiana Public Service Co.
(100)NPT-Western Kentucky Gas Co.
(120)NDL-Michigan Consolidated Gas Co.
(120)NPT-Equitable Gas Co.
(120)NPT-National Fuel Gas Supply Corp.
(120)NPT-Carnegie Natural Gas Co.
(120)NPT-Michigan Gas Storage Co.
```

DETAIL OF SUBSIDIARIES	PARENT
Columbia Gas Transmission Corp.	Columbia Gas System, Inc.
Inland Gas Co. Inc.	Columbia Gas System, Inc.
Consolidated Gas Supply Corp.	Consolidated Natural Gas
Panhandle Eastern Pipeline Co.	Panhandle Eastern Corp.
Ohio Valley Gas Corp.	Columbia Gas System, Inc.
East Ohio Gas Co.	Consolidated Natural Gas
River Gas Co.	Consolidated Natural Gas
Great Lakes Gas Transmission Co.	ANR Pipeline Co.
Trunkline Gas Co.	Panhandle Eastern Corp.
Columbia Gulf Transmission Co.	Columbia Gas System, Inc.

DAYTONA BEACH, FL

```
(  0)     Florida Gas Transmission Co.
(100)NDL-South Georgia Nautural Gas Co.
```

DECATUR, IL

```
(  0)     Natural Gas Pipeline Co. of America
(  0) PT-Central Illinois Public Service Co.
(  0) PT-Illinois Power Co.
(100)NDL-ANR Pipeline Co.
(100)NDL-Mississippi River Transmission Corp.
(100)NDL*Panhandle Eastern Corp.
(100)NDL-Midwestern Gas Transmission Co.
(100)NDL-Texas Gas Transmission Co.
(100)NPT-United Cities Gas Co.
(100)NPT-Central Illinois Light Co.
(100)NPT-Northern Illinois Gas Co.
(120)NDL-Texas Eastern Transmission Corp.
(120)NPT-Northern Indiana Public Service Co.
```

DETAIL OF SUBSIDIARIES	PARENT
Panhandle Eastern Pipeline Co.	Panhandle Eastern Corp.
Trunkline Gas Co.	Panhandle Eastern Corp.

DENVER, CO

```
(  0)     Panhandle Eastern Pipeline Co.
(  0)     Western Slope Gas Co.
(  0)     Colorado Interstate Gas Co.
(100)NDL-KN Energy Inc.
(100)NPT-Rocky Mountain Natural Gas Co., Inc.
(120)NDL*Northwest Energy Co.
(120)NDL-Kansas Power & Light Co.
(120)NDL-Northern Natural Gas Co.
(140)NDL-El Paso Natural Gas Co.
```

DETAIL OF SUBSIDIARIES	PARENT
Northwest Central Pipeline Corp.	Northwest Energy Co.
Northwest Pipeline Corp.	Northwest Energy Co.

DES MOINES, IA

```
(  0)     Natural Gas Pipeline Co. of America
(  0)     *Internorth Inc.
(100)NDL-ANR Pipeline Co.
(120)NDL-KN Energy Inc.
(120)NDL-Northwest Central Pipeline Corp.
(120)NDL-Panhandle Eastern Pipeline Co.
(120)NDL-Union Gas System Inc.
(120)NPT-Missouri Public Service Co.
(140)NDL-Southern Natural Gas Co.
```

DETAIL OF SUBSIDIARIES	PARENT
Northern Natural Gas Co.	Internorth Inc.
Northern Border Pipeline Co.	Internorth Inc.

DETROIT , MI

```
(  0)   *ANR Pipeline Co.
(  0)   *Panhandle Eastern Corp.
(  0)    Michigan Consolidated Gas Co.
(  0) PT-Michigan Gas Storage Co.
(100)NDL-Columbia Gas Transmission Corp.
(100)NDL-Tenneco Inc.
(100)NDL-Texas Gas Transmission Co.
(100)NPT*Consolidated Natural Gas Corp.
(100)NPT-Texas Eastern Transmission Corp.
(100)NPT-Transcontinental Gas Pipeline Corp.
(100)NPT-Northern Indiana Public Service Co.
(120)NPT-National Fuel Gas Supply Corp.
(120)NPT-Cincinnati Gas & Electric Co.
```

DETAIL OF SUBSIDIARIES	PARENT
Great Lakes Gas Transmission Co.	ANR Pipeline Co.
Panhandle Eastern Pipeline Co.	Panhandle Eastern Corp.
Trunkline Gas Co.	Panhandle Eastern Corp.
Consolidated Gas Supply Corp.	Consolidated Natural Gas
East Ohio Gas Co.	Consolidated Natural Gas

DUBUQUE, IA

```
(  0)   *Internorth Inc.
(100)NDL*ANR Pipeline Co.
(100)NDL-Panhandle Eastern Pipeline Co.
(100)NDL-Natural Gas Pipeline Co. of America
(100)NPT-Central Illinois Light Co.
(100)NPT-Northern Illinois Gas Co.
(100)NPT-Northern Indiana Public Service Co.
(120)NDL-Midwestern Gas Transmission Co.
```

DETAIL OF SUBSIDIARIES	PARENT
Northern Natural Gas Co.	Internorth Inc.
Wisconsin Natural Gas Co.	ANR Pipeline Co.
Northern Border Pipeline Co.	Internorth Inc.

DULUTH (MN-WI)

```
(  0)    Northern Natural Gas Co.
(100)NDL*ANR Pipeline Co.
(100)NDL-Midwestern Gas Transmission Co.
```

DETAIL OF SUBSIDIARIES	PARENT
Great Lakes Gas Transmission Co.	ANR Pipeline Co.

EAU CLAIRE, WI

    (0)   Midwestern Gas Transmission Co.
    (0)   *Internorth Inc.
    (100)NDL*ANR Pipeline Co.

    DETAIL OF SUBSIDIARIES   PARENT

    Northern Natural Gas Co.   Internorth Inc.
    Great Lakes Gas Transmission Co.   ANR Pipeline Co.
    Northern Border Pipeline Co.   Internorth Inc.

EL PASO, TX

    (0)   El Paso Natural Gas Co.
    (0)   Western Gas Interstate Co.
    (100)NDL-Natural Gas Pipeline Co. of America
    (140)NPT-Transwestern Pipeline Co.

ELKHART-GOSHEN, IN

    (0)   *Panhandle Eastern Corp.
    (0) PT-Northern Indiana Public Service Co.
    (100)NDL*ANR Pipeline Co.
    (100)NDL-Columbia Gas Transmission Corp.
    (100)NDL*Tenneco Inc.
    (100)NDL-Michigan Consolidated Gas Co.
    (100)NDL-Natural Gas Pipeline Co. of America
    (100)NDL-Texas Gas Transmission Co.
    (100)NPT*Consolidated Natural Gas Corp.
    (100)NPT-Michigan Gas Storage Co.
    (100)NPT-Northern Illinois Gas Co.
    (120)NPT-Cincinnati Gas & Electric Co.
    (140)NDL-Texas Eastern Transmission Corp.
    (140)NPT-Central Illinois Light Co.
    (140)NPT-Illinois Power Co.

    DETAIL OF SUBSIDIARIES   PARENT

    Trunkline Gas Co.   Panhandle Eastern Corp.
    Great Lakes Gas Transmission Co.   ANR Pipeline Co.
    Panhandle Eastern Pipeline Co.   Panhandle Eastern Corp.
    Midwestern Gas Transmission Co.   Tenneco Inc.
    East Ohio Gas Co.   Consolidated Natural Gas
    Wisconsin Natural Gas Co.   ANR Pipeline Co.
    Consolidated Gas Supply Corp.   Consolidated Natural Gas

ENID, OK

```
(  0)   *Oklahoma Natural Gas Co. (Oneok Inc.)
(100)NDL-Arkla Inc.
(100)NDL-Enserch Corp.
(100)NDL-Mississippi River Transmission Corp.
(100)NDL-Northwest Central Pipeline Corp.
(100)NDL-Panhandle Eastern Pipeline Co.
(100)NDL-Union Gas System Inc.
(100)NDL-Crab Run Gas Co.
(100)NDL-Kansas Power & Light Co.
(100)NDL-Producers Gas Co.
(100)NDL-Delhi Gas Pipeline Corp.
(100)NDL-Natural Gas Pipeline Co. of America
(100)NDL-Transok, Inc.
(100)NDL-Colorado Interstate Gas Co.
(100)NDL-Northern Natural Gas Co.
(120)NDL-Transwestern Pipeline Co.
(140)NDL-Arkansas Oklahoma Gas Co.
(140)NDL-El Paso Natural Gas Co.
(140)NPT-Mustang Fuel Corp.
(140)NPT-Ozark Gas Pipeline Corp.
(140)NPT-Red River Gas Pipeline Corp.
(140)NPT-Arkansas Western Gas Co.
```

DETAIL OF SUBSIDIARIES	PARENT
Ringwood Gathering Co.	Oklahoma Natural Gas Co.

ERIE, PA

```
(  0)   *National Fuel Gas Co.
(100)NDL-Columbia Gas Transmission Corp.
(100)NDL*Consolidated Natural Gas Corp.
(100)NDL-Equitable Gas Co.
(100)NDL-Tenneco Inc.
(100)NDL-Texas Eastern Transmission Corp.
(100)NDL-Transcontinental Gas Pipeline Corp.
(100)NDL-Carnegie Natural Gas Co.
(100)NDL-North Penn Gas Co.
(100)NPT-Rochester Gas & Electric Corp.
(120)NDL-Texas Gas Transmission Co.
```

DETAIL OF SUBSIDIARIES	PARENT
National Fuel Gas Supply Corp.	National Fuel Gas Co.
Consolidated Gas Supply Corp.	Consolidated Natural Gas
National Fuel Gas Distribution Corp	National Fuel Gas Co.
East Ohio Gas Co.	Consolidated Natural Gas
River Gas Co.	Consolidated Natural Gas

EVANSVILLE (IN-KY)

```
(  0)    Texas Eastern Transmission Corp.
(  0)    Texas Gas Transmission Co.
(100)NDL-ANR Pipeline Co.
(100)NDL*Columbia Gas System, Inc.
(100)NDL-Mississippi River Transmission Corp.
(100)NDL*Panhandle Eastern Corp.
(100)NDL*Tenneco Inc.
(100)NDL-Monterey Pipeline Co.
(100)NDL-Natural Gas Pipeline Co. of America
(100)NDL-Ohio River Pipeline Corp.
(100)NPT-United Cities Gas Co.
(100)NPT-Central Illinois Public Service Co.
(100)NPT-Illinois Power Co.
(100)NPT-Louisville Gas & Electric Co.
(100)NPT-Western Kentucky Gas Co.
(120)NPT-Central Illinois Light Co.
(120)NPT-Cincinnati Gas & Electric Co.
(120)NPT-Northern Illinois Gas Co.
(140)NDL-Associated Natural Gas Co.
```

DETAIL OF SUBSIDIARIES	PARENT
Panhandle Eastern Pipeline Co.	Panhandle Eastern Corp.
Trunkline Gas Co.	Panhandle Eastern Corp.
East Tennessee Natural Gas Co.	Tenneco Inc.
Midwestern Gas Transmission Co.	Tenneco Inc.
Columbia Gulf Transmission Co.	Columbia Gas System, Inc.
Tennessee Natural Gas Lines, Inc.	Tenneco Inc.
Columbia Gas Transmission Corp.	Columbia Gas System, Inc.
Inland Gas Co. Inc.	Columbia Gas System, Inc.
Ohio Valley Gas Corp.	Columbia Gas System, Inc.

FARGO-MOORHEAD (ND-MN)

```
(  0)    Midwestern Gas Transmission Co.
(100)NDL-Great Lakes Gas Transmission Co.
(100)NDL-Montana-Dakota Utilities Co.
(100)NDL*Internorth Inc.
```

DETAIL OF SUBSIDIARIES	PARENT
Northern Natural Gas Co.	Internorth Inc.
Northern Border Pipeline Co.	Internorth Inc.

FLORENCE, AL

(0)   Alabama-Tennessee Natural Gas Co.
(0)   *Tenneco Inc.
(0)   Texas Eastern Transmission Corp.
(100)NDL-ANR Pipeline Co.
(100)NDL-Trunkline Gas Co.
(100)NDL-Southern Natural Gas Co.
(100)NDL-Mississippi Valley Gas Co.
(100)NDL-United Gas Pipeline Co.
(100)NDL-Texas Gas Transmission Co.
(100)NPT-Columbia Gulf Transmission Co.
(100)NPT-United Cities Gas Co.
(100)NPT-Western Kentucky Gas Co.
(140)NDL-Arkla Inc.
(140)NDL-Transcontinental Gas Pipeline Corp.
(140)NDL-Associated Natural Gas Co.
(140)NPT-Southeast Alabama Gas District, The

DETAIL OF SUBSIDIARIES	PARENT
East Tennessee Natural Gas Co.	Tenneco Inc.
Tennessee Natural Gas Lines, Inc.	Tenneco Inc.

FORT LAUDERDALE-HOLLYWOOD-POMPANO BEACH, FL

(0)   Florida Gas Transmission Co.

FORT PIERCE, FL

(0)   Florida Gas Transmission Co.

FORT SMITH (AR-OK)

(0)   Arkansas Oklahoma Gas Co.
(0)   Arkla Inc.
(0)   *Oklahoma Natural Gas Co. (Oneok Inc.)
(0) PT-Mustang Fuel Corp.
(0) PT-Ozark Gas Pipeline Corp.
(0) PT-Arkansas Western Gas Co.
(100)NDL-Enserch Corp.
(100)NDL-Northwest Central Pipeline Corp.
(100)NDL-Texas Eastern Transmission Corp.
(100)NDL-Union Gas System Inc.
(100)NDL-Delhi Gas Pipeline Corp.
(100)NDL-Natural Gas Pipeline Co. of America
(100)NDL-Transok, Inc.
(100)NPT-Producers Gas Co.
(120)NDL-Mississippi River Transmission Corp.
(120)NPT-Columbia Gulf Transmission Co.
(140)NDL-United Gas Pipeline Co.

DETAIL OF SUBSIDIARIES	PARENT
Ringwood Gathering Co.	Oklahoma Natural Gas Co.

FORT WAYNE, IN

```
(  0)   *Panhandle Eastern Corp.
(  0) PT-Northern Indiana Public Service Co.
(100)NDL*ANR Pipeline Co.
(100)NDL*Columbia Gas System, Inc.
(100)NDL*Tenneco Inc.
(100)NDL-Texas Eastern Transmission Corp.
(100)NDL-Michigan Consolidated Gas Co.
(100)NDL-Natural Gas Pipeline Co. of America
(100)NDL-Texas Gas Transmission Co.
(100)NPT*Consolidated Natural Gas Corp.
(100)NPT-Michigan Gas Storage Co.
(100)NPT-Cincinnati Gas & Electric Co.
(100)NPT-Northern Illinois Gas Co.
(140)NPT-Transcontinental Gas Pipeline Corp.
(140)NPT-Central Illinois Light Co.
(140)NPT-Illinois Power Co.
```

DETAIL OF SUBSIDIARIES	PARENT
Panhandle Eastern Pipeline Co.	Panhandle Eastern Corp.
Great Lakes Gas Transmission Co.	ANR Pipeline Co.
Columbia Gas Transmission Corp.	Columbia Gas System, Inc.
Trunkline Gas Co.	Panhandle Eastern Corp.
Midwestern Gas Transmission Co.	Tenneco Inc.
Ohio Valley Gas Corp.	Columbia Gas System, Inc.
Consolidated Gas Supply Corp.	Consolidated Natural Gas
East Ohio Gas Co.	Consolidated Natural Gas

FORT WORTH-ARLINGTON, TX

(0)   Enserch Corp.
(0) PT-Southwestern Gas Pipeline Inc.
(100)NDL-Arkla Inc.
(100)NDL-Producers Gas Co.
(100)NDL-Natural Gas Pipeline Co. of America
(100)NDL*United Energy Resources Inc.
(100)NDL-Oklahoma Natural Gas Co. (Oneok Inc.)
(100)NDL*Houston Natural Gas Corp.
(100)NPT*El Paso Natural Gas Co.
(100)NPT-Western Gas Interstate Co.
(100)NPT-Winnie Pipeline Co.
(100)NPT-Esperanza Transmission Co.
(100)NPT-Texas Gas Transmission Co.
(100)NPT-Texacol Gas Services, Inc.
(100)NPT-Northern Natural Gas Co.
(120)NDL-KN Energy Inc.
(120)NPT-Valero Interstate Transmission Co.
(120)NPT-Delhi Gas Pipeline Corp.
(140)NDL-Mississippi River Transmission Corp.
(140)NDL-Northwest Central Pipeline Corp.
(140)NDL*Tenneco Inc.
(140)NDL-Transok, Inc.
(140)NPT-Texas Eastern Transmission Corp.

DETAIL OF SUBSIDIARIES	PARENT
United Gas Pipeline Co.	United Energy Resources
Houston Pipeline Co.	Houston Natural Gas Corp.
Intratex Gas Co.	Houston Natural Gas Corp.
Oasis Pipeline Co.	Houston Natural Gas Corp.
Channel Industries Gas Co.	Tenneco Inc.
Palo Duro Pipeline Co.	United Energy Resources
United Texas Transmission Co.	United Energy Resources
Odessa Natural Gas Corp.	El Paso Natural Gas Co.

GADSEN, AL

(0)   *Southern Natural Gas Co.
(100)NDL-Alabama-Tennessee Natural Gas Co.
(100)NDL*Tenneco Inc.
(100)NDL-Texas Eastern Transmission Corp.
(100)NDL-Transcontinental Gas Pipeline Corp.
(100)NDL-Texas Gas Transmission Co.
(100)NPT-Columbia Gulf Transmission Corp.
(100)NPT-United Cities Gas Co.
(100)NPT-Southeast Alabama Gas District, The

DETAIL OF SUBSIDIARIES	PARENT
East Tennessee Natural Gas Co.	Tenneco Inc.
South Georgia Nautral Gas Co.	Southern Natural Gas Co.
Tennessee Natural Gas Lines, Inc.	Tenneco Inc.

GAINESVILLE, FL

(0)   Florida Gas Transmission Co.
(100)NDL*Southern Natural Gas Co.

DETAIL OF SUBSIDIARIES   PARENT

South Georgia Nautural Gas Co.   Southern Natural Gas Co.

GALVESTON—TEXAS CITY, TX

(0)   Enserch Corp.
(0) PT-Seagull Pipeline Corp.
(100)NDL-Arkla Inc.
(100)NDL*Panhandle Eastern Corp.
(100)NDL*Tenneco Inc.
(100)NDL-Texas Eastern Transmission Corp.
(100)NDL-Crab Run Gas Co.
(100)NDL-West Lake Arthur Corp.
(100)NDL-Florida Gas Transmission Co.
(100)NDL-Natural Gas Pipeline Co. of America
(100)NDL*United Energy Resources Inc.
(100)NDL-Texas Gas Pipeline Co.
(100)NDL*Houston Natural Gas Corp.
(100)NPT-El Paso Natural Gas Co.
(100)NPT-Intrastate Gathering Corp.
(100)NPT-Southern Natural Gas Co.
(100)NPT-Transcontinental Gas Pipeline Corp.
(100)NPT-Valero Interstate Transmission Co.
(100)NPT-Shell Oil Co.
(100)NPT-Producers Gas Co.
(100)NPT-Delhi Gas Pipeline Corp.
(100)NPT-Sabine Pipeline Co.
(120)NDL-Louisiana Resources Co.
(140)NPT-Columbia Gulf Transmission Co.
(140)NPT-Mid-Louisiana Gas Co.
(140)NPT-Winnie Pipeline Co.
(140)NPT-Texas Gas Transmission Co.
(140)NPT-Northern Natural Gas Co.

DETAIL OF SUBSIDIARIES   PARENT

Trunkline Gas Co.   Panhandle Eastern Corp.
Trunkline Lng Co.   Panhandle Eastern Corp.
Channel Industries Gas Co.   Tenneco Inc.
United Gas Pipeline Co.   United Energy Resources
United Texas Transmission Co.   United Energy Resources
Valley Gas Transmission, Inc.   Houston Natural Gas Corp.
Houston Pipeline Co.   Houston Natural Gas Corp.
Louisiana Intrastate Gas Corp.   Tenneco Inc.
Intratex Gas Co.   Houston Natural Gas Corp.
Oasis Pipeline Co.   Houston Natural Gas Corp.

GARY-HAMMOND, IN

```
(  0)    Texas Gas Transmission Co.
(  0) PT-Northern Illinois Gas Co.
(  0) PT-Northern Indiana Public Service Co.
(100)NDL*ANR Pipeline Co.
(100)NDL*Panhandle Eastern Corp.
(100)NDL-Midwestern Gas Transmission Co.
(100)NDL-Michigan Consolidated Gas Co.
(100)NDL-Natural Gas Pipeline Co. of America
(100)NDL-Northern Natural Gas Co.
(100)NPT-Central Illinois Light Co.
(100)NPT-Illinois Power Co.
(120)NPT-Michigan Gas Storage Co.
(120)NPT-Central Illinois Public Service Co.
(140)NDL-Columbia Gas Transmission Corp.
(140)NPT-East Ohio Gas Co.
```

DETAIL OF SUBSIDIARIES	PARENT
Panhandle Eastern Pipeline Co.	Panhandle Eastern Corp.
Trunkline Gas Co.	Panhandle Eastern Corp.
Great Lakes Gas Transmission Co.	ANR Pipeline Co.
Wisconsin Natural Gas Co.	ANR Pipeline Co.

GRAND FORKS, ND

```
(  0)    Midwestern Gas Transmission Co.
(100)NDL-Montana-Dakota Utilities Co.
(120)NDL-Great Lakes Gas Transmission Co.
(120)NDL*Internorth Inc.
```

DETAIL OF SUBSIDIARIES	PARENT
Northern Border Pipeline Co.	Internorth Inc.
Northern Natural Gas Co.	Internorth Inc.

GREELEY, CO

```
(  0)    Western Slope Gas Co.
(  0)    Colorado Interstate Gas Co.
(100)NDL-KN Energy Inc.
(100)NDL-Panhandle Eastern Pipeline Co.
(120)NDL-Montana-Dakota Utilities Co.
(120)NPT-Rocky Mountain Natural Gas Co., Inc.
(140)NDL-Northern Natural Gas Co.
```

GREENSBORO-WINSTON-SALEM-HIGH POINT, NC

```
(  0)    *Transcontinental Gas Pipeline Corp.
(100)NDL*Columbia Gas System, Inc.
(100)NDL-Consolidated Gas Supply Corp.
(100)NDL-Southern Natural Gas Co.
(100)NDL*Tenneco Inc.
(100)NPT-United Cities Gas Co.
(100)NPT-Roanoke Gas Co.
(100)NPT*South Carolina Electric & Gas Co.
(120)NDL-Eastern Shore Natural Gas Co.
(120)NPT-South Jersey Gas Co.
(140)NDL-Kentucky-West Virginia Gas Co.
(140)NDL*Texas Eastern Corp.
(140)NDL-Carnegie Natural Gas Co.
```

DETAIL OF SUBSIDIARIES	PARENT
Columbia Gas Transmission Corp.	Columbia Gas System, Inc.
East Tennessee Natural Gas Co.	Tenneco Inc.
North Carolina Natural Gas Corp.	Tenneco Inc.
Public Service Co. of N.C., Inc.	Transcontinental Gas
Carolina Pipeline Co.	South Carolina Electric
Columbia Gulf Transmission Co.	Columbia Gas System, Inc.
Commonwealth Gas Pipeline Corp.	Columbia Gas System, Inc.
Inland Gas Co. Inc.	Columbia Gas System, Inc.
Algonquin Gas Transmission Co.	Texas Eastern Corp.
Texas Eastern Transmission Corp.	Texas Eastern Corp.

GREENVILLE-SPARTANBURG, SC

```
(  0)    *Transcontinental Gas Pipeline Corp.
(  0) PT*South Carolina Electric & Gas Co.
(100)NDL-Southern Natural Gas Co.
(100)NDL*Tenneco Inc.
(100)NPT-United Cities Gas Co.
```

DETAIL OF SUBSIDIARIES	PARENT
Carolina Pipeline Co.	South Carolina Electric
East Tennessee Natural Gas Co.	Tenneco Inc.
North Carolina Natural Gas Corp.	Tenneco Inc.
Public Service Co. of N.C., Inc.	Transcontinental Gas

HAMILTON—MIDDLETOWN, OH

```
(  0)    Texas Eastern Transmission Corp.
(  0)    Texas Gas Transmission Co.
(  0) PT-Cincinnati Gas & Electric Co.
(100)NDL-ANR Pipeline Co.
(100)NDL*Columbia Gas System, Inc.
(100)NDL*Consolidated Natural Gas Corp.
(100)NDL*Panhandle Eastern Corp.
(100)NDL*Tenneco Inc.
(100)NDL-Ohio River Pipeline Corp.
(100)NPT-Louisville Gas & Electric Co.
(100)NPT-Northern Indiana Public Service Co.
(100)NPT-Western Kentucky Gas Co.
(140)NDL-Kentucky-West Virginia Gas Co.
(140)NDL-Gas Transport Inc.
```

DETAIL OF SUBSIDIARIES   PARENT

Columbia Gas Transmission Corp.	Columbia Gas System, Inc.
Inland Gas Co. Inc.	Columbia Gas System, Inc.
Consolidated Gas Supply Corp.	Consolidated Natural Gas
Panhandle Eastern Pipeline Co.	Panhandle Eastern Corp.
Ohio Valley Gas Corp.	Columbia Gas System, Inc.
East Ohio Gas Co.	Consolidated Natural Gas
Trunkline Gas Co.	Panhandle Eastern Corp.
Midwestern Gas Transmission Co.	Tenneco Inc.
Columbia Gulf Transmission Co.	Columbia Gas System, Inc.
River Gas Co.	Consolidated Natural Gas

HARTFORD—N.BRIT.—MIDDLE.—BRIS.,CT

```
(  0)    *Tenneco Inc.
(  0)    *Texas Eastern Corp.
(100)NDL-Columbia Gas Transmission Corp.
(100)NDL-Consolidated Gas Supply Corp.
(100)NDL-Equitable Gas Co.
(100)NDL-Transcontinental Gas Pipeline Corp.
(100)NDL-Distrigas of Massachusetts Corp.
(100)NPT-Central Hudson Gas & Electric Corp.
(100)NPT-Niagara Mohawk Power Corp.
(120)NDL-North Penn Gas Co.
(140)NPT-South Jersey Gas Co.
```

DETAIL OF SUBSIDIARIES   PARENT

Algonquin Gas Transmission Co.	Texas Eastern Corp.
Granite State Gas Transmission, Inc	Tenneco Inc.
Texas Eastern Transmission Corp.	Texas Eastern Corp.
Northern Utilities, Inc., - ME	Tenneco Inc.

HOUMA—THIBODAUX, LA

```
(  0)    *Tenneco Inc.
(  0)     United Gas Pipeline Co.
(  0)     Texas Gas Transmission Co.
(  0) PT-Louisiana State Gas Corp.
(100)NDL-Arkla Inc.
(100)NDL-Southern Natural Gas Co.
(100)NDL-Texas Eastern Transmission Corp.
(100)NDL-Transcontinental Gas Pipeline Corp.
(100)NDL-Shell Oil Co.
(100)NDL-Louisiana Resources Co.
(100)NDL-Delta Gas Inc.
(100)NDL-Mid-Louisiana Gas Co.
(100)NDL-Monterey Pipeline Co.
(100)NDL-Natural Gas Pipeline Co. of America
(100)NDL-Northern Natural Gas Co.
(100)NPT-Columbia Gulf Transmission Co.
(100)NPT-Florida Gas Transmission Co.
(120)NDL*Panhandle Eastern Corp.
(120)NDL-Crab Run Gas Co.
(120)NDL-West Lake Arthur Corp.
(120)NPT-Sabine Pipeline Co.
(140)NDL-Valley Gas Transmission, Inc.
```

```
  DETAIL OF SUBSIDIARIES              PARENT

Louisiana Intrastate Gas Corp.      Tenneco Inc.
Trunkline Gas Co.                    Panhandle Eastern Corp.
Trunkline Lng Co.                    Panhandle Eastern Corp.
```

HOUSTON, TX

```
(  0)    Enserch Corp.
(  0)   *Tenneco Inc.
(  0)    Natural Gas Pipeline Co. of America
(  0)   *United Energy Resources Inc.
(  0)   *Houston Natural Gas Corp.
(100)NDL-Arkla Inc.
(100)NDL*Panhandle Eastern Corp.
(100)NDL-Southern Natural Gas Co.
(100)NDL-Texas Eastern Transmission Corp.
(100)NDL-Crab Run Gas Co.
(100)NDL-West Lake Arthur Corp.
(100)NDL-Louisiana Resources Co.
(100)NDL-Florida Gas Transmission Co.
(100)NDL-Texas Gas Pipeline Co.
(100)NDL-Texas Gas Transmission Co.
(100)NPT-El Paso Natural Gas Co.
(100)NPT-Intrastate Gathering Corp.
(100)NPT-Transcontinental Gas Pipeline Corp.
(100)NPT-Valero Interstate Transmission Co.
(100)NPT-Shell Oil Co.
(100)NPT-Seagull Pipeline Corp.
(100)NPT-Producers Gas Co.
(100)NPT-Delhi Gas Pipeline Corp.
(100)NPT-Sabine Pipeline Co.
(100)NPT-Winnie Pipeline Co.
(100)NPT-Texacol Gas Services, Inc.
(100)NPT-Northern Natural Gas Co.
(120)NPT-Columbia Gulf Transmission Co.
(120)NPT-Mid-Louisiana Gas Co.
(120)NPT-Esperanza Transmission Co.
(140)NDL-KN Energy Inc.
(140)NPT-Southwestern Gas Pipeline Inc.
```

DETAIL OF SUBSIDIARIES	PARENT
Channel Industries Gas Co.	Tenneco Inc.
United Texas Transmission Co.	United Energy Resources
Houston Pipeline Co.	Houston Natural Gas Corp.
Trunkline Gas Co.	Panhandle Eastern Corp.
Trunkline Lng Co.	Panhandle Eastern Corp.
United Gas Pipeline Co.	United Energy Resources
Valley Gas Transmission, Inc.	Houston Natural Gas Corp.
Intratex Gas Co.	Houston Natural Gas Corp.
Oasis Pipeline Co.	Houston Natural Gas Corp.
Louisiana Intrastate Gas Corp.	Tenneco Inc.

HUNTINGTON-ASHLAND (WV-KY-OH)

```
(  0)   *Columbia Gas System, Inc.
(  0)   *Tenneco Inc.
(100)NDL*Consolidated Natural Gas Corp.
(100)NDL*Equitable Gas Co.
(100)NDL-Gas Transport Inc.
(100)NDL-Panhandle Eastern Pipeline Co.
(100)NDL-Texas Eastern Transmission Corp.
(100)NDL-Carnegie Natural Gas Co.
(100)NDL-Ohio River Pipeline Corp.
(100)NDL-Texas Gas Transmission Co.
(100)NPT-United Cities Gas Co.
(100)NPT-Cincinnati Gas & Electric Co.
(100)NPT-Louisville Gas & Electric Co.
(100)NPT-Western Kentucky Gas Co.
(120)NPT-Roanoke Gas Co.
(140)NDL*Transcontinental Gas Pipeline Corp.
(140)NPT-ANR Pipeline Co.
(140)NPT-National Fuel Gas Supply Corp.
```

DETAIL OF SUBSIDIARIES	PARENT
Columbia Gas Transmission Corp.	Columbia Gas System, Inc.
Inland Gas Co. Inc.	Columbia Gas System, Inc.
Consolidated Gas Supply Corp.	Consolidated Natural Gas
Kentucky-West Virginia Gas Co.	Equitable Gas Co.
East Tennessee Natural Gas Co.	Tenneco Inc.
Columbia Gulf Transmission Co.	Columbia Gas System, Inc.
Ohio Valley Gas Corp.	Columbia Gas System, Inc.
East Ohio Gas Co.	Consolidated Natural Gas
River Gas Co.	Consolidated Natural Gas
Public Service Co. of N.C., Inc.	Transcontinental Gas

HUNTSVILLE, AL

```
(  0)    Alabama-Tennessee Natural Gas Co.
(100)NDL-Southern Natural Gas Co.
(100)NDL*Tenneco Inc.
(100)NDL-Texas Eastern Transmission Corp.
(100)NDL-Transcontinental Gas Pipeline Corp.
(100)NDL-United Gas Pipeline Co.
(100)NDL-Texas Gas Transmission Co.
(100)NPT-Columbia Gulf Transmission Co.
(100)NPT-United Cities Gas Co.
(100)NPT-Western Kentucky Gas Co.
(120)NDL-Mississippi Valley Gas Co.
(120)NPT-Southeast Alabama Gas District, The
(140)NDL-ANR Pipeline Co.
```

DETAIL OF SUBSIDIARIES	PARENT
East Tennessee Natural Gas Co.	Tenneco Inc.
Tennessee Natural Gas Lines, Inc.	Tenneco Inc.

INDIANAPOLIS, IN

```
(  0)   *Panhandle Eastern Corp.
(100)NDL-ANR Pipeline Co.
(100)NDL*Columbia Gas System, Inc.
(100)NDL*Tenneco Inc.
(100)NDL-Texas Eastern Transmission Corp.
(100)NDL-Natural Gas Pipeline Co. of America
(100)NDL-Ohio River Pipeline Corp.
(100)NDL-Texas Gas Transmission Co.
(100)NPT-Central Illinois Light Co.
(100)NPT-Cincinnati Gas & Electric Co.
(100)NPT-Illinois Power Co.
(100)NPT-Louisville Gas & Electric Co.
(100)NPT-Northern Illinois Gas Co.
(100)NPT-Northern Indiana Public Service Co.
(100)NPT-Western Kentucky Gas Co.
(120)NPT*Consolidated Natural Gas Corp.
(120)NPT-Central Illinois Public Service Co.
(140)NDL-Mississippi River Transmission Corp.
(140)NDL-Michigan Consolidated Gas Co.
(140)NPT-United Cities Gas Co.
```

DETAIL OF SUBSIDIARIES	PARENT
Panhandle Eastern Pipeline Co.	Panhandle Eastern Corp.
Columbia Gas Transmission Corp.	Columbia Gas System, Inc.
Inland Gas Co. Inc.	Columbia Gas System, Inc.
Trunkline Gas Co.	Panhandle Eastern Corp.
Midwestern Gas Transmission Co.	Tenneco Inc.
Ohio Valley Gas Corp.	Columbia Gas System, Inc.
Consolidated Gas Supply Corp.	Consolidated Natural Gas
East Ohio Gas Co.	Consolidated Natural Gas

JACKSON, MS

```
(  0)   Texas Eastern Transmission Corp.
(  0)   Mississippi Valley Gas Co.
(  0)   United Gas Pipeline Co.
(100)NDL-Arkla Inc.
(100)NDL-Mississippi River Transmission Corp.
(100)NDL-Trunkline Gas Co.
(100)NDL-Southern Natural Gas Co.
(100)NDL*Tenneco Inc.
(100)NDL-Transcontinental Gas Pipeline Corp.
(100)NDL-Shell Oil Co.
(100)NDL-Mid-Louisiana Gas Co.
(100)NDL-Monterey Pipeline Co.
(100)NDL-Texas Gas Transmission Co.
(100)NDL-Northern Natural Gas Co.
(100)NPT-Columbia Gulf Transmission Co.
(100)NPT-Florida Gas Transmission Co.
(100)NPT-Louisiana State Gas Corp.
(120)NDL-Valley Gas Transmission, Inc.
```

DETAIL OF SUBSIDIARIES	PARENT
Louisiana Intrastate Gas Corp.	Tenneco Inc.

JACKSON, TN

```
(  0)    Texas Gas Transmission Co.
(100)NDL-Alabama-Tennessee Natural Gas Co.
(100)NDL-ANR Pipeline Co.
(100)NDL-Arkla Inc.
(100)NDL-Trunkline Gas Co.
(100)NDL*Tenneco Inc.
(100)NDL-Texas Eastern Transmission Corp.
(100)NDL-Mississippi Valley Gas Co.
(100)NDL-Associated Natural Gas Co.
(100)NPT-Columbia Gulf Transmission Co.
(100)NPT-United Cities Gas Co.
(100)NPT-Western Kentucky Gas Co.
(120)NDL-Southern Natural Gas Co.
(140)NDL-Mississippi River Transmission Corp.
```

DETAIL OF SUBSIDIARIES	PARENT
East Tennessee Natural Gas Co.	Tenneco Inc.
Tennessee Natural Gas Lines, Inc.	Tenneco Inc.
Midwestern Gas Transmission Co.	Tenneco Inc.

JACKSONVILLE, FL

```
(  0)    Florida Gas Transmission Co.
(100)NDL*Southern Natural Gas Co.
```

DETAIL OF SUBSIDIARIES	PARENT
South Georgia Nautural Gas Co.	Southern Natural Gas Co.

JANESVILLE-BELOIT, WI

```
(  0)    *ANR Pipeline Co.
(  0)    *Internorth Inc.
(100)NDL-Midwestern Gas Transmission Co.
(100)NDL-Natural Gas Pipeline Co. of America
(100)NDL-Texas Gas Transmission Co.
(100)NPT-Northern Illinois Gas Co.
(100)NPT-Northern Indiana Public Service Co.
(120)NDL*Panhandle Eastern Corp.
(120)NPT-Central Illinois Light Co.
(140)NPT-Michigan Consolidated Gas Co.
```

DETAIL OF SUBSIDIARIES	PARENT
Northern Natural Gas Co.	Internorth Inc.
Wisconsin Natural Gas Co.	ANR Pipeline Co.
Northern Border Pipeline Co.	Internorth Inc.
Panhandle Eastern Pipeline Co.	Panhandle Eastern Corp.
Trunkline Gas Co.	Panhandle Eastern Corp.

JOHNSON CITY-KINGSPORT-BRISTOL (TN-VA)

```
(  0)   *Tenneco Inc.
(  0) PT-United Cities Gas Co.
(100)NDL*Columbia Gas System, Inc.
(100)NDL-Consolidated Gas Supply Corp.
(100)NDL-Kentucky-West Virginia Gas Co.
(100)NDL*Transcontinental Gas Pipeline Corp.
(100)NDL-Carnegie Natural Gas Co.
(100)NPT-Texas Eastern Transmission Corp.
(100)NPT-Roanoke Gas Co.
(100)NPT*South Carolina Electric & Gas Co.
(120)NDL-Southern Natural Gas Co.
```

DETAIL OF SUBSIDIARIES	PARENT
East Tennessee Natural Gas Co.	Tenneco Inc.
Columbia Gas Transmission Corp.	Columbia Gas System, Inc.
Inland Gas Co. Inc.	Columbia Gas System, Inc.
Columbia Gulf Transmission Co.	Columbia Gas System, Inc.
North Carolina Natural Gas Corp.	Tenneco Inc.
Public Service Co. of N.C., Inc.	Transcontinental Gas
Carolina Pipeline Co.	South Carolina Electric

JOLIET, IL

```
(  0)    Natural Gas Pipeline Co. of America
(  0) PT-Northern Illinois Gas Co.
(100)NDL*ANR Pipeline Co.
(100)NDL*Panhandle Eastern Corp.
(100)NDL-Midwestern Gas Transmission Co.
(100)NDL-Texas Gas Transmission Co.
(100)NDL-Northern Natural Gas Co.
(100)NPT-Central Illinois Light Co.
(100)NPT-Central Illinois Public Service Co.
(100)NPT-Illinois Power Co.
(100)NPT-Northern Indiana Public Service Co.
(120)NDL-Michigan Consolidated Gas Co.
```

DETAIL OF SUBSIDIARIES	PARENT
Panhandle Eastern Pipeline Co.	Panhandle Eastern Corp.
Trunkline Gas Co.	Panhandle Eastern Corp.
Wisconsin Natural Gas Co.	ANR Pipeline Co.

JOPLIN, MO

```
(  0)   *Northwest Energy Co.
(100)NDL-Arkansas Oklahoma Gas Co.
(100)NDL-Arkla Inc.
(100)NDL-KN Energy Inc.
(100)NDL-Panhandle Eastern Pipeline Co.
(100)NDL-Union Gas System Inc.
(100)NDL-Delhi Gas Pipeline Corp.
(100)NDL-Transok, Inc.
(100)NDL-Oklahoma Natural Gas Co. (Oneok Inc.)
(100)NDL-Northern Natural Gas Co.
(100)NPT-Mustang Fuel Corp.
(100)NPT-Missouri Public Service Co.
(100)NPT-Ozark Gas Pipeline Corp.
(100)NPT-Arkansas Western Gas Co.
(120)NDL-Natural Gas Pipeline Co. of America
(120)NPT-Kansas Power & Light Co.
(140)NDL-ANR Pipeline Co.
(140)NDL-Texas Eastern Transmission Corp.
```

```
   DETAIL OF SUBSIDIARIES                  PARENT

Northwest Central Pipeline Corp.      Northwest Energy Co.
Commercial Pipeline Corp.             Northwest Energy Co.
```

KANSAS CITY, MO

```
(  0)    KN Energy Inc.
(  0)   *Northwest Energy Co.
(  0)    Panhandle Eastern Pipeline Co.
(  0)    Union Gas System Inc.
(  0)    Northern Natural Gas Co.
(  0) PT-Missouri Public Service Co.
(100)NDL-ANR Pipeline Co.
(100)NDL-Arkla Inc.
(100)NDL-Kansas Power & Light Co.
(100)NDL-Natural Gas Pipeline Co. of America
(120)NDL-Mississippi River Transmission Corp.
(120)NDL-Transok, Inc.
(120)NDL-Oklahoma Natural Gas Co. (Oneok Inc.)
(120)NPT-Central Illinois Public Service Co.
(120)NPT-Illinois Power Co.
```

```
   DETAIL OF SUBSIDIARIES                  PARENT

Northwest Central Pipeline Corp.      Northwest Energy Co.
Commercial Pipeline Corp.             Northwest Energy Co.
```

KILLEEN-TEMPLE, TX

```
(  0)    Enserch Corp.
(  0) PT-Texas Gas Transmission Co.
(  0) PT-Texacol Gas Services, Inc.
(100)NDL-Arkla Inc.
(100)NDL*Tenneco Inc.
(100)NDL-Natural Gas Pipeline Co. of America
(100)NDL*United Energy Resources Inc.
(100)NDL*Houston Natural Gas Corp.
(100)NPT*El Paso Natural Gas Co.
(100)NPT-Intrastate Gathering Corp.
(100)NPT-Texas Eastern Transmission Corp.
(100)NPT-Valero Interstate Transmission Co.
(100)NPT-Seagull Pipeline Corp.
(100)NPT-Producers Gas Co.
(100)NPT-Delhi Gas Pipeline Corp.
(100)NPT-Western Gas Interstate Co.
(100)NPT-Winnie Pipeline Co.
(100)NPT-Southwestern Gas Pipeline Inc.
(100)NPT-Northern Natural Gas Co.
(120)NPT-Trunkline Gas Co.
(120)NPT-Southern Natural Gas Co.
(120)NPT-Esperanza Transmission Co.
(140)NDL-Florida Gas Transmission Co.
(140)NPT-Transcontinental Gas Pipeline Corp.
```

DETAIL OF SUBSIDIARIES	PARENT
Channel Industries Gas Co.	Tenneco Inc.
United Gas Pipeline Co.	United Energy Resources
United Texas Transmission Co.	United Energy Resources
Houston Pipeline Co.	Houston Natural Gas Corp.
Intratex Gas Co.	Houston Natural Gas Corp.
Oasis Pipeline Co.	Houston Natural Gas Corp.
Odessa Natural Gas Corp.	El Paso Natural Gas Co.
Palo Duro Pipeline Co.	United Energy Resources

KNOXVILLE, TN

```
(  0)    *Tenneco Inc.
(  0) PT-United Cities Gas Co.
(100)NDL*Columbia Gas System, Inc.
(100)NDL-Kentucky-West Virginia Gas Co.
(100)NDL-Southern Natural Gas Co.
(100)NDL*Transcontinental Gas Pipeline Corp.
(100)NDL-Texas Gas Transmission Co.
(100)NPT-Texas Eastern Transmission Corp.
(100)NPT-Carolina Pipeline Co.
(120)NDL-United Gas Pipeline Co.
(140)NDL-Alabama-Tennessee Natural Gas Co.
(140)NDL-Consolidated Gas Supply Corp.
(140)NDL-Carnegie Natural Gas Co.
(140)NDL-Ohio River Pipeline Corp.
(140)NPT-Louisville Gas & Electric Co.
(140)NPT-Western Kentucky Gas Co.
```

DETAIL OF SUBSIDIARIES	PARENT
East Tennessee Natural Gas Co.	Tenneco Inc.
Columbia Gas Transmission Corp.	Columbia Gas System, Inc.
Inland Gas Co. Inc.	Columbia Gas System, Inc.
Columbia Gulf Transmission Co.	Columbia Gas System, Inc.
North Carolina Natural Gas Corp.	Tenneco Inc.
Tennessee Natural Gas Lines, Inc.	Tenneco Inc.
Public Service Co. of N.C., Inc.	Transcontinental Gas

KOKOMO, IN

```
(  0)    *Panhandle Eastern Corp.
(100)NDL*ANR Pipeline Co.
(100)NDL*Columbia Gas System, Inc.
(100)NDL*Tenneco Inc.
(100)NDL-Texas Eastern Transmission Corp.
(100)NDL-Natural Gas Pipeline Co. of America
(100)NDL-Texas Gas Transmission Co.
(100)NPT-Central Illinois Light Co.
(100)NPT-Cincinnati Gas & Electric Co.
(100)NPT-Illinois Power Co.
(100)NPT-Northern Illinois Gas Co.
(100)NPT-Northern Indiana Public Service Co.
(120)NDL-Michigan Consolidated Gas Co.
(120)NDL-Ohio River Pipeline Corp.
(120)NPT*Consolidated Natural Gas Corp.
(120)NPT-Louisville Gas & Electric Co.
(120)NPT-Western Kentucky Gas Co.
(140)NPT-Michigan Gas Storage Co.
(140)NPT-Central Illinois Public Service Co.
```

DETAIL OF SUBSIDIARIES   PARENT

```
Panhandle Eastern Pipeline Co.        Panhandle Eastern Corp.
Columbia Gas Transmission Corp.       Columbia Gas System, Inc.
Trunkline Gas Co.                     Panhandle Eastern Corp.
Midwestern Gas Transmission Co.       Tenneco Inc.
Ohio Valley Gas Corp.                 Columbia Gas System, Inc.
Consolidated Gas Supply Corp.         Consolidated Natural Gas
East Ohio Gas Co.                     Consolidated Natural Gas
Great Lakes Gas Transmission Co.      ANR Pipeline Co.
Inland Gas Co. Inc.                   Columbia Gas System, Inc.
```

LA CROSSE, WI

```
(  0)    *Internorth Inc.
(100)NDL*ANR Pipeline Co.
(100)NDL-Midwestern Gas Transmission Co.
(120)NPT-Northern Illinois Gas Co.
(140)NDL-Natural Gas Pipeline Co. of America
```

DETAIL OF SUBSIDIARIES   PARENT

```
Northern Natural Gas Co.              Internorth Inc.
Wisconsin Natural Gas Co.             ANR Pipeline Co.
Northern Border Pipeline Co.          Internorth Inc.
```

LAFAYETTE, LA

```
(  0)     Southern Natural Gas Co.
(  0)    *Tenneco Inc.
(  0)    *United Energy Resources Inc.
(  0) PT-Columbia Gulf Transmission Co.
(100)NDL-Arkla Inc.
(100)NDL-Enserch Corp.
(100)NDL*Panhandle Eastern Corp.
(100)NDL-Texas Eastern Transmission Corp.
(100)NDL-Transcontinental Gas Pipeline Corp.
(100)NDL-Crab Run Gas Co.
(100)NDL-West Lake Arthur Corp.
(100)NDL-Shell Oil Co.
(100)NDL-Louisiana Resources Co.
(100)NDL-Delta Gas Inc.
(100)NDL-Mid-Louisiana Gas Co.
(100)NDL-Monterey Pipeline Co.
(100)NDL-Natural Gas Pipeline Co. of America
(100)NDL-Texas Gas Pipeline Co.
(100)NDL*Houston Natural Gas Corp.
(100)NDL-Texas Gas Transmission Co.
(100)NDL-Northern Natural Gas Co.
(100)NPT-Seagull Pipeline Corp.
(100)NPT-Florida Gas Transmission Co.
(100)NPT-Louisiana State Gas Corp.
(100)NPT-Sabine Pipeline Co.
(140)NDL-Mississippi Valley Gas Co.
```

DETAIL OF SUBSIDIARIES	PARENT
Louisiana Intrastate Gas Corp.	Tenneco Inc.
United Gas Pipeline Co.	United Energy Resources
Trunkline Gas Co.	Panhandle Eastern Corp.
Trunkline Lng Co.	Panhandle Eastern Corp.
Channel Industries Gas Co.	Tenneco Inc.
United Texas Transmission Co.	United Energy Resources
Valley Gas Transmission, Inc.	Houston Natural Gas Corp.
Houston Pipeline Co.	Houston Natural Gas Corp.

LAKE CHARLES, LA

```
(  0)   *Panhandle Eastern Corp.
(  0)    Texas Eastern Transmission Corp.
(  0)    Crab Run Gas Co.
(  0)    West Lake Arthur Corp.
(  0)   *United Energy Resources Inc.
(  0) PT-Sabine Pipeline Co.
(100)NDL-Arkla Inc.
(100)NDL-Enserch Corp.
(100)NDL-Southern Natural Gas Co.
(100)NDL*Tenneco Inc.
(100)NDL-Shell Oil Co.
(100)NDL-Louisiana Resources Co.
(100)NDL-Florida Gas Transmission Co.
(100)NDL-Mid-Louisiana Gas Co.
(100)NDL-Monterey Pipeline Co.
(100)NDL-Natural Gas Pipeline Co. of America
(100)NDL-Texas Gas Pipeline Co.
(100)NDL*Houston Natural Gas Corp.
(100)NDL-Texas Gas Transmission Co.
(100)NDL-Northern Natural Gas Co.
(100)NPT-Columbia Gulf Transmission Co.
(100)NPT-Transcontinental Gas Pipeline Corp.
(100)NPT-Seagull Pipeline Corp.
(120)NPT-Louisiana State Gas Corp.
(140)NDL-KN Energy Inc.
(140)NPT-Valero Interstate Transmission Co.
(140)NPT-Producers Gas Co.
(140)NPT-Delhi Gas Pipeline Corp.
```

DETAIL OF SUBSIDIARIES	PARENT
Trunkline Lng Co.	Panhandle Eastern Corp.
United Gas Pipeline Co.	United Energy Resources
Trunkline Gas Co.	Panhandle Eastern Corp.
Louisiana Intrastate Gas Corp.	Tenneco Inc.
Channel Industries Gas Co.	Tenneco Inc.
United Texas Transmission Co.	United Energy Resources
Valley Gas Transmission, Inc.	Houston Natural Gas Corp.
Houston Pipeline Co.	Houston Natural Gas Corp.

LAKELAND-WINTER HAVEN, FL

```
(  0)    Florida Gas Transmission Co.
```

LAREDO, TX

```
(  0)     Enserch Corp.
(  0)     Texacol Gas Services, Inc.
(  0) PT-Seagull Pipeline Corp.
(  0) PT-Delhi Gas Pipeline Corp.
(100)NDL*Tenneco Inc.
(100)NDL*Valero Interstate Transmission Co.
(100)NDL-Florida Gas Transmission Co.
(100)NDL*United Energy Resources Inc.
(100)NDL*Houston Natural Gas Corp.
(100)NPT-Trunkline Gas Co.
(100)NPT-Intrastate Gathering Corp.
(100)NPT-Transcontinental Gas Pipeline Corp.
(100)NPT-Winnie Pipeline Co.
(100)NPT-Esperanza Transmission Co.
(120)NPT-El Paso Natural Gas Co.
(120)NPT-Southern Natural Gas Co.
(120)NPT-Natural Gas Pipeline Co. of America
(140)NPT-Producers Gas Co.
(140)NPT-Texas Gas Transmission Co.
(140)NPT-Northern Natural Gas Co.
```

DETAIL OF SUBSIDIARIES	PARENT
United Texas Transmission Co.	United Energy Resources
Channel Industries Gas Co.	Tenneco Inc.
Rio Grande Valley Gas Co.	Valero Interstate Trans
United Gas Pipeline Co.	United Energy Resources
Valley Gas Transmission, Inc.	Houston Natural Gas Corp.
Houston Pipeline Co.	Houston Natural Gas Corp.
Intratex Gas Co.	Houston Natural Gas Corp.
Oasis Pipeline Co.	Houston Natural Gas Corp.

LAS CRUCES, NM

```
(  0)     El Paso Natural Gas Co.
(  0)     Western Gas Interstate Co.
(100)NPT-Transwestern Pipeline Co.
(120)NDL-Natural Gas Pipeline Co. of America
```

LAS VEGAS, NV

```
(  0)     Southwest Gas Corp.
(100)NDL-El Paso Natural Gas Co.
(100)NDL-Transwestern Pipeline Co.
(100)NDL-Pacific Gas & Electric Co.
(100)NDL*Pacific Lighting Corp.
```

DETAIL OF SUBSIDIARIES	PARENT
Pacific Interstate Transmission Co.	Pacific Lighting Corp.
Southern Calif. Gas Co.	Pacific Lighting Corp.
San Diego Gas & Electric Co.	Pacific Lighting Corp.

LAWRENCE, KS

```
(  0)   *Northwest Energy Co.
(100)NDL-ANR Pipeline Co.
(100)NDL-Arkla Inc.
(100)NDL-KN Energy Inc.
(100)NDL-Panhandle Eastern Pipeline Co.
(100)NDL-Union Gas System Inc.
(100)NDL-Kansas Power & Light Co.
(100)NDL-Natural Gas Pipeline Co. of America
(100)NDL-Northern Natural Gas Co.
(100)NPT-Missouri Public Service Co.
(140)NDL-Transok, Inc.
(140)NDL-Oklahoma Natural Gas Co. (Oneok Inc.)
```

```
   DETAIL OF SUBSIDIARIES                PARENT

Northwest Central Pipeline Corp.     Northwest Energy Co.
Commercial Pipeline Corp.            Northwest Energy Co.
```

LAWTON, OK

```
(  0)    Arkla Inc.
(100)NDL-El Paso Natural Gas Co.
(100)NDL-Enserch Corp.
(100)NDL-Mississippi River Transmission Corp.
(100)NDL-Northwest Central Pipeline Corp.
(100)NDL-Panhandle Eastern Pipeline Co.
(100)NDL-Union Gas System Inc.
(100)NDL-Crab Run Gas Co.
(100)NDL-Producers Gas Co.
(100)NDL-Delhi Gas Pipeline Corp.
(100)NDL-Natural Gas Pipeline Co. of America
(100)NDL-Transok, Inc.
(100)NDL*Oklahoma Natural Gas Co. (Oneok Inc.)
(100)NPT-United Gas Pipeline Co.
(100)NPT-Red River Gas Pipeline Corp.
(100)NPT-Southwestern Gas Pipeline Inc.
(100)NPT-Texas Gas Transmission Co.
(100)NPT-Texacol Gas Services, Inc.
(120)NDL-Transwestern Pipeline Co.
(120)NDL-Energas Co.
```

```
   DETAIL OF SUBSIDIARIES                PARENT

Ringwood Gathering Co.               Oklahoma Natural Gas Co.
```

LEXINGTON-FAYETTE, KY

```
( 0)    *Columbia Gas System, Inc.
( 0)    *Tenneco Inc.
(100)NDL*Consolidated Natural Gas Corp.
(100)NDL-Kentucky-West Virginia Gas Co.
(100)NDL-Panhandle Eastern Pipeline Co.
(100)NDL-Texas Eastern Transmission Corp.
(100)NDL-Ohio River Pipeline Corp.
(100)NDL-Texas Gas Transmission Co.
(100)NPT-United Cities Gas Co.
(100)NPT-Cincinnati Gas & Electric Co.
(100)NPT-Louisville Gas & Electric Co.
(100)NPT-Western Kentucky Gas Co.
(120)NDL-ANR Pipeline Co.
(120)NDL-Carnegie Natural Gas Co.
(140)NDL-Gas Transport Inc.
```

DETAIL OF SUBSIDIARIES	PARENT
Columbia Gas Transmission Corp.	Columbia Gas System, Inc.
Inland Gas Co. Inc.	Columbia Gas System, Inc.
Consolidated Gas Supply Corp.	Consolidated Natural Gas
East Tennessee Natural Gas Co.	Tenneco Inc.
Ohio Valley Gas Corp.	Columbia Gas System, Inc.
Midwestern Gas Transmission Co.	Tenneco Inc.
Columbia Gulf Transmission Co.	Columbia Gas System, Inc.
Tennessee Natural Gas Lines, Inc.	Tenneco Inc.
River Gas Co.	Consolidated Natural Gas

LINCOLN, NE

```
( 0)    Northern Natural Gas Co.
(100)NDL-ANR Pipeline Co.
(100)NDL-KN Energy Inc.
(100)NDL-Northwest Central Pipeline Corp.
(100)NDL-Panhandle Eastern Pipeline Co.
(100)NDL-Union Gas System Inc.
(100)NDL-Kansas Power & Light Co.
(100)NDL-Natural Gas Pipeline Co. of America
(100)NPT-Missouri Public Service Co.
```

LITTLE ROCK-N. LITTLE ROCK, AR

```
(  0)    Arkla Inc.
(  0)    Texas Eastern Transmission Corp.
(100)NDL-Arkansas Oklahoma Gas Co.
(100)NDL-Mississippi River Transmission Corp.
(100)NDL-Trunkline Gas Co.
(100)NDL*Tenneco Inc.
(100)NDL-Delhi Gas Pipeline Corp.
(100)NDL-Natural Gas Pipeline Co. of America
(100)NDL-Oklahoma Natural Gas Co. (Oneok Inc.)
(100)NDL-Texas Gas Transmission Co.
(100)NPT-Columbia Gulf Transmission Co.
(100)NPT-Mustang Fuel Corp.
(100)NPT-Mississippi Valley Gas Co.
(100)NPT-Ozark Gas Pipeline Corp.
(100)NPT-Arkansas Western Gas Co.
(120)NDL-Enserch Corp.
(120)NDL-Northwest Central Pipeline Corp.
(120)NDL-Mid-Louisiana Gas Co.
(120)NDL-United Gas Pipeline Co.
(120)NDL-Associated Natural Gas Co.
(120)NPT-Louisiana State Gas Corp.
(140)NDL-Southern Natural Gas Co.
(140)NDL-Union Gas System Inc.
(140)NDL-Transok, Inc.
```

```
 DETAIL OF SUBSIDIARIES              PARENT

Louisiana Intrastate Gas Corp.      Tenneco Inc.
```

LONGVIEW—MARSHALL, TX

```
(  0)    Arkla Inc.
(  0)    Enserch Corp.
(  0)    KN Energy Inc.
(  0)   *United Energy Resources Inc.
(  0) PT-Delhi Gas Pipeline Corp.
(100)NDL*Panhandle Eastern Corp.
(100)NDL*Tenneco Inc.
(100)NDL-Texas Eastern Transmission Corp.
(100)NDL-Mid-Louisiana Gas Co.
(100)NDL-Natural Gas Pipeline Co. of America
(100)NDL*Houston Natural Gas Corp.
(100)NDL-Texas Gas Transmission Co.
(100)NPT-Columbia Gulf Transmission Co.
(100)NPT-Louisiana State Gas Corp.
(100)NPT-Esperanza Transmission Co.
(100)NPT-Texacol Gas Services, Inc.
(120)NPT-Valero Interstate Transmission Co.
(120)NPT-Producers Gas Co.
(120)NPT-Southwestern Gas Pipeline Inc.
(140)NDL-Mississippi River Transmission Corp.
(140)NDL-Crab Run Gas Co.
(140)NDL-West Lake Arthur Corp.
(140)NDL-Texas Gas Pipeline Co.
(140)NPT-Southern Natural Gas Co.
(140)NPT-Shell Oil Co.
(140)NPT-Seagull Pipeline Corp.
(140)NPT-Sabine Pipeline Co.
```

DETAIL OF SUBSIDIARIES	PARENT
United Gas Pipeline Co.	United Energy Resources
Trunkline Gas Co.	Panhandle Eastern Corp.
Louisiana Intrastate Gas Corp.	Tenneco Inc.
Valley Gas Transmission, Inc.	Houston Natural Gas Corp.
Houston Pipeline Co.	Houston Natural Gas Corp.
Trunkline Lng Co.	Panhandle Eastern Corp.
Channel Industries Gas Co.	Tenneco Inc.
United Texas Transmission Co.	United Energy Resources

LOUISVILLE (KY-IN)

```
(  0)    Ohio River Pipeline Corp.
(  0)    Texas Gas Transmission Co.
(  0) PT-Louisville Gas & Electric Co.
(  0) PT-Western Kentucky Gas Co.
(100)NDL-ANR Pipeline Co.
(100)NDL*Columbia Gas System, Inc.
(100)NDL*Panhandle Eastern Corp.
(100)NDL*Tenneco Inc.
(100)NDL-Texas Eastern Transmission Corp.
(100)NPT-United Cities Gas Co.
(100)NPT-Cincinnati Gas & Electric Co.
(120)NDL-Kentucky-West Virginia Gas Co.
(140)NPT-Consolidated Gas Supply Corp.
(140)NPT-Central Illinois Light Co.
(140)NPT-Illinois Power Co.
(140)NPT-Northern Illinois Gas Co.
```

DETAIL OF SUBSIDIARIES	PARENT
Columbia Gas Transmission Corp.	Columbia Gas System, Inc.
Inland Gas Co. Inc.	Columbia Gas System, Inc.
Panhandle Eastern Pipeline Co.	Panhandle Eastern Corp.
East Tennessee Natural Gas Co.	Tenneco Inc.
Midwestern Gas Transmission Co.	Tenneco Inc.
Columbia Gulf Transmission Co.	Columbia Gas System, Inc.
Ohio Valley Gas Corp.	Columbia Gas System, Inc.
Tennessee Natural Gas Lines, Inc.	Tenneco Inc.
Trunkline Gas Co.	Panhandle Eastern Corp.

MACON-WARNER ROBINS, GA

```
(  0)    *Southern Natural Gas Co.
(100)NDL-Transcontinental Gas Pipeline Corp.
(100)NPT-United Cities Gas Co.
(100)NPT*South Carolina Electric & Gas Co.
(100)NPT-Southeast Alabama Gas District, The
(120)NDL-Florida Gas Transmission Co.
(140)NDL-East Tennessee Natural Gas Co.
```

DETAIL OF SUBSIDIARIES	PARENT
South Georgia Nautural Gas Co.	Southern Natural Gas Co.
Carolina Pipeline Co.	South Carolina Electric

MADISON, WI

```
(  0)    *ANR Pipeline Co.
(  0)    *Internorth Inc.
(100)NDL-Mississippi River Transmission Corp.
(100)NDL-Midwestern Gas Transmission Co.
(100)NDL-Natural Gas Pipeline Co. of America
(100)NPT-Northern Illinois Gas Co.
(100)NPT-Northern Indiana Public Service Co.
(120)NDL-Texas Gas Transmission Co.
(140)NDL-Panhandle Eastern Pipeline Co.
(140)NPT-Michigan Consolidated Gas Co.
(140)NPT-Central Illinois Light Co.
```

```
   DETAIL OF SUBSIDIARIES                   PARENT

Northern Natural Gas Co.                 Internorth Inc.
Wisconsin Natural Gas Co.                ANR Pipeline Co.
Northern Border Pipeline Co.             Internorth Inc.
```

MANCHESTER-NASHUA, NH

```
(  0)    *Tenneco Inc.
(100)NDL-Consolidated Gas Supply Corp.
(100)NDL*Texas Eastern Corp.
(100)NDL-Distrigas of Massachusetts Corp.
(100)NPT-Central Hudson Gas & Electric Corp.
(100)NPT-Niagara Mohawk Power Corp.
(120)NDL-Columbia Gas Transmission Corp.
(120)NDL-Equitable Gas Co.
(120)NDL-Transcontinental Gas Pipeline Corp.
```

```
   DETAIL OF SUBSIDIARIES                   PARENT

Granite State Gas Transmission, Inc   Tenneco Inc.
Algonquin Gas Transmission Co.        Texas Eastern Corp.
Northern Utilities, Inc., - ME        Tenneco Inc.
Texas Eastern Transmission Corp.      Texas Eastern Corp.
```

MANSFIELD, OH

```
(  0)    Texas Gas Transmission Co.
(100)NDL*ANR Pipeline Co.
(100)NDL*Columbia Gas System, Inc.
(100)NDL*Consolidated Natural Gas Corp.
(100)NDL-Equitable Gas Co.
(100)NDL-Gas Transport Inc.
(100)NDL*National Fuel Gas Co.
(100)NDL-Panhandle Eastern Pipeline Co.
(100)NDL-Tenneco Inc.
(100)NDL-Texas Eastern Transmission Corp.
(100)NDL-Carnegie Natural Gas Co.
(100)NDL-Michigan Consolidated Gas Co.
(100)NPT-Transcontinental Gas Pipeline Corp.
(100)NPT-Michigan Gas Storage Co.
(100)NPT-Cincinnati Gas & Electric Co.
(120)NPT-Northern Indiana Public Service Co.
```

DETAIL OF SUBSIDIARIES	PARENT
Great Lakes Gas Transmission Co.	ANR Pipeline Co.
Columbia Gas Transmission Corp.	Columbia Gas System, Inc.
Consolidated Gas Supply Corp.	Consolidated Natural Gas
National Fuel Gas Distribution Corp	National Fuel Gas Co.
National Fuel Gas Supply Corp.	National Fuel Gas Co.
Ohio Valley Gas Corp.	Columbia Gas System, Inc.
East Ohio Gas Co.	Consolidated Natural Gas
River Gas Co.	Consolidated Natural Gas
Inland Gas Co. Inc.	Columbia Gas System, Inc.
Columbia Gulf Transmission Co.	Columbia Gas System, Inc.

MCALLEN-EDINBURG-MISSION, TX

```
(  0)    *Valero Interstate Transmission Co.
(  0)    *United Energy Resources Inc.
(  0)    *Houston Natural Gas Corp.
(  0) PT-Intrastate Gathering Corp.
(  0) PT-Transcontinental Gas Pipeline Corp.
(  0) PT-Esperanza Transmission Co.
(100)NDL-Enserch Corp.
(100)NDL*Tenneco Inc.
(100)NDL-Florida Gas Transmission Co.
(100)NDL-Texacol Gas Services, Inc.
(100)NPT-Trunkline Gas Co.
(100)NPT-Seagull Pipeline Corp.
(100)NPT-Delhi Gas Pipeline Corp.
(140)NPT-El Paso Natural Gas Co.
(140)NPT-Southern Natural Gas Co.
(140)NPT-Natural Gas Pipeline Co. of America
```

DETAIL OF SUBSIDIARIES	PARENT
Rio Grande Valley Gas Co.	Valero Interstate Trans
United Gas Pipeline Co.	United Energy Resources
Valley Gas Transmission, Inc.	Houston Natural Gas Corp.
Channel Industries Gas Co.	Tenneco Inc.
Houston Pipeline Co.	Houston Natural Gas Corp.
United Texas Transmission Co.	United Energy Resources

MEDFORD, OR

```
(  0)    *Northwest Energy Co.
(100)NDL*Pacific Gas & Electric Co.
(100)NPT-Northwest Natural Gas Corp.
```

DETAIL OF SUBSIDIARIES   PARENT

```
Northwest Pipeline Corp.              Northwest Energy Co.
Pacific Gas Transmission Co.          Pacific Gas & Electric Co.
Southwest Gas Corp.                   Northwest Energy Co.
```

MELBOURNE—TITUSVILLE—PALM BAY, FL

```
(  0)    Florida Gas Transmission Co.
```

MEMPHIS (TN—AR—MS)

```
(  0)    Trunkline Gas Co.
(  0)    Texas Gas Transmission Co.
(  0) PT-Columbia Gulf Transmission Co.
(100)NDL-Alabama-Tennessee Natural Gas Co.
(100)NDL-ANR Pipeline Co.
(100)NDL-Arkla Inc.
(100)NDL-Mississippi River Transmission Corp.
(100)NDL-Southern Natural Gas Co.
(100)NDL*Tenneco Inc.
(100)NDL-Texas Eastern Transmission Corp.
(100)NDL-Mississippi Valley Gas Co.
(100)NDL-Associated Natural Gas Co.
(100)NPT-United Cities Gas Co.
(100)NPT-Natural Gas Pipeline Co. of America
(120)NDL-United Gas Pipeline Co.
(120)NPT-Western Kentucky Gas Co.
(140)NPT-Transcontinental Gas Pipeline Corp.
```

DETAIL OF SUBSIDIARIES   PARENT

```
East Tennessee Natural Gas Co.        Tenneco Inc.
Tennessee Natural Gas Lines, Inc.     Tenneco Inc.
```

MIAMI—HIALEAH, FL

```
(  0)    Florida Gas Transmission Co.
```

MIDDLESEX-SOMERSET-HUNTERDON, NJ

```
(  0)    Equitable Gas Co.
(  0)    *Texas Eastern Corp.
(100)NDL-Columbia Gas Transmission Corp.
(100)NDL-Consolidated Gas Supply Corp.
(100)NDL-Tenneco Inc.
(100)NDL-Transcontinental Gas Pipeline Corp.
(100)NDL*Washington Gas Light Co.
(100)NDL-Eastern Shore Natural Gas Co.
(100)NDL-North Penn Gas Co.
(100)NPT-Central Hudson Gas & Electric Corp.
(100)NPT-Niagara Mohawk Power Corp.
(100)NPT-South Jersey Gas Co.
```

DETAIL OF SUBSIDIARIES	PARENT
Texas Eastern Transmission Corp.	Texas Eastern Corp.
Algonquin Gas Transmission Co.	Texas Eastern Corp.
Frederick Gas Co.	Washington Gas Light Co.

MILWAUKEE, WI

```
(  0)    *ANR Pipeline Co.
(100)NDL-Midwestern Gas Transmission Co.
(100)NDL-Natural Gas Pipeline Co. of America
(100)NDL-Texas Gas Transmission Co.
(100)NDL-Northern Natural Gas Co.
(100)NPT-Michigan Consolidated Gas Co.
(100)NPT-Northern Illinois Gas Co.
(100)NPT-Northern Indiana Public Service Co.
(120)NDL-Panhandle Eastern Pipeline Co.
(140)NPT-Central Illinois Light Co.
```

DETAIL OF SUBSIDIARIES	PARENT
Wisconsin Natural Gas Co.	ANR Pipeline Co.

MINNEAPOLIS-ST. PAUL (MN-WI)

```
(  0)    Midwestern Gas Transmission Co.
(  0)    *Internorth Inc.
(100)NDL*ANR Pipeline Co.
```

DETAIL OF SUBSIDIARIES	PARENT
Northern Natural Gas Co.	Internorth Inc.
Great Lakes Gas Transmission Co.	ANR Pipeline Co.
Northern Border Pipeline Co.	Internorth Inc.

MOBILE, AL

```
(  0)    United Gas Pipeline Co.
(100)NDL-Southern Natural Gas Co.
(100)NDL*Tenneco Inc.
(100)NDL-Transcontinental Gas Pipeline Corp.
(100)NDL-Shell Oil Co.
(100)NDL-Florida Gas Transmission Co.
(100)NDL-Monterey Pipeline Co.
(100)NPT-Columbia Gulf Transmission Co.
(100)NPT-Louisiana State Gas Corp.
(100)NPT-Okaloosa County Gas District
(100)NPT-Southeast Alabama Gas District, The
(120)NDL-Texas Eastern Transmission Corp.
(120)NDL-Mississippi Valley Gas Co.
(140)NDL-Mid-Louisiana Gas Co.
(140)NDL-Texas Gas Transmission Co.
(140)NDL-Northern Natural Gas Co.
```

```
DETAIL OF SUBSIDIARIES                 PARENT

Louisiana Intrastate Gas Corp.     Tenneco Inc.
```

MONROE, LA

```
(  0)    Arkla Inc.
(  0)    *Tenneco Inc.
(  0)    Mid-Louisiana Gas Co.
(  0)    United Gas Pipeline Co.
(  0)    Texas Gas Transmission Co.
(  0) PT-Louisiana State Gas Corp.
(100)NDL-Enserch Corp.
(100)NDL-KN Energy Inc.
(100)NDL-Mississippi River Transmission Corp.
(100)NDL*Panhandle Eastern Corp.
(100)NDL-Southern Natural Gas Co.
(100)NDL-Texas Eastern Transmission Corp.
(100)NDL-Transcontinental Gas Pipeline Corp.
(100)NDL-Mississippi Valley Gas Co.
(100)NDL-Natural Gas Pipeline Co. of America
(100)NDL-Valley Gas Transmission, Inc.
(100)NPT-Columbia Gulf Transmission Co.
(100)NPT-Delhi Gas Pipeline Corp.
(120)NDL-Monterey Pipeline Co.
(120)NDL-Northern Natural Gas Co.
(140)NDL-Crab Run Gas Co.
(140)NDL-West Lake Arthur Corp.
(140)NPT-Shell Oil Co.
(140)NPT-Sabine Pipeline Co.
```

```
DETAIL OF SUBSIDIARIES                 PARENT

Louisiana Intrastate Gas Corp.     Tenneco Inc.
Trunkline Gas Co.                  Panhandle Eastern Corp.
Trunkline Lng Co.                  Panhandle Eastern Corp.
```

MONTGOMERY, AL

```
(  0)    *Southern Natural Gas Co.
(  0)  PT-Southeast Alabama Gas District, The
(100)NDL*Tenneco Inc.
(100)NDL-Transcontinental Gas Pipeline Corp.
(100)NDL-Florida Gas Transmission Co.
(100)NDL-United Gas Pipeline Co.
(100)NPT-United Cities Gas Co.
(100)NPT-Mississippi Valley Gas Co.
(100)NPT-Okaloosa County Gas District
(120)NDL-Alabama-Tennessee Natural Gas Co.
(140)NDL-Texas Eastern Transmission Corp.
```

DETAIL OF SUBSIDIARIES   PARENT

South Georgia Nautural Gas Co.   Southern Natural Gas Co.
East Tennessee Natural Gas Co.   Tenneco Inc.

MUNCIE, IN

```
(  0)    *ANR Pipeline Co.
(100)NDL*Columbia Gas System, Inc.
(100)NDL*Panhandle Eastern Corp.
(100)NDL*Tenneco Inc.
(100)NDL-Texas Eastern Transmission Corp.
(100)NDL-Ohio River Pipeline Corp.
(100)NDL-Texas Gas Transmission Co.
(100)NPT*Consolidated Natural Gas Corp.
(100)NPT-Cincinnati Gas & Electric Co.
(100)NPT-Louisville Gas & Electric Co.
(100)NPT-Northern Illinois Gas Co.
(100)NPT-Northern Indiana Public Service Co.
(100)NPT-Western Kentucky Gas Co.
(120)NDL-Michigan Consolidated Gas Co.
(120)NDL-Natural Gas Pipeline Co. of America
(120)NPT-Michigan Gas Storage Co.
(140)NPT-Central Illinois Light Co.
(140)NPT-Illinois Power Co.
```

DETAIL OF SUBSIDIARIES   PARENT

Columbia Gas Transmission Corp.   Columbia Gas System, Inc.
Panhandle Eastern Pipeline Co.   Panhandle Eastern Corp.
Trunkline Gas Co.   Panhandle Eastern Corp.
Midwestern Gas Transmission Co.   Tenneco Inc.
Ohio Valley Gas Corp.   Columbia Gas System, Inc.
Consolidated Gas Supply Corp.   Consolidated Natural Gas
East Ohio Gas Co.   Consolidated Natural Gas
Great Lakes Gas Transmission Co.   ANR Pipeline Co.
Inland Gas Co. Inc.   Columbia Gas System, Inc.

NASHVILLE, TN

```
(  0)    *Tenneco Inc.
(  0)     Texas Gas Transmission Co.
(  0) PT-United Cities Gas Co.
(100)NDL-Alabama-Tennessee Natural Gas Co.
(100)NDL-ANR Pipeline Co.
(100)NDL*Columbia Gas System, Inc.
(100)NDL-Trunkline Gas Co.
(100)NDL-Southern Natural Gas Co.
(100)NDL-Texas Eastern Transmission Corp.
(100)NDL-Ohio River Pipeline Corp.
(100)NDL-United Gas Pipeline Co.
(100)NPT-Louisville Gas & Electric Co.
(100)NPT-Western Kentucky Gas Co.
(120)NDL-Mississippi Valley Gas Co.
(140)NDL-Arkla Inc.
(140)NDL-Transcontinental Gas Pipeline Corp.
(140)NDL-Associated Natural Gas Co.
```

```
 DETAIL OF SUBSIDIARIES                PARENT

 East Tennessee Natural Gas Co.        Tenneco Inc.
 Columbia Gulf Transmission Co.        Columbia Gas System, Inc.
 Tennessee Natural Gas Lines, Inc.     Tenneco Inc.
 Midwestern Gas Transmission Co.       Tenneco Inc.
 Columbia Gas Transmission Corp.       Columbia Gas System, Inc.
 Inland Gas Co. Inc.                   Columbia Gas System, Inc.
```

NASSAU-SUFFOLK, NY

```
(  0)     Transcontinental Gas Pipeline Corp.
(100)NDL-Columbia Gas Transmission Corp.
(100)NDL-Consolidated Gas Supply Corp.
(100)NDL-Equitable Gas Co.
(100)NDL-Tenneco Inc.
(100)NDL*Texas Eastern Corp.
(100)NDL-North Penn Gas Co.
(100)NPT-Central Hudson Gas & Electric Corp.
(100)NPT-Niagara Mohawk Power Corp.
(100)NPT-South Jersey Gas Co.
(120)NDL-Eastern Shore Natural Gas Co.
```

```
 DETAIL OF SUBSIDIARIES                PARENT

 Algonquin Gas Transmission Co.        Texas Eastern Corp.
 Texas Eastern Transmission Corp.      Texas Eastern Corp.
```

N.BEDFORD—FALL R.—ATTLEBORO, MA

```
(  0)    *Texas Eastern Corp.
(100)NDL*Tenneco Inc.
(100)NDL-Distrigas of Massachusetts Corp.
(120)NDL-Columbia Gas Transmission Corp.
(120)NDL-Consolidated Gas Supply Corp.
(120)NDL-Equitable Gas Co.
(120)NDL-Transcontinental Gas Pipeline Corp.
(120)NPT-Central Hudson Gas & Electric Corp.
(120)NPT-Niagara Mohawk Power Corp.
```

DETAIL OF SUBSIDIARIES	PARENT
Algonquin Gas Transmission Co.	Texas Eastern Corp.
Granite State Gas Transmission, Inc	Tenneco Inc.
Northern Utilities, Inc., – ME	Tenneco Inc.
Texas Eastern Transmission Corp.	Texas Eastern Corp.

N.HAVEN—WATERBURY—MER., CT

```
(  0)    *Tenneco Inc.
(  0)    *Texas Eastern Corp.
(100)NDL-Columbia Gas Transmission Corp.
(100)NDL-Consolidated Gas Supply Corp.
(100)NDL-Equitable Gas Co.
(100)NDL-Transcontinental Gas Pipeline Corp.
(100)NDL-Distrigas of Massachusetts Corp.
(100)NDL-North Penn Gas Co.
(100)NPT-Central Hudson Gas & Electric Corp.
(100)NPT-Niagara Mohawk Power Corp.
(120)NPT-South Jersey Gas Co.
```

DETAIL OF SUBSIDIARIES	PARENT
Algonquin Gas Transmission Co.	Texas Eastern Corp.
Granite State Gas Transmission, Inc	Tenneco Inc.
Texas Eastern Transmission Corp.	Texas Eastern Corp.
Northern Utilities, Inc., – ME	Tenneco Inc.

N.LONDON—NORWICH, CT

```
(  0)    *Texas Eastern Corp.
(100)NDL-Columbia Gas Transmission Corp.
(100)NDL-Consolidated Gas Supply Corp.
(100)NDL-Equitable Gas Co.
(100)NDL*Tenneco Inc.
(100)NDL-Transcontinental Gas Pipeline Corp.
(100)NDL-Distrigas of Massachusetts Corp.
(100)NPT-Central Hudson Gas & Electric Corp.
(100)NPT-Niagara Mohawk Power Corp.
(140)NDL-North Penn Gas Co.
```

DETAIL OF SUBSIDIARIES	PARENT
Algonquin Gas Transmission Co.	Texas Eastern Corp.
Granite State Gas Transmission, Inc	Tenneco Inc.
Texas Eastern Transmission Corp.	Texas Eastern Corp.
Northern Utilities, Inc., – ME	Tenneco Inc.

NEW ORLEANS, LA

```
(  0)   *Tenneco Inc.
(  0)    Shell Oil Co.
(  0)    United Gas Pipeline Co.
(  0) PT-Columbia Gulf Transmission Co.
(  0) PT-Louisiana State Gas Corp.
(100)NDL-Arkla Inc.
(100)NDL-Southern Natural Gas Co.
(100)NDL-Texas Eastern Transmission Corp.
(100)NDL-Transcontinental Gas Pipeline Corp.
(100)NDL-Louisiana Resources Co.
(100)NDL-Mississippi Valley Gas Co.
(100)NDL-Delta Gas Inc.
(100)NDL-Florida Gas Transmission Co.
(100)NDL-Mid-Louisiana Gas Co.
(100)NDL-Monterey Pipeline Co.
(100)NDL-Natural Gas Pipeline Co. of America
(100)NDL-Texas Gas Transmission Co.
(100)NDL-Northern Natural Gas Co.
(120)NDL*Panhandle Eastern Corp.
(140)NDL-Crab Run Gas Co.
(140)NDL-West Lake Arthur Corp.
(140)NPT-Okaloosa County Gas District
(140)NPT-Sabine Pipeline Co.
```

```
   DETAIL OF SUBSIDIARIES                PARENT

Louisiana Intrastate Gas Corp.       Tenneco Inc.
Trunkline Gas Co.                    Panhandle Eastern Corp.
Trunkline Lng Co.                    Panhandle Eastern Corp.
```

NEW YORK, NY

```
(  0)    Equitable Gas Co.
(  0)   *Tenneco Inc.
(  0)   *Texas Eastern Corp.
(  0)    Transcontinental Gas Pipeline Corp.
(100)NDL-Columbia Gas Transmission Corp.
(100)NDL-Consolidated Gas Supply Corp.
(100)NDL-Eastern Shore Natural Gas Co.
(100)NDL-North Penn Gas Co.
(100)NPT-Central Hudson Gas & Electric Corp.
(100)NPT-Niagara Mohawk Power Corp.
(100)NPT-South Jersey Gas Co.
(120)NDL-Distrigas of Massachusetts Corp.
(120)NPT-Frederick Gas Co.
```

```
   DETAIL OF SUBSIDIARIES                PARENT

Algonquin Gas Transmission Co.       Texas Eastern Corp.
Texas Eastern Transmission Corp.     Texas Eastern Corp.
Granite State Gas Transmission, Inc  Tenneco Inc.
```

NEWARK, NJ

    (0)   Tenneco Inc.
    (0)   *Texas Eastern Corp.
    (100)NDL-Columbia Gas Transmission Corp.
    (100)NDL-Consolidated Gas Supply Corp.
    (100)NDL-Equitable Gas Co.
    (100)NDL-Transcontinental Gas Pipeline Corp.
    (100)NDL-Eastern Shore Natural Gas Co.
    (100)NDL-North Penn Gas Co.
    (100)NPT-Central Hudson Gas & Electric Corp.
    (100)NPT-Niagara Mohawk Power Corp.
    (100)NPT-South Jersey Gas Co.
    (120)NPT-Frederick Gas Co.

     DETAIL OF SUBSIDIARIES   PARENT

    Algonquin Gas Transmission Co.   Texas Eastern Corp.
    Texas Eastern Transmission Corp.   Texas Eastern Corp.

NIAGARA FALLS, NY

    (0)   *National Fuel Gas Co.
    (0)   Tenneco Inc.
    (100)NDL-Columbia Gas Transmission Corp.
    (100)NDL-Consolidated Gas Supply Corp.
    (100)NDL-Transcontinental Gas Pipeline Corp.
    (100)NDL-North Penn Gas Co.
    (100)NPT-Niagara Mohawk Power Corp.
    (100)NPT-Rochester Gas & Electric Corp.
    (120)NPT-Equitable Gas Co.

     DETAIL OF SUBSIDIARIES   PARENT

    National Fuel Gas Distribution Corp National Fuel Gas Co.
    National Fuel Gas Supply Corp.   National Fuel Gas Co.

OCALA, FL

    (0)   Florida Gas Transmission Co.
    (100)NDL*Southern Natural Gas Co.

     DETAIL OF SUBSIDIARIES   PARENT

    South Georgia Nautural Gas Co.   Southern Natural Gas Co.

ODESSA, TX

```
(  0)   *El Paso Natural Gas Co.
(  0)    Energas Co.
(  0)   *Pioneer Corp.
(  0) PT-Red River Gas Pipeline Corp.
(100)NDL-Enserch Corp.
(100)NDL-Transwestern Pipeline Co.
(100)NDL-Natural Gas Pipeline Co. of America
(100)NDL-Palo Duro Pipeline Co.
(100)NDL*Houston Natural Gas Corp.
(100)NDL*Coastal Corp.
(100)NPT-Producers Gas Co.
(100)NPT-Western Gas Interstate Co.
(100)NPT-Northern Natural Gas Co.
```

```
 DETAIL OF SUBSIDIARIES                  PARENT

West Texas Gathering Co.          Pioneer Corp.
Odessa Natural Gas Corp.          El Paso Natural Gas Co.
Valley Gas Transmission, Inc.     Houston Natural Gas Corp.
Colorado Interstate Gas Co.       Coastal Corp.
Texacol Gas Services, Inc.        Coastal Corp.
Intratex Gas Co.                  Houston Natural Gas Corp.
```

OKLAHOMA CITY, OK

```
(  0)    Northwest Central Pipeline Corp.
(  0)    Transok, Inc.
(  0)   *Oklahoma Natural Gas Co. (Oneok Inc.)
(100)NDL-Arkansas Oklahoma Gas Co.
(100)NDL-Arkla Inc.
(100)NDL-Enserch Corp.
(100)NDL-Mississippi River Transmission Corp.
(100)NDL-Panhandle Eastern Pipeline Co.
(100)NDL-Union Gas System Inc.
(100)NDL-Crab Run Gas Co.
(100)NDL-Kansas Power & Light Co.
(100)NDL-Producers Gas Co.
(100)NDL-Delhi Gas Pipeline Corp.
(100)NDL-Natural Gas Pipeline Co. of America
(100)NDL*Coastal Corp.
(100)NDL-Northern Natural Gas Co.
(100)NPT-Mustang Fuel Corp.
(100)NPT-United Gas Pipeline Co.
(100)NPT-Ozark Gas Pipeline Corp.
(100)NPT-Arkansas Western Gas Co.
(100)NPT-Texas Gas Transmission Co.
(120)NDL-El Paso Natural Gas Co.
(120)NDL-Transwestern Pipeline Co.
(120)NPT-Red River Gas Pipeline Corp.
(140)NDL-Energas Co.
(140)NPT-Southwestern Gas Pipeline Inc.
```

```
 DETAIL OF SUBSIDIARIES                  PARENT

Ringwood Gathering Co.            Oklahoma Natural Gas Co.
Texacol Gas Services, Inc.       Coastal Corp.
Colorado Interstate Gas Co.      Coastal Corp.
```

OMAHA (NE-IA)

```
(  0)    Northern Natural Gas Co.
(100)NDL-ANR Pipeline Co.
(100)NDL-KN Energy Inc.
(100)NDL-Northwest Central Pipeline Corp.
(100)NDL-Kansas Power & Light Co.
(100)NDL-Natural Gas Pipeline Co. of America
(120)NDL-Panhandle Eastern Pipeline Co.
(120)NDL-Union Gas System Inc.
(120)NPT-Missouri Public Service Co.
```

ORANGE COUNTY, NY

```
(  0)    Columbia Gas Transmission Corp.
(  0) PT-Central Hudson Gas & Electric Corp.
(100)NDL-Consolidated Gas Supply Corp.
(100)NDL-Equitable Gas Co.
(100)NDL*Tenneco Inc.
(100)NDL*Texas Eastern Corp.
(100)NDL-Transcontinental Gas Pipeline Corp.
(100)NDL-North Penn Gas Co.
(100)NPT-Niagara Mohawk Power Corp.
(100)NPT-South Jersey Gas Co.
(120)NDL-Eastern Shore Natural Gas Co.
(140)NDL-Distrigas of Massachusetts Corp.
(140)NPT-Frederick Gas Co.
```

```
  DETAIL OF SUBSIDIARIES              PARENT

Algonquin Gas Transmission Co.      Texas Eastern Corp.
Texas Eastern Transmission Corp.    Texas Eastern Corp.
Granite State Gas Transmission, Inc Tenneco Inc.
```

ORLANDO, FL

```
(  0)    Florida Gas Transmission Co.
(140)NDL-South Georgia Nautural Gas Co.
```

PANAMA CITY, FL

```
(  0)    Florida Gas Transmission Co.
(100)NDL*Southern Natural Gas Co.
(100)NDL-United Gas Pipeline Co.
(100)NPT-Transcontinental Gas Pipeline Corp.
(100)NPT-United Cities Gas Co.
(100)NPT-Okaloosa County Gas District
(100)NPT-Southeast Alabama Gas District, The
```

```
  DETAIL OF SUBSIDIARIES              PARENT

South Georgia Nautural Gas Co.      Southern Natural Gas Co.
```

PARKERSBURG-MARIETTA (WV-OH)

```
(  0)   *Columbia Gas System, Inc.
(  0)    Gas Transport Inc.
(100)NDL*Consolidated Natural Gas Corp.
(100)NDL*Equitable Gas Co.
(100)NDL*National Fuel Gas Co.
(100)NDL*Tenneco Inc.
(100)NDL-Texas Eastern Transmission Corp.
(100)NDL-Carnegie Natural Gas Co.
(100)NDL-Texas Gas Transmission Co.
(100)NPT-Transcontinental Gas Pipeline Corp.
(100)NPT-Cincinnati Gas & Electric Co.
(120)NDL-Panhandle Eastern Pipeline Co.
(140)NPT-ANR Pipeline Co.
(140)NPT-Roanoke Gas Co.
```

```
   DETAIL OF SUBSIDIARIES                 PARENT

Columbia Gas Transmission Corp.      Columbia Gas System, Inc.
River Gas Co.                        Consolidated Natural Gas
Inland Gas Co. Inc.                  Columbia Gas System, Inc.
Consolidated Gas Supply Corp.        Consolidated Natural Gas
National Fuel Gas Supply Corp.       National Fuel Gas Co.
Columbia Gulf Transmission Co.       Columbia Gas System, Inc.
East Ohio Gas Co.                    Consolidated Natural Gas
Kentucky-West Virginia Gas Co.       Equitable Gas Co.
National Fuel Gas Distribution Corp  National Fuel Gas Co.
Ohio Valley Gas Corp.                Columbia Gas System, Inc.
East Tennessee Natural Gas Co.       Tenneco Inc.
```

PASCAGOULA, MS

```
(  0)    United Gas Pipeline Co.
(100)NDL-Southern Natural Gas Co.
(100)NDL*Tenneco Inc.
(100)NDL-Texas Eastern Transmission Corp.
(100)NDL-Transcontinental Gas Pipeline Corp.
(100)NDL-Shell Oil Co.
(100)NDL-Delta Gas Inc.
(100)NDL-Florida Gas Transmission Co.
(100)NDL-Mid-Louisiana Gas Co.
(100)NDL-Monterey Pipeline Co.
(100)NDL-Texas Gas Transmission Co.
(100)NDL-Northern Natural Gas Co.
(100)NPT-Columbia Gulf Transmission Co.
(100)NPT-Louisiana State Gas Corp.
(100)NPT-Okaloosa County Gas District
(120)NDL-Mississippi Valley Gas Co.
```

```
   DETAIL OF SUBSIDIARIES                 PARENT

Louisiana Intrastate Gas Corp.       Tenneco Inc.
```

PENSACOLA, FL

(0)   Florida Gas Transmission Co.
(0)   United Gas Pipeline Co.
(0) PT-Okaloosa County Gas District
(100)NDL*Southern Natural Gas Co.
(100)NDL*Tenneco Inc.
(100)NDL-Transcontinental Gas Pipeline Corp.
(100)NPT-Southeast Alabama Gas District, The
(120)NPT-United Cities Gas Co.
(140)NDL-Shell Oil Co.
(140)NPT-Columbia Gulf Transmission Co.
(140)NPT-Mississippi Valley Gas Co.
(140)NPT-Monterey Pipeline Co.
(140)NPT-Louisiana State Gas Corp.

  DETAIL OF SUBSIDIARIES   PARENT

South Georgia Nautural Gas Co.   Southern Natural Gas Co.
Louisiana Intrastate Gas Corp.   Tenneco Inc.

PEORIA, IL

(0)   *Panhandle Eastern Corp.
(0) PT-Central Illinois Light Co.
(100)NDL*ANR Pipeline Co.
(100)NDL-Mississippi River Transmission Corp.
(100)NDL-Midwestern Gas Transmission Co.
(100)NDL-Natural Gas Pipeline Co. of America
(100)NDL-Texas Gas Transmission Co.
(100)NDL*Internorth Inc.
(100)NPT-United Cities Gas Co.
(100)NPT-Central Illinois Public Service Co.
(100)NPT-Illinois Power Co.
(100)NPT-Northern Illinois Gas Co.
(100)NPT-Northern Indiana Public Service Co.

  DETAIL OF SUBSIDIARIES   PARENT

Panhandle Eastern Pipeline Co.   Panhandle Eastern Corp.
Trunkline Gas Co.   Panhandle Eastern Corp.
Northern Natural Gas Co.   Internorth Inc.
Northern Border Pipeline Co.   Internorth Inc.
Wisconsin Natural Gas Co.   ANR Pipeline Co.

PHILADELPHIA (PA-NJ)

```
(  0)    *Texas Eastern Corp.
(  0)     Transcontinental Gas Pipeline Corp.
(  0) PT-South Jersey Gas Co.
(100)NDL-Columbia Gas Transmission Corp.
(100)NDL-Consolidated Gas Supply Corp.
(100)NDL-Equitable Gas Co.
(100)NDL-Tenneco Inc.
(100)NDL*Washington Gas Light Co.
(100)NDL-Eastern Shore Natural Gas Co.
(100)NDL-North Penn Gas Co.
(100)NPT-Central Hudson Gas & Electric Corp.
(120)NPT-Niagara Mohawk Power Corp.
```

DETAIL OF SUBSIDIARIES	PARENT
Texas Eastern Transmission Corp.	Texas Eastern Corp.
Algonquin Gas Transmission Co.	Texas Eastern Corp.
Shenandoah Gas Co.	Washington Gas Light Co.
Frederick Gas Co.	Washington Gas Light Co.

PHOENIX, AZ

```
(  0)     El Paso Natural Gas Co.
(100)NDL-Southwest Gas Corp.
(100)NDL-Transwestern Pipeline Co.
(100)NDL-Pacific Gas & Electric Co.
(100)NDL*Pacific Lighting Corp.
```

DETAIL OF SUBSIDIARIES	PARENT
Pacific Interstate Transmission Co.	Pacific Lighting Corp.
Southern Calif. Gas Co.	Pacific Lighting Corp.

PINE BLUFF, AR

```
(  0)    Arkla Inc.
(  0)    Mississippi River Transmission Corp.
(  0) PT-Columbia Gulf Transmission Co.
(100)NDL-Trunkline Gas Co.
(100)NDL*Tenneco Inc.
(100)NDL-Texas Eastern Transmission Corp.
(100)NDL-Mississippi Valley Gas Co.
(100)NDL-Mid-Louisiana Gas Co.
(100)NDL-Natural Gas Pipeline Co. of America
(100)NDL-United Gas Pipeline Co.
(100)NDL-Texas Gas Transmission Co.
(100)NPT-Delhi Gas Pipeline Corp.
(100)NPT-Louisiana State Gas Corp.
(120)NDL-Arkansas Oklahoma Gas Co.
(120)NDL-Southern Natural Gas Co.
(120)NPT-Transcontinental Gas Pipeline Corp.
(120)NPT-Mustang Fuel Corp.
(120)NPT-Ozark Gas Pipeline Corp.
(120)NPT-Oklahoma Natural Gas Co. (Oneok Inc.)
(120)NPT-Arkansas Western Gas Co.
(140)NDL-Enserch Corp.
(140)NDL-KN Energy Inc.
(140)NDL-Associated Natural Gas Co.
(140)NDL-Valley Gas Transmission, Inc.
```

```
DETAIL OF SUBSIDIARIES             PARENT

Louisiana Intrastate Gas Corp.     Tenneco Inc.
```

PITTSBURG, PA

```
(  0)   *Columbia Gas System, Inc.
(  0)   *Consolidated Natural Gas Corp.
(  0)    Equitable Gas Co.
(  0)   *Tenneco Inc.
(  0)    Texas Eastern Transmission Corp.
(  0)    Carnegie Natural Gas Co.
(100)NDL-Gas Transport Inc.
(100)NDL*National Fuel Gas Co.
(100)NDL-Transcontinental Gas Pipeline Corp.
(100)NDL*Washington Gas Light Co.
(100)NDL-North Penn Gas Co.
(100)NDL-Texas Gas Transmission Co.
(140)NPT-Roanoke Gas Co.
```

DETAIL OF SUBSIDIARIES   PARENT

Columbia Gas Transmission Corp.	Columbia Gas System, Inc.
Consolidated Gas Supply Corp.	Consolidated Natural Gas
East Ohio Gas Co.	Consolidated Natural Gas
National Fuel Gas Distribution Corp	National Fuel Gas Co.
National Fuel Gas Supply Corp.	National Fuel Gas Co.
Shenandoah Gas Co.	Washington Gas Light Co.
River Gas Co.	Consolidated Natural Gas
Columbia Gulf Transmission Co.	Columbia Gas System, Inc.
Commonwealth Gas Pipeline Corp.	Columbia Gas System, Inc.
Frederick Gas Co.	Washington Gas Light Co.
Inland Gas Co. Inc.	Columbia Gas System, Inc.
East Tennessee Natural Gas Co.	Tenneco Inc.

PITTSFIELD, MA

```
(  0)   *Tenneco Inc.
(  0)   *Texas Eastern Corp.
(100)NDL-Columbia Gas Transmission Corp.
(100)NDL-Consolidated Gas Supply Corp.
(100)NDL-Equitable Gas Co.
(100)NDL-Transcontinental Gas Pipeline Corp.
(100)NDL-Distrigas of Massachusetts Corp.
(100)NPT-Central Hudson Gas & Electric Corp.
(100)NPT-Niagara Mohawk Power Corp.
(120)NDL-North Penn Gas Co.
(140)NPT-South Jersey Gas Co.
```

DETAIL OF SUBSIDIARIES   PARENT

Algonquin Gas Transmission Co.	Texas Eastern Corp.
Granite State Gas Transmission, Inc	Tenneco Inc.
Texas Eastern Transmission Corp.	Texas Eastern Corp.
Northern Utilities, Inc., - ME	Tenneco Inc.

PORTSMOUTH–DOVER–ROCH., NH

```
(  0)   *Tenneco Inc.
(100)NDL-Consolidated Gas Supply Corp.
(100)NDL-Algonquin Gas Transmission Co.
(100)NDL-Distrigas of Massachusetts Corp.
(100)NPT-Central Hudson Gas & Electric Corp.
(100)NPT-Niagara Mohawk Power Corp.
```

```
 DETAIL OF SUBSIDIARIES              PARENT

Granite State Gas Transmission, Inc  Tenneco Inc.
Northern Utilities, Inc., - ME       Tenneco Inc.
```

POUGHKEEPSIE, NY

```
(  0)   *Tenneco Inc.
(  0) PT-Central Hudson Gas & Electric Corp.
(100)NDL-Columbia Gas Transmission Corp.
(100)NDL-Consolidated Gas Supply Corp.
(100)NDL-Equitable Gas Co.
(100)NDL*Texas Eastern Corp.
(100)NDL-Transcontinental Gas Pipeline Corp.
(100)NDL-Distrigas of Massachusetts Corp.
(100)NDL-North Penn Gas Co.
(100)NPT-Niagara Mohawk Power Corp.
(100)NPT-South Jersey Gas Co.
```

```
 DETAIL OF SUBSIDIARIES              PARENT

Granite State Gas Transmission, Inc  Tenneco Inc.
Algonquin Gas Transmission Co.       Texas Eastern Corp.
Texas Eastern Transmission Corp.     Texas Eastern Corp.
Northern Utilities, Inc., - ME       Tenneco Inc.
```

PROV.–PAWTUCKET–WOONSOCKET, RI

```
(  0)   *Tenneco Inc.
(  0)   *Texas Eastern Corp.
(100)NDL-Columbia Gas Transmission Corp.
(100)NDL-Consolidated Gas Supply Corp.
(100)NDL-Equitable Gas Co.
(100)NDL-Transcontinental Gas Pipeline Corp.
(100)NDL-Distrigas of Massachusetts Corp.
(100)NPT-Central Hudson Gas & Electric Corp.
(100)NPT-Niagara Mohawk Power Corp.
```

```
 DETAIL OF SUBSIDIARIES              PARENT

Algonquin Gas Transmission Co.       Texas Eastern Corp.
Granite State Gas Transmission, Inc  Tenneco Inc.
Texas Eastern Transmission Corp.     Texas Eastern Corp.
Northern Utilities, Inc., - ME       Tenneco Inc.
```

PUEBLO, CO

```
(  0)    Colorado Interstate Gas Co.
(100)NDL-KN Energy Inc.
(100)NDL-Panhandle Eastern Pipeline Co.
(100)NDL-Kansas Power & Light Co.
(100)NDL-Western Slope Gas Co.
(100)NDL-Northern Natural Gas Co.
(120)NDL-Mountain Fuel Supply Co.
(120)NDL-Western Gas Interstate Co.
(120)NPT-Rocky Mountain Natural Gas Co., Inc.
(140)NDL*Northwest Energy Co.
(140)NDL-Energas Co.
```

DETAIL OF SUBSIDIARIES   PARENT

```
Northwest Central Pipeline Corp.      Northwest Energy Co.
Northwest Pipeline Corp.              Northwest Energy Co.
```

RAPID CITY, SD

```
(  0)    Montana-Dakota Utilities Co.
(100)NDL-Mountain Fuel Supply Co.
(100)NDL-Panhandle Eastern Pipeline Co.
(100)NDL-Colorado Interstate Gas Co.
(120)NDL-KN Energy Inc.
(140)NPT-Northern Border Pipeline Co.
```

READING, PA

```
(  0)    *Consolidated Natural Gas Corp.
(100)NDL-Columbia Gas Transmission Corp.
(100)NDL-Equitable Gas Co.
(100)NDL-Tenneco Inc.
(100)NDL*Texas Eastern Corp.
(100)NDL-Transcontinental Gas Pipeline Corp.
(100)NDL*Washington Gas Light Co.
(100)NDL-Eastern Shore Natural Gas Co.
(100)NDL-North Penn Gas Co.
(100)NPT-Central Hudson Gas & Electric Corp.
(100)NPT-South Jersey Gas Co.
(140)NDL-National Fuel Gas Supply Corp.
(140)NDL-Carnegie Natural Gas Co.
(140)NPT-Niagara Mohawk Power Corp.
```

DETAIL OF SUBSIDIARIES   PARENT

```
Consolidated Gas Supply Corp.        Consolidated Natural Gas
Algonquin Gas Transmission Co.       Texas Eastern Corp.
Texas Eastern Transmission Corp.     Texas Eastern Corp.
Frederick Gas Co.                    Washington Gas Light Co.
Shenandoah Gas Co.                   Washington Gas Light Co.
East Ohio Gas Co.                    Consolidated Natural Gas
```

RENO, NV

```
(  0)   *Northwest Energy Co.
(100)NDL*Pacific Gas & Electric Co.
(100)NPT-Shell Oil Co.
(120)NPT-Pacific Lighting Corp.
```

DETAIL OF SUBSIDIARIES	PARENT
Southwest Gas Corp.	Northwest Energy Co.
Pacific Gas Transmission Co.	Pacific Gas & Electric Co.
Northwest Pipeline Corp.	Northwest Energy Co.

RICHLAND-KENNEWICK-PASCO, WA

```
(  0)    Northwest Pipeline Corp.
(  0) PT-Pacific Gas Transmission Co.
(100)NPT-Northwest Natural Gas Corp.
```

RIVERSIDE-SAN BERNADINO, CA

```
(  0)    Southwest Gas Corp.
(  0)    Transwestern Pipeline Co.
(  0)    Pacific Gas & Electric Co.
(  0)   *Pacific Lighting Corp.
(100)NDL-El Paso Natural Gas Co.
```

DETAIL OF SUBSIDIARIES	PARENT
Pacific Interstate Transmission Co.	Pacific Lighting Corp.
Southern Calif. Gas Co.	Pacific Lighting Corp.
Pacific Interstate Offshore Co.	Pacific Lighting Corp.
Pacific Offshore Pipeline Co.	Pacific Lighting Corp.
San Diego Gas & Electric Co.	Pacific Lighting Corp.

ROANOKE, VA

```
(  0)   *Columbia Gas System, Inc.
(  0)   *Tenneco Inc.
(  0) PT-Roanoke Gas Co.
(100)NDL*Consolidated Natural Gas Corp.
(100)NDL*Transcontinental Gas Pipeline Corp.
(100)NDL*Washington Gas Light Co.
(100)NDL-Pacific Gas & Electric Co.
(100)NDL-Carnegie Natural Gas Co.
(100)NPT-United Cities Gas Co.
(120)NDL*Equitable Gas Co.
(120)NDL-Texas Eastern Transmission Corp.
(120)NPT-ANR Pipeline Co.
(140)NDL-Gas Transport Inc.
```

DETAIL OF SUBSIDIARIES	PARENT
Columbia Gas Transmission Corp.	Columbia Gas System, Inc.
East Tennessee Natural Gas Co.	Tenneco Inc.
Consolidated Gas Supply Corp.	Consolidated Natural Gas
Columbia Gulf Transmission Co.	Columbia Gas System, Inc.
Commonwealth Gas Pipeline Corp.	Columbia Gas System, Inc.
North Carolina Natural Gas Corp.	Tenneco Inc.
Public Service Co. of N.C., Inc.	Transcontinental Gas
Inland Gas Co. Inc.	Columbia Gas System, Inc.
Shenandoah Gas Co.	Washington Gas Light Co.
Kentucky-West Virginia Gas Co.	Equitable Gas Co.
East Ohio Gas Co.	Consolidated Natural Gas
River Gas Co.	Consolidated Natural Gas

ROCHESTER, NY

```
(  0)   Consolidated Gas Supply Corp.
(  0)   *National Fuel Gas Co.
(  0) PT-Rochester Gas & Electric Corp.
(100)NDL-Columbia Gas Transmission Corp.
(100)NDL-Tenneco Inc.
(100)NDL-Transcontinental Gas Pipeline Corp.
(100)NDL-North Penn Gas Co.
(100)NPT-Equitable Gas Co.
(100)NPT-Central Hudson Gas & Electric Corp.
(100)NPT-Niagara Mohawk Power Corp.
```

DETAIL OF SUBSIDIARIES	PARENT
National Fuel Gas Distribution Corp	National Fuel Gas Co.
National Fuel Gas Supply Corp.	National Fuel Gas Co.

SACRAMENTO, CA

```
(  0)   Southwest Gas Corp.
(  0)   *Pacific Gas & Electric Co.
(  0) PT-Shell Oil Co.
(120)NPT-Pacific Lighting Corp.
```

DETAIL OF SUBSIDIARIES	PARENT
Standard Pacific Gas Line Inc.	Pacific Gas & Electric Co.

ST. CLOUD, MN

```
(  0)    Northern Natural Gas Co.
(100)NDL-Great Lakes Gas Transmission Co.
(100)NDL-Midwestern Gas Transmission Co.
```

ST. JOSEPH, MO

```
(  0)    *Northwest Energy Co.
(100)NDL-ANR Pipeline Co.
(100)NDL-KN Energy Inc.
(100)NDL-Panhandle Eastern Pipeline Co.
(100)NDL-Union Gas System Inc.
(100)NDL-Kansas Power & Light Co.
(100)NDL-Natural Gas Pipeline Co. of America
(100)NDL-Northern Natural Gas Co.
(100)NPT-Missouri Public Service Co.
(140)NDL-Arkla Inc.
```

DETAIL OF SUBSIDIARIES	PARENT
Northwest Central Pipeline Corp.	Northwest Energy Co.
Commercial Pipeline Corp.	Northwest Energy Co.

ST. LOUIS (MO-IL)

```
(  0)    Mississippi River Transmission Corp.
(  0)    Natural Gas Pipeline Co. of America
(  0) PT-Central Illinois Public Service Co.
(  0) PT-Illinois Power Co.
(100)NDL-ANR Pipeline Co.
(100)NDL*Panhandle Eastern Corp.
(100)NDL*Tenneco Inc.
(100)NDL-Texas Eastern Transmission Corp.
(100)NDL-Monterey Pipeline Co.
(100)NDL-Associated Natural Gas Co.
(100)NDL-Texas Gas Transmission Co.
(100)NPT-United Cities Gas Co.
(100)NPT-Central Illinois Light Co.
(100)NPT-Northern Illinois Gas Co.
(100)NPT-Western Kentucky Gas Co.
(120)NDL-KN Energy Inc.
(120)NDL-Northwest Central Pipeline Corp.
(120)NDL-Union Gas System Inc.
(120)NDL-Northern Natural Gas Co.
(120)NPT-Missouri Public Service Co.
```

DETAIL OF SUBSIDIARIES	PARENT
Panhandle Eastern Pipeline Co.	Panhandle Eastern Corp.
Trunkline Gas Co.	Panhandle Eastern Corp.
Midwestern Gas Transmission Co.	Tenneco Inc.

SALT LAKE CITY-OGDEN, UT

```
(  0)    Mountain Fuel Supply Co.
(100)NDL-Northwest Pipeline Corp.
(100)NDL-Pacific Gas Transmission Co.
(100)NDL-Colorado Interstate Gas Co.
(120)NDL-El Paso Natural Gas Co.
```

SAN ANGELO, TX

```
(  0)    Enserch Corp.
(  0) PT-Texacol Gas Services, Inc.
(  0) PT-Northern Natural Gas Co.
(100)NDL*El Paso Natural Gas Co.
(100)NDL-Energas Co.
(100)NDL*United Energy Resources Inc.
(100)NDL*Pioneer Corp.
(100)NDL*Houston Natural Gas Corp.
(100)NPT-Producers Gas Co.
(100)NPT-Western Gas Interstate Co.
(100)NPT-Red River Gas Pipeline Corp.
(100)NPT-Southwestern Gas Pipeline Inc.
(120)NPT-Texas Gas Transmission Co.
(140)NPT-Intrastate Gathering Corp.
(140)NPT-Winnie Pipeline Co.
```

```
   DETAIL OF SUBSIDIARIES                PARENT

   Odessa Natural Gas Corp.             El Paso Natural Gas Co.
   Palo Duro Pipeline Co.               United Energy Resources
   West Texas Gathering Co.             Pioneer Corp.
   Valley Gas Transmission, Inc.        Houston Natural Gas Corp.
   Intratex Gas Co.                     Houston Natural Gas Corp.
   United Gas Pipeline Co.              United Energy Resources
   Oasis Pipeline Co.                   Houston Natural Gas Corp.
```

SANTA BARBARA-SANTA MARIA-LOMPOC, CA

```
(  0)    *Pacific Lighting Corp.
(100)NDL-Southwest Gas Corp.
(100)NDL-Transwestern Pipeline Co.
(100)NDL*Pacific Gas & Electric Co.
```

```
   DETAIL OF SUBSIDIARIES                PARENT

   Pacific Interstate Offshore Co.      Pacific Lighting Corp.
   Pacific Offshore Pipeline Co.        Pacific Lighting Corp.
   Pacific Interstate Transmission Co.  Pacific Lighting Corp.
   Southern Calif. Gas Co.              Pacific Lighting Corp.
   Standard Pacific Gas Line Inc.       Pacific Gas & Electric Co.
   San Diego Gas & Electric Co.         Pacific Lighting Corp.
```

SARASOTA, FL

```
(  0)    Florida Gas Transmission Co.
```

SAVANNAH, GA

```
(  0)   *Southern Natural Gas Co.
(100)NDL-Transcontinental Gas Pipeline Corp.
(100)NDL-Florida Gas Transmission Co.
(100)NPT*South Carolina Electric & Gas Co.
```

```
  DETAIL OF SUBSIDIARIES              PARENT

South Georgia Nautural Gas Co.       Southern Natural Gas Co.
Carolina Pipeline Co.                South Carolina Electric
```

SCRANTON-WILKES-BARRE, PA

```
(  0)    Transcontinental Gas Pipeline Corp.
(100)NDL-Columbia Gas Transmission Corp.
(100)NDL*Consolidated Natural Gas Corp.
(100)NDL-Equitable Gas Co.
(100)NDL*National Fuel Gas Co.
(100)NDL-Tenneco Inc.
(100)NDL*Texas Eastern Corp.
(100)NDL*Washington Gas Light Co.
(100)NDL-Eastern Shore Natural Gas Co.
(100)NDL-North Penn Gas Co.
(100)NPT-Central Hudson Gas & Electric Corp.
(100)NPT-Niagara Mohawk Power Corp.
(100)NPT-Rochester Gas & Electric Corp.
(100)NPT-South Jersey Gas Co.
(140)NDL-Carnegie Natural Gas Co.
```

```
  DETAIL OF SUBSIDIARIES              PARENT

Consolidated Gas Supply Corp.        Consolidated Natural Gas
National Fuel Gas Distribution Corp  National Fuel Gas Co.
National Fuel Gas Supply Corp.       National Fuel Gas Co.
Algonquin Gas Transmission Co.       Texas Eastern Corp.
Texas Eastern Transmission Corp.     Texas Eastern Corp.
Frederick Gas Co.                    Washington Gas Light Co.
Shenandoah Gas Co.                   Washington Gas Light Co.
East Ohio Gas Co.                    Consolidated Natural Gas
```

SEATTLE, WA

```
(  0)    Northwest Pipeline Corp.
(100)NPT-Pacific Gas Transmission Co.
(100)NPT-Northwest Natural Gas Corp.
```

SHARON, PA

```
(  0)    *National Fuel Gas Co.
(100)NDL-Columbia Gas Transmission Corp.
(100)NDL*Consolidated Natural Gas Corp.
(100)NDL-Equitable Gas Co.
(100)NDL-Tenneco Inc.
(100)NDL-Texas Eastern Transmission Corp.
(100)NDL-Transcontinental Gas Pipeline Corp.
(100)NDL-Carnegie Natural Gas Co.
(100)NDL-North Penn Gas Co.
(100)NDL-Texas Gas Transmission Co.
(120)NDL-Gas Transport Inc.
(140)NPT-Rochester Gas & Electric Corp.
```

DETAIL OF SUBSIDIARIES	PARENT
National Fuel Gas Distribution Corp	National Fuel Gas Co.
National Fuel Gas Supply Corp.	National Fuel Gas Co.
Consolidated Gas Supply Corp.	Consolidated Natural Gas
East Ohio Gas Co.	Consolidated Natural Gas
River Gas Co.	Consolidated Natural Gas

SHERMAN-DENISON, TX

```
(  0)    Enserch Corp.
(100)NDL-Arkla Inc.
(100)NDL-KN Energy Inc.
(100)NDL-Northwest Central Pipeline Corp.
(100)NDL-Producers Gas Co.
(100)NDL-Delhi Gas Pipeline Corp.
(100)NDL-Natural Gas Pipeline Co. of America
(100)NDL-United Gas Pipeline Co.
(100)NDL-Transok, Inc.
(100)NDL-Oklahoma Natural Gas Co. (Oneok Inc.)
(100)NPT-Southwestern Gas Pipeline Inc.
(100)NPT-Esperanza Transmission Co.
(100)NPT-Houston Pipeline Co.
(100)NPT-Texas Gas Transmission Co.
(100)NPT-Texacol Gas Services, Inc.
(120)NDL-Mississippi River Transmission Corp.
(120)NDL-Union Gas System Inc.
(140)NDL-Arkansas Oklahoma Gas Co.
(140)NDL-Crab Run Gas Co.
(140)NPT-Mustang Fuel Corp.
(140)NPT-Ozark Gas Pipeline Corp.
(140)NPT-Arkansas Western Gas Co.
```

SHREVEPORT, LA

```
(  0)    Arkla Inc.
(  0)   *United Energy Resources Inc.
(100)NDL-Enserch Corp.
(100)NDL-KN Energy Inc.
(100)NDL*Panhandle Eastern Corp.
(100)NDL*Tenneco Inc.
(100)NDL-Texas Eastern Transmission Corp.
(100)NDL-Mid-Louisiana Gas Co.
(100)NDL-Natural Gas Pipeline Co. of America
(100)NDL*Houston Natural Gas Corp.
(100)NDL-Texas Gas Transmission Co.
(100)NPT-Columbia Gulf Transmission Co.
(100)NPT-Delhi Gas Pipeline Corp.
(100)NPT-Louisiana State Gas Corp.
(100)NPT-Esperanza Transmission Co.
(120)NDL-Mississippi River Transmission Corp.
(120)NDL-Crab Run Gas Co.
(120)NDL-West Lake Arthur Corp.
(120)NDL-Texas Gas Pipeline Co.
(120)NPT-Southern Natural Gas Co.
(120)NPT-Shell Oil Co.
(120)NPT-Seagull Pipeline Corp.
(120)NPT-Sabine Pipeline Co.
(120)NPT-Texacol Gas Services, Inc.
(140)NDL-Arkansas Oklahoma Gas Co.
(140)NPT-Mustang Fuel Corp.
(140)NPT-Ozark Gas Pipeline Corp.
(140)NPT-Oklahoma Natural Gas Co. (Oneok Inc.)
(140)NPT-Arkansas Western Gas Co.
```

DETAIL OF SUBSIDIARIES   PARENT

United Gas Pipeline Co.	United Energy Resources
Trunkline Gas Co.	Panhandle Eastern Corp.
Louisiana Intrastate Gas Corp.	Tenneco Inc.
Valley Gas Transmission, Inc.	Houston Natural Gas Corp.
Houston Pipeline Co.	Houston Natural Gas Corp.
Trunkline Lng Co.	Panhandle Eastern Corp.
Channel Industries Gas Co.	Tenneco Inc.
United Texas Transmission Co.	United Energy Resources

SIOUX CITY (IA-NE)

```
(  0)    Northern Natural Gas Co.
(100)NDL-KN Energy Inc.
(100)NDL-Natural Gas Pipeline Co. of America
(140)NDL-ANR Pipeline Co.
```

SIOUX FALLS, SD

```
(  0)    Northern Natural Gas Co.
(100)NDL-KN Energy Inc.
(140)NDL-Midwestern Gas Transmission Co.
```

SPRINGFIELD, IL

```
(  0)   *Panhandle Eastern Corp.
(  0) PT-Central Illinois Light Co.
(  0) PT-Central Illinois Public Service Co.
(  0) PT-Illinois Power Co.
(100)NDL-ANR Pipeline Co.
(100)NDL-Mississippi River Transmission Corp.
(100)NDL-Midwestern Gas Transmission Co.
(100)NDL-Natural Gas Pipeline Co. of America
(100)NDL-Texas Gas Transmission Co.
(100)NPT-United Cities Gas Co.
(100)NPT-Northern Illinois Gas Co.
(140)NDL-Columbia Gas Transmission Corp.
(140)NDL-Texas Eastern Transmission Corp.
(140)NDL-Monterey Pipeline Co.
(140)NDL-Associated Natural Gas Co.
(140)NDL*Internorth Inc.
(140)NPT-Northern Indiana Public Service Co.
```

```
  DETAIL OF SUBSIDIARIES                   PARENT

Panhandle Eastern Pipeline Co.      Panhandle Eastern Corp.
Trunkline Gas Co.                   Panhandle Eastern Corp.
Northern Natural Gas Co.            Internorth Inc.
Northern Border Pipeline Co.        Internorth Inc.
```

SPRINGFIELD, MO

```
(  0)   *Northwest Energy Co.
(100)NDL-Arkansas Oklahoma Gas Co.
(100)NDL-Arkla Inc.
(100)NDL-KN Energy Inc.
(100)NDL-Panhandle Eastern Pipeline Co.
(100)NDL-Union Gas System Inc.
(100)NDL-Transok, Inc.
(100)NDL-Oklahoma Natural Gas Co. (Oneok Inc.)
(100)NDL-Northern Natural Gas Co.
(100)NPT-Mustang Fuel Corp.
(100)NPT-Delhi Gas Pipeline Corp.
(100)NPT-Missouri Public Service Co.
(100)NPT-Ozark Gas Pipeline Corp.
(100)NPT-Arkansas Western Gas Co.
(120)NDL-Mississippi River Transmission Corp.
(120)NDL-Texas Eastern Transmission Corp.
(120)NDL-Natural Gas Pipeline Co. of America
(120)NPT-Central Illinois Public Service Co.
(120)NPT-Illinois Power Co.
(140)NDL-Associated Natural Gas Co.
```

```
  DETAIL OF SUBSIDIARIES                   PARENT

Northwest Central Pipeline Corp.    Northwest Energy Co.
Commercial Pipeline Corp.           Northwest Energy Co.
```

SPRINGFIELD, MA

```
(  0)    *Tenneco Inc.
(100)NDL-Columbia Gas Transmission Corp.
(100)NDL-Consolidated Gas Supply Corp.
(100)NDL-Equitable Gas Co.
(100)NDL*Texas Eastern Corp.
(100)NDL-Transcontinental Gas Pipeline Corp.
(100)NDL-Distrigas of Massachusetts Corp.
(100)NPT-Central Hudson Gas & Electric Corp.
(100)NPT-Niagara Mohawk Power Corp.
(120)NDL-North Penn Gas Co.
```

DETAIL OF SUBSIDIARIES	PARENT
Granite State Gas Transmission, Inc	Tenneco Inc.
Algonquin Gas Transmission Co.	Texas Eastern Corp.
Texas Eastern Transmission Corp.	Texas Eastern Corp.
Northern Utilities, Inc., - ME	Tenneco Inc.

TALLAHASSEE, FL

```
(  0)    *Southern Natural Gas Co.
(  0)     Florida Gas Transmission Co.
(100)NPT-United Cities Gas Co.
(100)NPT-Okaloosa County Gas District
(100)NPT-Southeast Alabama Gas District, The
(120)NDL-United Gas Pipeline Co.
(120)NPT-Transcontinental Gas Pipeline Corp.
```

DETAIL OF SUBSIDIARIES	PARENT
South Georgia Nautural Gas Co.	Southern Natural Gas Co.

TAMPA-ST.PETERSBURG-CLEARWATER, FL

```
(  0)     Florida Gas Transmission Co.
(120)NDL-South Georgia Nautural Gas Co.
```

TERRE HAUTE, IN

```
(  0)    Texas Gas Transmission Co.
(100)NDL-ANR Pipeline Co.
(100)NDL*Columbia Gas System, Inc.
(100)NDL-Mississippi River Transmission Corp.
(100)NDL*Panhandle Eastern Corp.
(100)NDL*Tenneco Inc.
(100)NDL-Texas Eastern Transmission Corp.
(100)NDL-Natural Gas Pipeline Co. of America
(100)NDL-Ohio River Pipeline Corp.
(100)NPT-United Cities Gas Co.
(100)NPT-Central Illinois Light Co.
(100)NPT-Central Illinois Public Service Co.
(100)NPT-Cincinnati Gas & Electric Co.
(100)NPT-Illinois Power Co.
(100)NPT-Louisville Gas & Electric Co.
(100)NPT-Northern Illinois Gas Co.
(100)NPT-Western Kentucky Gas Co.
(120)NPT-Northern Indiana Public Service Co.
```

DETAIL OF SUBSIDIARIES	PARENT
Columbia Gas Transmission Corp.	Columbia Gas System, Inc.
Panhandle Eastern Pipeline Co.	Panhandle Eastern Corp.
Trunkline Gas Co.	Panhandle Eastern Corp.
Midwestern Gas Transmission Co.	Tenneco Inc.
Ohio Valley Gas Corp.	Columbia Gas System, Inc.
Inland Gas Co. Inc.	Columbia Gas System, Inc.

TEXARKANA, (TX-AR)

```
(  0)    Arkla Inc.
(100)NDL-Arkansas Oklahoma Gas Co.
(100)NDL-Enserch Corp.
(100)NDL-KN Energy Inc.
(100)NDL-Mississippi River Transmission Corp.
(100)NDL*Tenneco Inc.
(100)NDL-Texas Eastern Transmission Corp.
(100)NDL-Delhi Gas Pipeline Corp.
(100)NDL-Mid-Louisiana Gas Co.
(100)NDL-Natural Gas Pipeline Co. of America
(100)NDL-United Gas Pipeline Co.
(100)NDL-Oklahoma Natural Gas Co. (Oneok Inc.)
(100)NDL*Houston Natural Gas Corp.
(100)NDL-Texas Gas Transmission Co.
(100)NPT-Columbia Gulf Transmission Co.
(100)NPT-Mustang Fuel Corp.
(100)NPT-Louisiana State Gas Corp.
(100)NPT-Ozark Gas Pipeline Corp.
(100)NPT-Arkansas Western Gas Co.
(100)NPT-Esperanza Transmission Co.
(100)NPT-Texacol Gas Services, Inc.
(140)NDL-Northwest Central Pipeline Corp.
(140)NDL-Trunkline Gas Co.
(140)NDL-Transok, Inc.
(140)NPT-Producers Gas Co.
(140)NPT-Southwestern Gas Pipeline Inc.
```

```
DETAIL OF SUBSIDIARIES            PARENT

Louisiana Intrastate Gas Corp.    Tenneco Inc.
Valley Gas Transmission, Inc.     Houston Natural Gas Corp.
Houston Pipeline Co.              Houston Natural Gas Corp.
```

TOLEDO, OH

```
( 0)    *ANR Pipeline Co.
( 0)    *Columbia Gas System, Inc.
( 0)    *Panhandle Eastern Corp.
(100)NDL*Consolidated Natural Gas Corp.
(100)NDL-Tenneco Inc.
(100)NDL-Texas Eastern Transmission Corp.
(100)NDL-Michigan Consolidated Gas Co.
(100)NDL-Texas Gas Transmission Co.
(100)NPT-National Fuel Gas Supply Corp.
(100)NPT-Transcontinental Gas Pipeline Corp.
(100)NPT-Michigan Gas Storage Co.
(100)NPT-Cincinnati Gas & Electric Co.
(100)NPT-Northern Indiana Public Service Co.
(140)NPT-Equitable Gas Co.
(140)NPT-Carnegie Natural Gas Co.
(140)NPT-Northern Illinois Gas Co.
```

DETAIL OF SUBSIDIARIES   PARENT

Columbia Gas Transmission Corp.	Columbia Gas System, Inc.
Panhandle Eastern Pipeline Co.	Panhandle Eastern Corp.
East Ohio Gas Co.	Consolidated Natural Gas
Great Lakes Gas Transmission Co.	ANR Pipeline Co.
Consolidated Gas Supply Corp.	Consolidated Natural Gas
Trunkline Gas Co.	Panhandle Eastern Corp.
Ohio Valley Gas Corp.	Columbia Gas System, Inc.
River Gas Co.	Consolidated Natural Gas

TOPEKA, KS

```
( 0)    *Northwest Energy Co.
(100)NDL-ANR Pipeline Co.
(100)NDL-Arkla Inc.
(100)NDL-KN Energy Inc.
(100)NDL-Panhandle Eastern Pipeline Co.
(100)NDL-Union Gas System Inc.
(100)NDL-Kansas Power & Light Co.
(100)NDL-Natural Gas Pipeline Co. of America
(100)NPT-Missouri Public Service Co.
(140)NDL-Transok, Inc.
(140)NDL-Oklahoma Natural Gas Co. (Oneok Inc.)
```

DETAIL OF SUBSIDIARIES   PARENT

Northwest Central Pipeline Corp.	Northwest Energy Co.
Commercial Pipeline Corp.	Northwest Energy Co.

TUCSON, AZ

```
(  0)    El Paso Natural Gas Co.
(  0)    Southwest Gas Corp.
(100)NDL-Transwestern Pipeline Co.
(100)NDL-Pacific Gas & Electric Co.
(100)NDL*Pacific Lighting Corp.
```

DETAIL OF SUBSIDIARIES   PARENT

```
Pacific Interstate Transmission Co.   Pacific Lighting Corp.
Southern Calif. Gas Co.               Pacific Lighting Corp.
```

TULSA, OK

```
(  0)    *Northwest Energy Co.
(  0)     Union Gas System Inc.
(  0)     Transok, Inc.
(  0)    *Oklahoma Natural Gas Co. (Oneok Inc.)
(100)NDL-Arkansas Oklahoma Gas Co.
(100)NDL-Arkla Inc.
(100)NDL-Enserch Corp.
(100)NDL-Mississippi River Transmission Corp.
(100)NDL-Panhandle Eastern Pipeline Co.
(100)NDL-Kansas Power & Light Co.
(100)NDL-Producers Gas Co.
(100)NDL-Delhi Gas Pipeline Corp.
(100)NDL-Natural Gas Pipeline Co. of America
(100)NDL-Northern Natural Gas Co.
(100)NPT-Mustang Fuel Corp.
(100)NPT-Ozark Gas Pipeline Corp.
(100)NPT-Arkansas Western Gas Co.
(120)NDL-KN Energy Inc.
(120)NDL-Crab Run Gas Co.
(120)NPT-Missouri Public Service Co.
(140)NDL-ANR Pipeline Co.
(140)NDL-Texas Eastern Transmission Corp.
```

DETAIL OF SUBSIDIARIES   PARENT

```
Northwest Central Pipeline Corp.    Northwest Energy Co.
Ringwood Gathering Co.              Oklahoma Natural Gas Co.
Commercial Pipeline Corp.          Northwest Energy Co.
```

TUSCALOOSA, AL

```
(  0)   *Southern Natural Gas Co.
(100)NDL-Alabama-Tennessee Natural Gas Co.
(100)NDL*Tenneco Inc.
(100)NDL-Texas Eastern Transmission Corp.
(100)NDL-Transcontinental Gas Pipeline Corp.
(100)NDL-Mississippi Valley Gas Co.
(100)NDL-United Gas Pipeline Co.
(100)NPT-Carolina Pipeline Co.
(100)NPT-Southeast Alabama Gas District, The
(120)NPT-United Cities Gas Co.
(140)NDL-Trunkline Gas Co.
(140)NDL-Florida Gas Transmission Co.
(140)NDL-Texas Gas Transmission Co.
(140)NPT-Columbia Gulf Transmission Co.
(140)NPT-Okaloosa County Gas District
```

DETAIL OF SUBSIDIARIES	PARENT
East Tennessee Natural Gas Co.	Tenneco Inc.
South Georgia Nautural Gas Co.	Southern Natural Gas Co.

TYLER, TX

```
(  0)    Enserch Corp.
(  0)   *United Energy Resources Inc.
(  0) PT-Esperanza Transmission Co.
(100)NDL-Arkla Inc.
(100)NDL-KN Energy Inc.
(100)NDL*Tenneco Inc.
(100)NDL-Natural Gas Pipeline Co. of America
(100)NDL*Houston Natural Gas Corp.
(100)NDL-Texas Gas Transmission Co.
(100)NPT-Valero Interstate Transmission Co.
(100)NPT-Producers Gas Co.
(100)NPT-Delhi Gas Pipeline Corp.
(100)NPT-Southwestern Gas Pipeline Inc.
(100)NPT-Texacol Gas Services, Inc.
(120)NDL-Trunkline Gas Co.
(120)NDL-Texas Eastern Transmission Corp.
(120)NDL-Texas Gas Pipeline Co.
(120)NPT-Southern Natural Gas Co.
(120)NPT-Seagull Pipeline Corp.
(120)NPT-Sabine Pipeline Co.
(140)NPT-Columbia Gulf Transmission Co.
(140)NPT-Mid-Louisiana Gas Co.
(140)NPT-Winnie Pipeline Co.
(140)NPT-Northern Natural Gas Co.
```

```
  DETAIL OF SUBSIDIARIES              PARENT

United Gas Pipeline Co.            United Energy Resources
Louisiana Intrastate Gas Corp.    Tenneco Inc.
Houston Pipeline Co.              Houston Natural Gas Corp.
Channel Industries Gas Co.        Tenneco Inc.
United Texas Transmission Co.      United Energy Resources
Valley Gas Transmission, Inc.     Houston Natural Gas Corp.
Intratex Gas Co.                  Houston Natural Gas Corp.
Oasis Pipeline Co.                Houston Natural Gas Corp.
```

VANCOUVER, WA

```
(  0)    Northwest Pipeline Corp.
(  0) PT-Northwest Natural Gas Corp.
(120)NPT-Pacific Gas Transmission Co.
```

VICTORIA, TX

```
(  0)    Enserch Corp.
(  0)   *United Energy Resources Inc.
(  0) PT-El Paso Natural Gas Co.
(  0) PT-Trunkline Gas Co.
(  0) PT-Intrastate Gathering Corp.
(  0) PT-Southern Natural Gas Co.
(  0) PT-Delhi Gas Pipeline Corp.
(100)NDL*Tenneco Inc.
(100)NDL*Valero Interstate Transmission Co.
(100)NDL-Florida Gas Transmission Co.
(100)NDL-Natural Gas Pipeline Co. of America
(100)NDL*Houston Natural Gas Corp.
(100)NPT-Arkla Inc.
(100)NPT-Texas Eastern Transmission Corp.
(100)NPT-Transcontinental Gas Pipeline Corp.
(100)NPT-Seagull Pipeline Corp.
(100)NPT-Producers Gas Co.
(100)NPT-Winnie Pipeline Co.
(100)NPT-Esperanza Transmission Co.
(100)NPT-Texas Gas Transmission Co.
(100)NPT-Northern Natural Gas Co.
(120)NDL-Texacol Gas Services, Inc.
```

```
  DETAIL OF SUBSIDIARIES              PARENT

United Gas Pipeline Co.            United Energy Resources
Channel Industries Gas Co.        Tenneco Inc.
United Texas Transmission Co.      United Energy Resources
Valley Gas Transmission, Inc.     Houston Natural Gas Corp.
Houston Pipeline Co.              Houston Natural Gas Corp.
Intratex Gas Co.                  Houston Natural Gas Corp.
Oasis Pipeline Co.                Houston Natural Gas Corp.
Rio Grande Valley Gas Co.         Valero Interstate Trans
```

WACO, TX

```
(  0)    Enserch Corp.
(  0) PT-Texacol Gas Services, Inc.
(100)NDL-Arkla Inc.
(100)NDL*Tenneco Inc.
(100)NDL-Natural Gas Pipeline Co. of America
(100)NDL*United Energy Resources Inc.
(100)NDL*Houston Natural Gas Corp.
(100)NPT-Intrastate Gathering Corp.
(100)NPT-Texas Eastern Transmission Corp.
(100)NPT-Valero Interstate Transmission Co.
(100)NPT-Producers Gas Co.
(100)NPT-Delhi Gas Pipeline Corp.
(100)NPT-Winnie Pipeline Co.
(100)NPT-Southwestern Gas Pipeline Inc.
(100)NPT-Esperanza Transmission Co.
(100)NPT-Texas Gas Transmission Co.
(100)NPT-Northern Natural Gas Co.
(120)NDL-KN Energy Inc.
(140)NPT-El Paso Natural Gas Co.
(140)NPT-Seagull Pipeline Corp.
(140)NPT-Western Gas Interstate Co.
```

DETAIL OF SUBSIDIARIES	PARENT
Channel Industries Gas Co.	Tenneco Inc.
United Gas Pipeline Co.	United Energy Resources
United Texas Transmission Co.	United Energy Resources
Houston Pipeline Co.	Houston Natural Gas Corp.
Intratex Gas Co.	Houston Natural Gas Corp.
Oasis Pipeline Co.	Houston Natural Gas Corp.

WASHINGTON (DC-MD-VA)

```
(  0)   *Columbia Gas System, Inc.
(  0)    Transcontinental Gas Pipeline Corp.
(  0)   *Washington Gas Light Co.
(100)NDL*Consolidated Natural Gas Corp.
(100)NDL-Equitable Gas Co.
(100)NDL*Tenneco Inc.
(100)NDL-Texas Eastern Transmission Corp.
(100)NDL-Carnegie Natural Gas Co.
(100)NDL-Eastern Shore Natural Gas Co.
(100)NDL-North Penn Gas Co.
(100)NPT-South Jersey Gas Co.
(120)NPT-Roanoke Gas Co.
```

DETAIL OF SUBSIDIARIES	PARENT
Columbia Gas Transmission Corp.	Columbia Gas System, Inc.
Consolidated Gas Supply Corp.	Consolidated Natural Gas
Shenandoah Gas Co.	Washington Gas Light Co.
Commonwealth Gas Pipeline Corp.	Columbia Gas System, Inc.
East Ohio Gas Co.	Consolidated Natural Gas
Frederick Gas Co.	Washington Gas Light Co.
East Tennessee Natural Gas Co.	Tenneco Inc.

WATERLOO—CEDAR FALLS, IA

```
(  0)   *Internorth Inc.
(100)NDL*ANR Pipeline Co.
(100)NDL-Natural Gas Pipeline Co. of America
(120)NDL-Midwestern Gas Transmission Co.
(140)NPT-Northern Illinois Gas Co.
```

```
 DETAIL OF SUBSIDIARIES                PARENT

Northern Natural Gas Co.              Internorth Inc.
Northern Border Pipeline Co.          Internorth Inc.
Wisconsin Natural Gas Co.             ANR Pipeline Co.
```

WAUSAU, WI

```
(  0)   *ANR Pipeline Co.
(100)NDL-Midwestern Gas Transmission Co.
(100)NDL-Northern Natural Gas Co.
```

```
 DETAIL OF SUBSIDIARIES                PARENT

Great Lakes Gas Transmission Co.      ANR Pipeline Co.
Wisconsin Natural Gas Co.             ANR Pipeline Co.
```

WEST PALM BEACH—BOCA RATON—DELRAY BEACH, FL

```
(  0)   Florida Gas Transmission Co.
(140)NDL-Texas Eastern Transmission Corp.
```

WHEELING (WV-OH)

```
(  0)   *Columbia Gas System, Inc.
(100)NDL*Consolidated Natural Gas Corp.
(100)NDL-Equitable Gas Co.
(100)NDL-Gas Transport Inc.
(100)NDL*National Fuel Gas Co.
(100)NDL*Tenneco Inc.
(100)NDL-Texas Eastern Transmission Corp.
(100)NDL-Carnegie Natural Gas Co.
(100)NDL-North Penn Gas Co.
(100)NDL-Texas Gas Transmission Co.
(100)NPT-Transcontinental Gas Pipeline Corp.
(120)NDL*Washington Gas Light Co.
(120)NPT-Cincinnati Gas & Electric Co.
(140)NDL-ANR Pipeline Co.
(140)NDL-Panhandle Eastern Pipeline Co.
(140)NPT-Roanoke Gas Co.
```

DETAIL OF SUBSIDIARIES	PARENT
Columbia Gas Transmission Corp.	Columbia Gas System, Inc.
East Ohio Gas Co.	Consolidated Natural Gas
River Gas Co.	Consolidated Natural Gas
Inland Gas Co. Inc.	Columbia Gas System, Inc.
Consolidated Gas Supply Corp.	Consolidated Natural Gas
National Fuel Gas Distribution Corp	National Fuel Gas Co.
National Fuel Gas Supply Corp.	National Fuel Gas Co.
Columbia Gulf Transmission Co.	Columbia Gas System, Inc.
East Tennessee Natural Gas Co.	Tenneco Inc.
Shenandoah Gas Co.	Washington Gas Light Co.
Commonwealth Gas Pipeline Corp.	Columbia Gas System, Inc.

WICHITA, KS

```
(  0)     Arkla Inc.
(  0)    *Northwest Energy Co.
(  0)     Natural Gas Pipeline Co. of America
(  0)     Northern Natural Gas Co.
(100)NDL-ANR Pipeline Co.
(100)NDL-KN Energy Inc.
(100)NDL-Panhandle Eastern Pipeline Co.
(100)NDL-Union Gas System Inc.
(100)NDL-Kansas Power & Light Co.
(100)NDL-Producers Gas Co.
(100)NDL-Delhi Gas Pipeline Corp.
(100)NDL-Transok, Inc.
(100)NDL*Oklahoma Natural Gas Co. (Oneok Inc.)
(100)NPT-Missouri Public Service Co.
(120)NDL-Colorado Interstate Gas Co.
```

DETAIL OF SUBSIDIARIES	PARENT
Northwest Central Pipeline Corp.	Northwest Energy Co.
Commercial Pipeline Corp.	Northwest Energy Co.
Ringwood Gathering Co.	Oklahoma Natural Gas Co.

WILLIAMSPORT, PA

```
(  0)    Transcontinental Gas Pipeline Corp.
(100)NDL-Columbia Gas Transmission Corp.
(100)NDL*Consolidated Natural Gas Corp.
(100)NDL-Equitable Gas Co.
(100)NDL*National Fuel Gas Co.
(100)NDL-Tenneco Inc.
(100)NDL*Texas Eastern Corp.
(100)NDL*Washington Gas Light Co.
(100)NDL-North Penn Gas Co.
(100)NPT-Central Hudson Gas & Electric Corp.
(100)NPT-Niagara Mohawk Power Corp.
(100)NPT-Rochester Gas & Electric Corp.
(100)NPT-South Jersey Gas Co.
(120)NDL-Carnegie Natural Gas Co.
(120)NDL-Eastern Shore Natural Gas Co.
```

DETAIL OF SUBSIDIARIES	PARENT
Consolidated Gas Supply Corp.	Consolidated Natural Gas
National Fuel Gas Distribution Corp	National Fuel Gas Co.
National Fuel Gas Supply Corp.	National Fuel Gas Co.
Algonquin Gas Transmission Co.	Texas Eastern Corp.
Texas Eastern Transmission Corp.	Texas Eastern Corp.
Frederick Gas Co.	Washington Gas Light Co.
East Ohio Gas Co.	Consolidated Natural Gas
Shenandoah Gas Co.	Washington Gas Light Co.

WILMINGTON (DE-NJ-MD)

```
(  0)    Transcontinental Gas Pipeline Corp.
(  0)    Eastern Shore Natural Gas Co.
(  0) PT-South Jersey Gas Co.
(100)NDL*Columbia Gas System, Inc.
(100)NDL-Consolidated Gas Supply Corp.
(100)NDL-Equitable Gas Co.
(100)NDL-Tenneco Inc.
(100)NDL*Texas Eastern Corp.
(100)NDL*Washington Gas Light Co.
(100)NDL-North Penn Gas Co.
(120)NPT-Central Hudson Gas & Electric Corp.
```

DETAIL OF SUBSIDIARIES	PARENT
Columbia Gas Transmission Corp.	Columbia Gas System, Inc.
Algonquin Gas Transmission Co.	Texas Eastern Corp.
Texas Eastern Transmission Corp.	Texas Eastern Corp.
Shenandoah Gas Co.	Washington Gas Light Co.
Frederick Gas Co.	Washington Gas Light Co.
Commonwealth Gas Pipeline Corp.	Columbia Gas System, Inc.

WORCH.-FITCHBURG-LEOMINSTER,MA

```
(  0)   *Tenneco Inc.
(  0)   *Texas Eastern Corp.
(100)NDL-Columbia Gas Transmission Corp.
(100)NDL-Consolidated Gas Supply Corp.
(100)NDL-Equitable Gas Co.
(100)NDL*Transcontinental Gas Pipeline Corp.
(100)NDL-Distrigas of Massachusetts Corp.
(100)NPT-Central Hudson Gas & Electric Corp.
(100)NPT-Niagara Mohawk Power Corp.
```

DETAIL OF SUBSIDIARIES	PARENT
Algonquin Gas Transmission Co.	Texas Eastern Corp.
Granite State Gas Transmission, Inc	Tenneco Inc.
Texas Eastern Transmission Corp.	Texas Eastern Corp.
Northern Utilities, Inc., - ME	Tenneco Inc.
Public Service Co. of N.C., Inc.	Transcontinental Gas

NOTES

CHAPTER 1

1. In competitive markets, any attempt by one firm to raise price arbitrarily will be unsuccessful. Conceptually, the competitive responses of incumbent firms and potential entrants can be broken down into three effects. Without changing their scale of plant, incumbent firms will initially respond by increasing output (i.e., the short-run effect). The aggregate impact of this increase in output is to reduce the market price. If the market price does not completely fall to its original equilibrium level, excess profits will encourage incumbent firms to expand (i.e., the scale effect) and new firms to enter (i.e., the numbers effect). Ultimately, aggregate output will expand to fully offset the initial reduction in output and to restore price to its long-run equilibrium level.

2. See, for example, Broadman and Montgomery (1983), pp. 15-17 and pp. 67-68; and Carpenter, Jacoby, and Wright (1982), p. 8.

3. For discussions of entry in the context of antitrust analysis of mergers, see U.S. Department of Justice (1984b), p. S-6; B. F. Goodrich Co., FTC Docket no. 9159, slip op. at 27 (March 15, 1988); and "Federal Trade Commission Statement Concerning Horizontal Mergers," Antitrust & Trade Regulation Report, Special Supplement, no. 1069, June 17, 1982.

4. U.S. Department of Justice (1984b).

5. See Scheffman and Spiller (1987), pp. 3-6.

6. For a detailed analysis of factors that could affect the ability to establish, maintain, and adjust a collusive agreement, see Coate (1985).

7. Mead (1984), p. 27.

8. Ibid., p. 27.

9. Ibid., p. 35.

10. Broadman (1986), p. 136.

11. Ibid. Broadman does, however, recommend that entry and exit regulations be eliminated. See Broadman (1987), pp. 35-37.

12. In addition to natural gas studies, at least two major studies on competition in crude oil pipeline markets also take a very narrow view of entry. The NERA study (1983) considers only pipelines that pass through the market but make no sales as potential entrants. Nearby pipelines located outside the market are ignored. The exclusion of nearby suppliers, however, is based on a weak analysis of barriers to entry (pp. 83-89). As a result, the study concludes that markets are highly concentrated and subject to monopoly pricing (p. 122).

The Department of Justice (1986) evaluated federally regulated oil pipelines to determine whether continued regulation was warranted. The study attempts to determine whether incumbent suppliers would possess substantial market power in a deregulated market. The study concluded that most pipelines would not be able to profitably reduce output substantially below current levels and, therefore, most pipelines should not be regulated. Perhaps due to data limitations, the study does not consider potential entry (p. 20). The market power of pipelines may therefore be overestimated and a stronger conclusion on the competitiveness of markets may be warranted.

13. This simplification allows us to focus on the issue of competition among pipelines without attempting to estimate the economic effects of regulations that may or may not remain in force.

One possible extension of the present study is to factor in the time taken to secure regulatory approvals (i.e., the "regulatory lag") to enter a new market or to expand service in an old market. Long regulatory lags tend to reduce the number of potential entrants and reduce competition in the market. Thus, the competitive impact of changes in regulatory lags on potential entry can be estimated using the same methodology developed in this study.

14. Divertible gas or throughput refers to the ability of pipelines to reduce the gas delivered to some customers and to profitably divert it to other customers. Industrial users, for example, may agree to interruptible service contracts that provide gas at prices substantially below the price of uninterruptible or "firm" service. In the event that industrial service is temporarily interrupted due to a strong residential peak demand, the user is generally able to switch to an alternative fuel such as residual fuel oil or coal.

Divertible gas is also created by contract expirations between pipelines and the LDCs. As supply contracts expire, the pipeline has the option of diverting gas from former customers to new customers.

15. The initial supply response we consider is the reallocation of available gas, throughout the pipeline's entire network, among the highest-valued customers. On the other hand, if the pipeline decides to contract for additional gas supplies, the construction of additional trunk-line capacity (e.g., looping), the installation of more powerful compressors, and the corresponding regulatory requirements are expected to take longer than the time required to construct the hookup between the trunk line and the new market.

16. U.S. Department of Justice (1984b), p. S-6.

17. See Demsetz (1968), pp. 55-65; and Goldberg (1976), pp. 426-48.

18. For example, if the contract length is shorter than the useful life of the pipeline, the short-run profits on one contract may not be sufficient to yield a competitive return on the total pipeline investment if future contracts (i.e., sales) are lost to more competitive rivals.

19. Another determinant of market performance is the existence of entry barriers. By analyzing the ability of major interstate pipelines to hook up to nearby markets, however, we hope to avoid any debate on the extent of entry barriers into the pipeline industry. Except in the short run, the decision to enter a new market will therefore be based primarily on the expected rate of return on the pipeline investment necessary to connect an existing main line system to a nearby local market. The only entry barrier that will be explicitly considered is regulation that directly affects the operation of natural gas pipelines.

20. For a careful review of such issues, see Broadman and Montgomery (1983).

21. I consider the Herfindahl-Hirschman Index (HHI) of less than 2500 as unconcentrated. The calculations are also performed for HHIs of under 1800, one of the benchmarks in the DOJ's Merger Guidelines, which does not change the major conclusions. I use the 2500 HHI level (equivalent to the existence of four equal-sized firms) because a recent DOJ study of pipelines suggests this level is the appropriate threshold for indicating whether regulation is warranted. DOJ argues that a HHI level greater than the 1800 threshold used to evaluate mergers is justified, since the issue is whether to continue regulation--not whether a merger creates a competitive concern. The increased market power implicit in the higher HHI (of 2500) is expected to be small relative to the administrative and resource distortion costs of pipeline regulation. Thus, from a social welfare viewpoint, the cost savings from discontinuing the regulatory apparatus is likely to exceed the costs of additional market power implicit in the HHI of 2500. See U.S. Department of Justice (1984a), pp. 28-29, and (1986), pp. 29-30.

The HHI is calculated by summing the squares of the individual market shares of all firms in the market. A market, for example, consisting of four firms with market shares of 45 percent, 30 percent, 20 percent, and 5 percent has a HHI of 3350 (= 2025 + 900 + 400 + 25).

22. The present study was unable to adequately quantify this competitive factor. Although econometric studies show that fuel switching is statistically significant for residential and industrial users, the coefficients of the cross-elasticity estimates are low, indicating that switching may be economically insignificant. Furthermore, engineering studies that suggest that industrial users will switch to alternative fuels in response to higher gas prices are not available for the residential sector. Development of a formal model of residential gas consumption is beyond the scope of this study.

Another possibility is that the remaining 11 markets reflect an upward bias in our construction and operation cost estimates rather than a lack of potential competition. Given that our cost estimates for a pipeline hookup are designed for larger markets, it is also possible that a smaller hookup would significantly reduce that associated construction and operation costs and thereby enable some nearby suppliers to consider entry.

CHAPTER 2

1. Helms (1974), p. 5; and Gonzales (1972), pp. 57-58.

2. Tiratsoo (1979), p. 2 and pp. 59-82.

3. DOE/EIA (1982), pp. 11-18.

4. Ibid., p. 12.

5. A detailed description of the origin of natural gas and the production process can be found in Tiratsoo (1979), Chapters 1 and 2; and in Adelman (1962).

6. Tiratsoo (1979), p. 245.

7. Ibid., pp. 251-52.

8. Ibid., p. 246. The proposed "Alcan" pipeline, a 4,753 mile pipeline from Alaska to Canada with feeder lines into the United States, for example, will require 975,000 horsepower of main line gas compression generated by 30 pumping stations to maintain a system pressure of 1,260 pounds per square inch; ibid., pp. 251-52.

9. Broadman and Montgomery (1983), p. 6.

10. Wellisz (1963), p. 31.

11. Broadman and Montgomery (1983), p. 6.

12. For an analysis of peak and off-peak pricing and the adverse effects of price regulations, see Rosenberg (1967), pp. 159-68.

13. Although Congress often considered imposing *common carrier* requirements on interstate natural gas pipelines, such a regulation was never enacted. Therefore, natural gas pipelines remain private carriers, typically owning the gas they transport. Oil pipelines, on the other hand, became common carriers with the passage of the Hepburn Act, in 1906. [See Tussing and Barlow (1984), pp. 96-98].

14. In 1983, the sample year for our pipeline delivery dataset, most LDCs did not purchase gas directly from the wellhead and then contract for transportation services with pipelines. There are exceptions, however. Stingray, Northern Border, and Trailblazer, for example, are just transporters. Since the mid-1980s, transportation sales have steadily increased and sales for resale (i.e., sales from pipelines to LDCs) have gradually declined.

15. DOE/EIA (1984c), p. 31.

16. Thus, the traditional broker function of pipelines is currently being challenged. Similarly, the right of a LDC to refuse to transport gas for commercial and industrial customers in their service area has also been challenged recently. In private litigation, a group of Washington, DC hospitals have sued the Washington Gas Light Co. on antitrust grounds for the abuse of its monopoly position in the distribution of gas in the Washington metropolitan area. On the state level, about eight states have required that LDCs transport gas for customers. See Tucker (1986).

17. DOE/EIA (1982), p. 15.

18. Ibid., p. 16.

19. Tiratsoo (1979), p. 247.

20. Broadman and Montgomery (1983), p. 6.

21. Electric utilities may generate electricity with turbines or with base load steam plants, which are often fueled by natural gas; Tiratsoo (1979), pp. 18-19; and Fink and Carroll (1968), Section 8: "Power Plants." For a discussion of electric power system planning and supply costs, see Munasingle (1979), Chapter 8.

22. If the pipeline also owns a LDC, however, main line sales may be subject to state regulation.

23. Dillard and Levine (1983), p. 3; and DOE/EIA (1983b), p. xvii.

24. DOE/EIA (1984c), p. 45.

25. Between 1816 and 1836, seven major U.S. cities introduced some form of gas: Baltimore, New York, Boston, New Orleans, Louisville, Pittsburgh, and Philadelphia. Tussing and Barlow (1984), p. 13.

26. A natural monopoly implies that costs are minimized if one company rather than several competing companies serve the entire market.

27. Two subsequent pipeline building "booms" virtually completed the pipeline system in the United States. One occurred during World War II, for national security purposes, and the other took place during the postwar expansion and lasted until the mid-1960s. See Tussing and Barlow (1984), pp. 25-50.

28. Tussing and Barlow (1984), pp. 207-8. The SEC continues to regulate the LDCs ("sales at retail") today. During the post-1935 divestiture wave, the SEC had jurisdiction over holding companies that owned both LDCs and pipelines.

29. Ibid., p. 208.

30. These provisions are discussed on p. 17, *infra.*

31. The pipelines were a *monopsony,* or single buyer, at the wellhead or point of origin and a *monopoly,* or single seller, at the "city gate" or delivery end. Thus, the logic of the Natural Gas Act (NGA) was to allow market forces to operate at the wellhead and to regulate the sales to consumers. See Tussing and Barlow (1982), p. 16.

32. This approach to regulatory ratemaking determines a price based on the actual costs of production, including a "normal" profit. An increase in the cost of an input will therefore justify an increase in the regulated price.

33. The problem was that

production in interstate markets began to fall short of contractual demands by greater amounts each year. Pipeline shipments were curtailed; that is, they delivered less than the contractually agreed upon amounts to downstream customers. For the period from September 1976 to August 1977, net curtailments of contracted interstate gas deliveries amounted to about 3.77 Tcf, a significant amount considering that the total supply of natural gas was about 19 Tcf for that period.

Braeutigam and Hubbard (1986), p. 143.

34. Tussing and Barlow (1984), p. 109.

35. The major provisions of the NGPA were the following:

First, the Federal Energy Regulatory Commission (FERC) was granted regulatory control over intrastate as well as interstate wellhead prices. Second, the Act contained a time schedule for the deregulation of new and old gas produced from "high-cost" sources. . .and it indicated a set of wellhead prices to be in effect for the new gas during the transition to deregulation. Old gas prices will remain regulated indefinitely. Third, the Act provided a set of rules under which the interstate pipelines must pass along the higher costs incurred with the purchase of "high-cost" gas to selected large industrial customers. This is known as the "incremental pricing" provision of the Act.

Braeutigam and Hubbard (1986), p. 151.

36. Subjecting intrastate pipelines to federal price regulation does not imply that the two classes of pipelines are treated identically. For instance, the NGPA maintained the ban against intrastate pipelines purchasing outer continental shelf gas. The original restriction was contained in the Submerged Lands Act and the Outer Continental Shelf Act. See Tussing and Barlow (1984), pp. 61-62, and Jacoby and Wright (1983), pp. 133-37.

37. Jacoby and Wright (1983), p. 133; and Braeutigam and Hubbard (1986), pp. 152-54.

38. Jacoby and Wright (1983), p. 135.

39. Once a pipeline decides to simply transport gas owned by others, FERC Orders 436/500 of the NGPA then requires the pipeline to offer this option to all of its customers. Customers of a pipeline that transports gas under Orders 436/500 were allowed to gradually reduce their contract demands with the pipeline, purchase gas directly from the wellhead, and contract for transportation.

40. The purchases of new and deep gas were not uniform across pipelines, as old gas still represented between 30 percent and 80 percent of an individual pipeline's "take" of gas in 1982. Likewise, deregulated deep gas contracts ranged from 0 percent to 15 percent of a pipeline's load. The prices also showed great variation in this period, since old gas contracts ranged from 68 cents to $1.78 per Mcf. In sharp contrast, deep gas contracts sold from $7.00 to $8.00 per Mcf, and the regulated categories of new gas, where available, sold at approximately $3.00 per Mcf. See Broadman and Montgomery (1983), pp. 10-11; and Tussing and Barlow (1984), p. 173.

41. Broadman and Montgomery (1983), p. 11.

42. Between 1978 (the year the NGPA was passed) and 1981, the average residential user reduced natural gas consumption by 14 percent. See Tussing and Barlow (1984), p. 143.

43. Broadman and Montgomery (1983), p. 9.

44. A mild winter, a recession, and a reduced demand by industrial users with dual-fuel capability (i.e., those who could switch to the cheaper residual fuel oil) all contributed to the price decline of natural gas.

45. Tussing and Barlow (1984), p. 173.

46. Minimum bill refers to a class of provisions under which pipelines charge customers when the minimum volume of contracted gas is not taken by the customer. Typical minimum bill formulas require that a predetermined percentage of a yearly or monthly volume be purchased.

47. Whereas residential customers can substantially reduce their gas purchases from the LDC, the LDC faces the minimum bill requirement with its pipeline suppliers. Consequently, a reduction in residential demand may result in the LDC's being unable to meet its minimum bill requirement.

48. One factor contributing to downwardly rigid city-gate prices was the inconsistency between partial deregulation at the wellhead and the prevailing pipeline regulation at the city gate. At the wellhead, the price of deregulated deep gas was falling; yet, the city-gate price was rising. To illustrate, consider the quantities and average prices of the three major categories of gas. In 1981, the weighted average cost of gas (WACOG) would have been

$$\text{WACOG} = .62(\$1.22_{\text{old}}) + .34(\$2.89_{\text{new}}) + .04(\$6.58_{\text{deep}}) = \$2.00 \text{ per Mcf.}$$

By the end of 1984, however, market conditions resulted in a lower price of deep gas, but the price escalation clauses pushed old and new gas prices upward. In 1984, the new WACOG would have equaled

$$\text{WACOG} = .48(\$1.45_{\text{old}}) + .43(\$3.65_{\text{new}}) + .09(\$5.35_{\text{deep}}) = \$2.74 \text{ per Mcf.}$$

In fact, the inconsistency in movements between the wellhead and city-gate prices was observed from 1981 through 1984. It created a minor political furor as the average price at the city gate continued to creep upward while visible decreases occurred in the price of deregulated deep gas. Finally, in 1985, after further declines in the price of deep gas, the WACOG ultimately declined. [Average prices and quantities are only reported for the entire industry. Their use in this example is simply to explain the WACOG phenomenon. See DOE/EIA (1985b), pp. 11-13.]

49. It could be argued that this perverse incentive of the PGA is actually a result of the general ratemaking procedure. During the 1978-82 period, the calculation of the WACOG under the general ratemaking methodology also encouraged pipelines to buy deregulated gas and LNG at prices as high as $10.00 per Mcf and roll it in with the low (regulated) price of old gas.

50. FERC Order 380, passed on May 25, 1984, essentially eliminated the "commodity charge" provisions in interstate pipeline contracts. Commodity charges are variable costs to the LDC, payable to the pipeline, and based on the volume of gas the LDC "takes" in a given contract period. See DOE/EIA (1984b), pp. vi-ix.

51. *Associated Gas Distributors v. Federal Energy Regulatory Commission*, 824 F2d 981 (D.C. Cir 1987), pp. 981-1046.

CHAPTER 3

1. Department of Justice (1984b), pp. S-2 and S-3, including footnotes.

2. The product and geographic markets are interrelated. The ability of consumers to switch to alternative products will depend, in part, on the location of the consumers and on the location of the suppliers of competing products. See Ibid., p. S-2, n. 5.

3. The residual demand curve is the demand faced by a hypothetical producer group in a particular area and is determined by the prices charged by the producer group, variables affecting demand, and variables affecting the costs of competing producers not in the group.

4. See Scheffman and Spiller (1987).

5. Although we do not have the data to estimate econometrically the residual demand for each market, the underlying principles are used to analyze the behavior of the colluding group and its rivals.

6. For an intuitive analysis see Ordover and Wall (1989), pp. 20-25. A more technical analysis is provided by Baker and Bresnahan (1984), (1985), and (1988).

7. This approximation is also reasonable if the product supplied by sellers outside the colluding group is highly inelastic.

8. FERC (1984), "General Instructions," p. iii.

9. DOE/EIA (1982), p. 13.

10. This characterization is valid at least through 1983, our base year. Since the early 1980s, however, sales for resale have been declining and transportation service has been increasing.

11. Nonetheless, this distinction is important for pipeline regulation policy. In contrast to wellhead markets, the limited number of current suppliers in delivery markets suggests the possibility of significant market power in the transportation of gas. Consequently, proponents of regulation fear that the market power of current pipelines in a deregulated market would result in higher transport fees and, in turn, higher delivered prices of gas. See, for example, Broadman (1987), pp. 31-36.

12. Only a small percentage of natural gas is moved by truck. Virtually all natural gas consumed in the United States is moved by pipeline. [The Secretary of Transportation and the Secretary of Energy (1980), p. 101, Hereafter referred to as NETS.] Although LNG has been successfully transported in tanker-trailers with gas-equivalent capacities of 220 Mcf, transportation by truck remains insignificant.

LNG has been imported into the United States from Nigeria, Algeria, and Japan via ocean tanker. In 1980, the standard LNG carrier had a gas-equivalent carrying capacity of 15.9 billion cubic feet (Bcf) and a construction cost of $150 million (in 1978 dollars). The cost of ocean tanker transport has been estimated at $.29/Mcf and $.50/Mcf for distances of 3,000 miles and 6,000 miles, respectively. [Tiratsoo (1979), p. 285; and Schwendtner (1977), pp. 52-60.] Most imported LNG is regasified at marine terminals and transported to end markets via pipeline. One minor exception is the use of barges [with 280 million cubic feet (MMcf) gas-equivalent capacities] to move LNG along the shallow waterways between East Coast LNG terminals. [Tiratsoo (1979), p. 283; and NETS, p. 106.]

13. DOE/EIA (1983a, p. 45) estimate that these three energy uses account for nearly 95 percent of all gas use in the residential sector.

14. See, for example, Tussing and Barlow (1984), pp. 163-64.

15. Since any profit-maximizing monopolist operates in the elastic portion of his demand curve, some substitution of competing products is expected to occur. Thus, the cross-elasticity coefficient is always greater than zero. The problem or confusion

with a cross-elasticity coefficient greater than zero is determining whether it is *sufficiently* greater than zero to indicate separate product markets. This issue is avoided by use of the market demand elasticity. See Landes and Posner (1981), pp. 960-62.

As can be seen in Table 3.1, the cross-elasticity of demand between natural gas and its principal substitutes (electricity and residual fuel oil) is substantially less than one. Some pipeline analysts consider a cross-price-elasticity coefficient greater than one to indicate strong substitutes. See Mead (1984), p. 32. As shown in Table 3.1, however, the highest cross-elasticity coefficient is between natural gas and electricity (.327); in addition, four other studies find lower elasticity coefficients.

In defining the relevant product market, note that the low cross-elasticities imply that the market demand for natural gas is a good proxy for the "residual demand" curve. See the discussion at p. 20, *supra*.

16. DOE/EIA (1983a), pp. 115-16.

17. For a discussion of the adaptability of gas boilers, see Rice and Rosaler (1983).

18. Long-run elasticity estimates may also account for the substitution of other inputs (such as labor and capital) and changes in interruptible service contracts that are profit-maximizing given the change in the price of natural gas. See, for example, Joskow and Baughman (1976), who estimate the long-run market demand elasticity at -.81 compared to the short-run estimate of -.07.

Technically, all the reported long-run elasticity estimates are biased upward. This is because all the long-run demand studies cited hold the price of substitute products constant. The degree of substitution is therefore overestimated because the subsequent increase in the price of strong substitutes such as fuel oil (due to the price increase of natural gas) will reduce the quantity demanded of fuel oil and increase the demand for natural gas. Thus, the initial increase in the price of natural gas will result in a smaller reduction in output.

19. Both data and time limitations do not permit consideration of markets based on LDC service areas. Alternatives available to LDCs within a given metropolitan area, however, are considered in our analysis of the market.

20. This assumes that the LDC does not own pipelines connecting two or more local service areas. It is common for an LDC's distribution system to be segmented into two or three distinct parts, each with different sources of gas supply.

21. Although a pipeline may serve cities that are geographically close to one another, the pipeline is likely to face a different set of rivals, including potential entrants, in each city. Thus, the market power of a pipeline in one market is not a reliable indicator of its market power in another market.

22. Note, however, that the *possibility* of nearby pipelines hooking up to a market in question can exert a competitive influence in that market. There is no inconsistency with a nearby pipeline not having a physical hookup into a local market (i.e., the short run) and the same nearby pipeline affecting the pricing decisions of current suppliers in the local market (i.e., the intermediate run).

23. Salop (1987), p. 7.

24. An alternative is to define markets on the basis of each major city plus the nearby areas also served by the LDCs serving the major city. Data on LDC service areas, however, are not readily available.

25. Although some major studies of crude oil pipelines define local markets as Department of Commerce, Bureau of Economic Analysis (BEA) Economic Areas, we believe that MSAs are more appropriate for natural gas pipelines. [See, for example, NETS, pp. 16-18; and U.S. Department of Justice (1986), pp. 20-23].

BEAs are based on employment and commuting patterns. Wherever possible, the BEA includes the place of work and the place of residence of its labor force. [U.S. Department of Commerce (1977), p. 1.] Since each BEA includes an MSA and its surrounding area, it is larger than an MSA. When products are easily transported by truck to the user, it may be appropriate to consider the BEA as a possible local market because it represents the maximum area that can be served by a competitive trucking industry.

Although trucks are often used to carry petroleum products to make small deliveries over short distances, (e.g., up to 50 miles), natural gas is not trucked to local markets in significant volumes. [See DOJ (1986), pp. 17 and 21; and NERA (1983), pp. 64-65.] For this reason, we believe that the larger BEA regions do not represent the smallest possible geographic market for natural gas. Some pipeline studies support our view. For example, two studies of crude oil pipelines defined product delivery markets as MSAs: Hansen (1980) and Mitchell (1982), cited in NERA (1983), p. 53.

26. Since we are concerned with the possibility of anticompetitive effects due to pipeline deregulation, we identify the smallest group of products and geographic area that are subject to market power. In this sense, our market definition is consistent with the DOJ "Merger Guidelines" definition of an antitrust market. See Scheffman and Spiller (1987), pp. 125-27.

Some natural gas *antitrust* markets (MSAs) may be smaller than *economic* markets. This is because deliveries originating within the MSA and transported to neighboring areas do not influence the size of the antitrust market--but they could expand the economic market. More technically, a high supply elasticity between an initial market boundary (MSA) and a nearby region is ignored for antitrust purposes, but it could determine a larger economic market (e.g., if the prices in the two areas tend toward uniformity). Hence, Elzinga-Hogarty criteria ("little-in-from-outside" and "little-out-from-inside") and Horowitz and Stigler price tests may indicate an economic market larger than an MSA. See, for example, Elzinga and Hogarty (1973), pp. 45-81; Horowitz (1981), pp. 1-16; and Stigler and Sherwin (1985), pp. 555-85.

27. A modified dominant firm model is used to analyze the behavior of the colluding group and its competitive fringe: The dominant firm may be comprised of more than one firm; fringe suppliers are limited to small current suppliers; and potential entrants attempt to gain admission into the dominant firm or colluding group.

28. The merger of two smaller pipelines in a local gas market may be procompetitive if it reduces the market power of the dominant firm. For a comprehensive review of the debates on market concentration, economic performance, and horizontal merger policy, see Pautler (1983), pp. 571-651.

29. The determination of the relevant antitrust market suggests what group of firms might possibly collude.

30. See Stigler (1964), pp. 44-61.

31. Whether a group of firms can effectively collude in a relevant market depends on more than just market concentration. For example, the nature of the product, the volatility of market demand and supply, the characteristics of buyers, and several other factors will influence the likelihood of collusion. See Coate (1985).

32. For a discussion of the relationship between collusion and the HHI, see Kwoka (1985), pp. 927-31.

33. Alternatively, the Herfindahl measure can be constructed so that the market shares sum to 1.00 rather than 100. In this case, the highest value of the HHI is 1.0 rather than 10000.

34. Some analysts characterize this attribute of the HHI more technically as the ability to account for the variation in the distribution of market shares. See, for example, Miller (1982), pp. 595-98.

35. Examples of both limitations implicit in the four-firm concentration index are provided in Weinstock (1982), pp. 285-301.

36. In this study, the term *nearby supplier* indicates that a pipeline is located within 140 miles of a market. (Why the distance requirement is set at 140 miles is explained in Chapter 5.) If the nearby supplier is too small to threaten a cartel if denied membership, it is not considered a potential entrant.

37. Current suppliers, by definition, are already located in the market and therefore need only meet the remaining size requirement to warrant their inclusion in the colluding group.

38. The estimation procedure will be explained in Chapter 5.

39. FERC, *FERC Reports*, "Ozark Gas Transmission System," Docket no. CP78-532, 16 FERC para. 61,099 (October 9, 1981), p. 61,190.

40. FERC, *FERC Reports*, "Ozark Gas Transmission System," Docket nos. CP78-532-000, CP82-416-000, CP78-532-008, and CP82-129-001, 22 FERC para. 61,334 (March 21, 1983), pp. 61,575-76.

41. Five to ten percent is considered a "small but significant and nontransitory increase in price," which is consistent with the DOJ's definition of relevant product and geographic markets. The 1984 revisions clarify that the "five-percent test" is not an inflexible standard to be used in every case. See U.S. Department of Justice (1984b), p. S-2, including n. 7. Also see Bronsteen (1984), p. 617.

42. During the 1982-84 period, however, the demand for natural gas steadily declined. [DOE/EIA (1984a), p. 26.] At the same time, pipelines began to transport gas for other pipelines. Rather than buy or sell gas, the pipelines now transport gas from the seller (producer) to the purchaser (LDC or end-user) for a fee. This relatively new service is offered during peak demand periods and appears to account for an increasing share of annual deliveries. Over the 1979-83 heating seasons, transportation for others averaged 25 percent of total sales (Ibid., pp. 39-40 and 49-50). Thus, both the decline in demand and the growing volume of transportation service for others represent new sources of throughput that are potentially divertible into new markets.

During the off-peak period, on the other hand, pipelines generally have excess capacity. Nearby pipelines therefore have the capacity to expand into new markets to offer off-peak service. As a result, the competitive problem, if any, is more likely to occur during peak demand periods.

43. The potential entrant is assumed to contract with customers in the new market before construction of the pipeline hookup. In this way, the winning bidder of a supply contract (i.e., the new entrant) can avoid making an extremely specialized investment in the pipeline hookup until the contract is formally awarded. Long-term contracts with minimum payment clauses limit the ability of customers to lower price by threatening to withdraw their business. See Mulherin (1984).

Equally important, such contracts would also limit the ability of the colluding group to lower price after the entrant completes construction, thereby generating excess capacity in the new hookup and imposing losses on the entrant. The potential opportunistic behavior due to the firm-specific nature of natural gas wells and pipelines is also recognized in Hubbard and Weiner (1986), p. 72.

44. The same space is offered to interruptible customers who pay commodity charges on the space actually used. Interruptible service contracts usually extend over several years. In this way, the pipeline attempts to generate both demand and commodity charges on its total pipeline capacity. Historically, FERC has allowed four methods of assigning a pipeline's costs to demand and commodity charges. See DOE/EIA (1984b), pp. 3-5.

45. Given regulated prices, pipelines have an incentive to sell all their capacity to firm demand customers. Absent regulation, it may be profitable to reserve some capacity for customers who are willing to pay a substantial ("haste") premium for service. Such premiums are prohibited under current regulation.

46. Another method of expanding capacity to serve new markets is to add compression along the supplier's trunk line or to loop the line to move a greater volume of gas per unit time. Data limitations preclude consideration of these possibilities.

47. The estimate of peak period interruptible deliveries is based on data contained in the *FERC Form No. 2: Annual Report of Major Natural Gas Companies*. Since interruptible sales during any one peak day demand period may vary due to unusually warm weather, short-run declines in demand, or other factors, peak period interruptible sales will be estimated for several years (e.g., 1982-84).

48. See, for example, Mead (1984), Broadman (1986), NERA (1983), and Department of Justice (1984a) and (1986).

49. Present regulations that may prevent an underground storage operator from utilizing its capacity in excess of "certificated" or authorized capacity or from expanding its service area (as authorized in its certificate-of-need application) are ignored.

50. As in the case of a nearby pipeline, the storage operator must be independent of the colluding group of suppliers if it is to be considered a potential entrant into the market. Similarly, if the storage operator is dependent on a single pipeline for its supply, it is treated as a subsidiary of the supplying pipeline. Depending on the collusive price in the new market, the storage operator, the LDC (customer), or nearby pipelines may be willing to construct the hookup between the storage facility and the new market. Thus, the storage operator is not necessarily dependent on an existing

hookup owned by a member of the colluding group.

51. DOE/EIA (1984b) conducted a survey of minimum bill provisions in contracts between interstate pipelines and their customers for the year 1981. In the process, EIA collected information on a large sample of service contracts between pipelines and their customers, which are on file at the FERC. The sample of contracts was expanded in subsequent years to include 666 resale, 217 industrial, and 366 transportation contracts. The expanded sample was made available to the FTC Bureau of Economics.

Ten-year contracts are common in industries with highly durable assets. See, for example, Masten and Crocker (1985), p. 1084; Goldberg and Erickson (1982); and Carney (1978), pp. 197-230. One of the most recent studies of natural gas pipelines suggests that contract terms of one to five years are replacing the longer terms typical of older contracts. See Broadman (1986), p. 122.

52. The entry ratio measures a subset of potential entry markets: the percentage of potential entry markets that the pipeline can enter simultaneously. Nearby markets that cannot be entered by the pipeline in question are not relevant.

53. That is, a pipeline with an entry ratio of 20 percent.

54. The win ratio may be adjusted upward to account for the cost or "risk" of winning more than the average number of bids. That is, if the bidder wins more service contracts than can be fulfilled, he may incur transaction costs to withdraw one or more of his bids. If the average win ratio is increased by two standard deviations, for example, there is only a 5 percent chance that the bidder cannot fulfill his potential supply obligations.

55. A sensitivity analysis will be performed using several different win ratios. One possibility is to set the firm's win ratio equal to the industry average win ratio across all markets and bids.

56. DOE/EIA (1984a), Appendix B.

57. The failure of a 1982 Department of Energy pipeline study to account for subsidiary relationships between pipelines serving the same market, for example, was criticized by NERA. See DOE/EIA (1982); and NERA (1983), p. 45.

58. See also, Chapter 4, p. 257, n. 13, *infra*.

59. An alternative measure that assigns the profit-maximizing cartel output to each member in proportion to his capacity (relative to the total capacity of the cartel) is difficult to interpret in natural gas pipeline markets. Since each pipeline serves several different markets, it is difficult to determine what proportion of each member's total system capacity is available to serve each individual market.

60. This procedure does not suppress information about the size of individual colluders. Although the physical capacity of all colluders may not be identical, the bargaining power of each colluder is approximately the same. Since each colluder is powerful enough to destroy the cartel on his own, the assumption is that cartel output and profit must be shared equally to minimize recalcitrant behavior.

In the short run, the use of the HHI remains sensitive to the size of the competitive fringe. In the intermediate run, however, there is no competitive fringe: all current suppliers join the colluding group. (See Chapter 5.)

CHAPTER 4

1. Local producers of natural gas represent another type of current supplier. Where local supplies are available, some buyers construct private pipelines and purchase directly from the field (or producer), thereby avoiding the need to buy from interstate pipelines. The inability to develop production data on an MSA basis render such estimates highly unreliable. The omission of this type of supplier, however, is not expected to be significant, since MSAs in gas-producing areas are served by numerous suppliers and therefore the likelihood of collusive behavior is low.

2. Department of Commerce (1979).

3. OMB has recently completed a comprehensive review of the nation's Standard Metropolitan Statistical Areas (SMSAs). The new definitions reflect the application of published MSA standards to demographic data drawn from the 1980 decennial census. The previous term *SMSA* has been shortened to *MSA* and a new area termed *PMSA* (Primary Metropolitan Statistical Area) has been introduced. The overall geographic area covered by the SMSA definitions is now roughly approximated by the sum of the MSA and the PMSA areas. MSAs and PMSAs do not overlap. It should also be noted that we used *NECMAs* (New England County Metropolitan Areas) instead of the numerous subcounty MSAs for the New England region. A detailed explanation for these changes is provided in "Primary Listing of MSAs," OMB-83-20, 84-16, and 84-24, Office of Management and Budget (1983-84). We can simplify the discussion without any loss in generality by using the term *MSA* to denote any one of the three geographic classifications.

4. "Natural Gas Pipelines of the United States and Canada" Penwell (1982).

5. To my knowledge, this is the first study to compile pipeline transmission data on such a disaggregated, geographical basis.

6. FERC (1984). Our sample year is 1983. The FERC Form 2 annual reports represent the best pipeline receipts data available.

7. Since our major concern is that the pipeline's *size* (i.e., its total system deliveries across all markets) not be underestimated, we attempted to allocate TVP deliveries in only one case. For each pipeline that reported TVP *and* MSA-specific deliveries in the same region (e.g., within the same state), TVP deliveries were assigned to MSAs in the same proportion as the MSA-specific deliveries. The remaining TVP deliveries were added to the sum of all MSA and county-specific deliveries to determine the pipeline's *total* transmission system deliveries.

MSA-specific sales plus TVP sales equal current sales. Hence, if pipelines report TVP sales in a market, MSA-specific sales will underestimate current sales. The corresponding market shares of the current suppliers, however, will not be significantly biased if suppliers report approximately the same percentage of TVP deliveries.

8. Approximately 25 additional companies filed a FERC Form 2 but either reported no deliveries or failed to identify city or county destinations.

9. In some states, however, LDCs also own substantial pipeline transmission systems and have alternative sources of gas supplies. In such cases, pipeline deliveries by an LDC into a local market are included in our analysis. The LDCs that are deleted from our sample are identified with an asterisk (*) in Table 4.1.

10. Intrastate pipeline delivery data were requested from the appropriate state regulatory authority in each of the seven major natural gas-producing states: Texas, Oklahoma, Louisiana, Kansas, California, Mississippi, and Colorado.

11. Although our market sample accounts for only 66 percent of all MSAs (208/314), it represents almost 90 percent (7.6/8.7 Tcf) of total gas purchases by distributors and municipalities in 1983. [DOE/EIA (1985b), p. 54.] More importantly, the 208 markets represent output subject to FERC regulation. Deregulation at the federal level will therefore not affect the 106 smaller markets. Consequently, the 106 markets are not relevant to our analysis.

12. The FERC Form 2 contains information on different types of deliveries. Some deliveries tend to be regulated (e.g., sales for resale), whereas others are not (e.g., industrial sales). For our purposes, we consider sales for resale, industrial sales, and transportation for others.

13. Ownership in a joint venture pipeline, or in a partially owned subsidiary, is assigned to that joint venturer who owns another pipeline operating in the same area as the joint venture. Thus, the joint venture is considered an independent supplier only in those markets that are not also served by pipelines owned by any of the joint venturers. This assignment of ownership tends to increase the market share of the joint venturer who also serves the market through wholly owned pipelines. As a result, the corresponding HHI may be overestimated. Such a procedure, however, avoids the complex analysis required to properly determine the controlling partner.

14. Although intrastate pipelines are not included in Appendix B because of confidentiality commitments, the market share of each major intrastate pipeline within each leading gas-producing state is included in the HHI computations summarized in Table 4.2 and in all similar tables. Reporting intrastate pipelines account for 13.3 percent of total MSA-specific deliveries.

15. As explained in Appendix C, cartel output will be one-half the aggregate output supplied by the cartel members had they behaved competitively.

16. Summing the squares of the short-run current market shares for the two colluders and the single fringe supplier yields $1600 + 1600 + 400 = 3600$.

If the colluding group sets a cartel price, however, the fringe supply is likely to increase. In the intermediate run, we therefore estimate the ability of fringe suppliers to generate sufficient divertible gas to gain admission into the cartel. We find that all fringe suppliers in the short run are potential entrants in the intermediate run.

17. The assumption that each potential colluder shares equally in the cartel output may reduce the market share of the largest colluding supplier. On the other hand, the countervailing assumption that small suppliers (i.e., suppliers too small to gain admission into the cartel on their own) can combine and jointly attempt to gain admission into the colluding group tends to increase the market share of the group of small suppliers. Empirically, the net effect of these two assumptions is found to produce a HHI that is not significantly different than the HHI based on the sales of each current supplier. As will be shown in the next two chapters, the superiority of our methodology lies in its ability to account for potential entrants.

18. Department of Justice (1984a), pp. 28-30, and (1986), pp. 29-31; and Untiet (1987), pp. 18-19.

19. The NERA study, for example, considers three HHI categories depending upon the estimated risk of monopoly rates if oil pipeline markets are deregulated: below 2500 (low risk), 2500 to 4999 (moderate risk), and 5000 to 10000 (high risk). NERA (1983), pp. 92-95 and p. 121. Thus, at least two major pipeline studies use a 2500 HHI threshold to indicate significant market power among current suppliers. In order to highlight the impact of potential entry on market concentration, we also use the same HHI threshold value. We do have the capability, however, of selecting alternative threshold values and computing the corresponding HHI distributions.

20. See Chapter 3, p. 38, *supra*. A recent study by Morris (1988) suggests that three pipelines serving a market are as effective a control on price as is government regulation. Kwoka (1979 and 1984) has found that the share distribution among the largest three firms in an industry is an important determinant of market power. If the third firm is sufficiently large, it can significantly limit market power in contrast to the fourth firm, which appears to have no effect. When scale economies are present, Kwoka and Ravenscraft (1986) find rivalry between the two leading firms may be sufficient. Evidence that markets with three or four sellers tend to converge to the competitive outcome, or equilibrium, is also provided by a wide range of research in the laboratory study of market behavior and performance. See Plott (1982), pp. 1493-523; Smith and Williams (1981), pp. 467-74; and Smith et al. (1982), pp. 58-77.

In addition, applicants and intervenors in some recent FERC proceedings are also using the HHI threshold of 2500. See, for example, *Buckeye Pipeline Company, L.P.*, Docket nos. IS87-14-000, et al.

21. Mead (1984), Table 2: "4-Firm Concentration Ratios for Gas Pipeline Delivery Capacity, by State, 1979," pp. 19-20.

22. The HHI distribution based on sales by current suppliers and the HHI distribution based on the number of colluding firms plus fringe suppliers are virtually identical. Except for four markets, the number of markets in each HHI interval (shown in Table 4.2) are the same. Thus, our methodology does not lead to lower levels of concentration in the short run than suggested by the sales approach.

23. The new entrant is assumed to contract with customers in the new market before construction of the pipeline hookup. See Chapter 3, p. 254, n. 43; and Chapter 6, pp. 73-74.

24. For a discussion of the relationship between open and closed markets and monopoly pricing, see Alchian and Allen (1969), pp. 140-42.

CHAPTER 5

1. The fundamental difference between the intermediate run and the long run is therefore a matter of degree: the *number* of potential entrants (or bidders) into the local market. All nearby suppliers are potential entrants in the long run.

2. Construction time is less than one year. See Table 5.1, columns entitled Date of Commission Order and Date of Completion, *infra;* and p. 31, *supra*.

3. Mathematically,

$$R = E + (R - E - D)(T) + I,$$

where

R = annual revenues,
E = annual maintenance and operating costs,
D = annual depreciation allowance,
T = tax rate, and
I = amortized construction costs.

Since R is the product of the annual volume (V) delivered through the new hookup and the unit transport fee (t), the minimum required t can be determined by first solving the above equation for R (given E, D, T, and I), then substituting R and V into Vt = R and solving for t. For a similar analysis of the Trans-Alaskan pipeline project for transporting crude oil from Prudhoe Bay to various markets, see Adelman, Bradley, and Norman (1971), pp. 33-79.

4. Pipeline diameters of 30 inches or more are usually used in the construction of long-distance trunk lines rather than in the construction of the shorter and smaller spur lines (or feeder lines) between the trunk line and the local market. Large-diameter pipeline projects (i.e., 30 inches and over) are therefore excluded.

5. Docket nos. CP84-222, CP83-210, CP80-481, and CP82-143.

6. A Box-Cox test was performed to determine whether the explanatory variables should be expressed in log-linear or log-log form. The regression results were invariant with respect to either form of the explanatory variables.

7. The estimating equation is as follows:

$$C = -115.756 + 34.235 \, Ln(DI) + 7.459 \, Ln(L)$$
$$\quad (-3.327) \quad (3.055) \quad\quad\quad (7.398) \quad\quad\quad\quad\quad r^2 = .70$$

where

C   = total construction costs (in millions of dollars),
Ln(DI) = log diameter of pipeline (in inches), and
Ln(L) = log length of pipeline (in miles).

The numbers in parentheses are t-values. Both explanatory variables are statistically significant at the .01 level of confidence. The incremental construction cost for a 100-mile hookup is estimated by $(C_2 - C_1) = 7.459 \, Ln[(L_1 + 100)/L_1)]$. Using the *median* pipeline length (L_1) of 22.09 miles (before the expansion or hookup) determines an incremental cost of $12.8 million.

The median pipeline length is used instead of the mean length to avoid the influence of a few large observations that may influence the mean length. Although the incremental cost is $9.9 million if the *mean* length is used, we use the higher construction cost estimate of $12.8 million. Further, the incremental cost based on the median pipeline length of the sample of 30 small pipelines is likely to overestimate the true incremental cost, since all the pipelines in the study currently own more than 22 miles of transmission capacity.

Note that the incremental cost $(C_2 - C_1)$ is used rather than the total cost (C).

Since all the competitors or potential competitors in our analysis currently own and operate trunk lines, we are concerned only with the incremental costs of adding spur lines to the existing pipeline transmission network of each competitor.

8. We do not consider an upper or lower bound on our point estimate. Using an upper bound would reduce the error of deregulating a market when regulation is appropriate. If potential entry is overestimated and the market is deregulated, suppliers may be able to reduce output, charge supracompetitive prices, and impose a welfare cost on society. On the other hand, using a lower bound would reduce the error that regulation is continued when deregulation is appropriate. In this event, society unnecessarily bears the direct and indirect costs of regulation. Since we are equally concerned about both types of errors, we use the point estimate.

The regression estimate is superior to an estimate based on the weighted average cost of the same projects because many of the projects are less than 100-140 miles in length. Consequently, the economies of scale accounted for by the weighted average cost approach are likely to correspond to a much smaller pipeline length.

The weighted average cost can be computed by dividing the total construction cost of all 30 projects by the total length of all 30 projects. Using the corresponding column totals in Table 5.1, $381,489,841 divided by 1,090.80 miles yields $349,734 per mile or $34,973,400 per 100 miles. All costs are measured in 1983 dollars.

9. Assuming a useful life of the hookup of 20 years and a real, after-tax rate of return on investment of 4 percent, annual revenues of $0.94 million [=(.0735)($12.8 million)] are needed to generate a present value of $12.8 million, which equals the total construction cost estimate. On the other hand, if the useful life of the hookup is increased to 30 years, the amortized annual cost falls to $0.74 million. (Depreciation is computed on a straight-line basis.)

We approximate the real, after-tax, private rate of capitalization by the corporate bond yields adjusted for inflation and corporate income taxes. In 1983, the Moody's Baa highest monthly bond yield was 13.95 percent. The rate of inflation in 1983, measured by the implicit GNP deflator, was 3.8 percent and the maximum corporate tax rate was 46.0 percent. The real after-tax bond yield was therefore 3.73 percent [= (13.95)(1.00 - .46) - 3.80]. We round up and use a 4.0 percent discount factor. Council of Economic Advisors (1986), pp. 256 and 333; and *Information Please Almanac*: 1988, p. 81.

10. If new pipelines have lower operating or maintenance costs, the EIA data will overestimate these costs. This bias, however, tends to reduce the number of potential entrants and to increase the HHI.

11. Major pipelines are not included in the sample because their greater volume (of gas transported) tends to reduce operating costs. For the lower volumes usually transmitted in spur lines, we therefore exclude major pipelines to avoid grossly underestimating these costs.

12. From Table 5.2, $37,599,745 divided by 18,137 miles (columns 2 + 3) yields $2,073 per mile, or $207,310 per 100 miles.

13. The regression equation is

$$E = -519,827 + 3,545(L) + 1,520(F)$$
$$\quad\;\; (1.691) \quad\;\; (10.059) \quad\; (3.626) \qquad\qquad\qquad r^2 = .87,$$

where

      E = maintenance and operating expenses,

      L = transmission pipeline length (miles), and

      F = field and storage lines (miles).

The t-values are shown in parentheses. Assuming that the length of the field or gathering lines remains constant, the incremental costs $(E_2 - E_1)$ associated with an increase in transmission length is 3,545(L). Substituting $L = 100$ miles yields $(E_2 - E_1)$ = \$354,500.

14. See *supra*, n. 8, p. 260.

15. Mathematically, the tax base $= (R - E - D)$ and the corresponding tax liability $= (R - E - D)(T)$.

16. These cost estimates are substituted into the equation in n. 3, p. 259, *supra*. Straight-line depreciation (D) over a 30 year life is computed on the initial \$12.8 million pipeline investment.

17. This approach is preferred to solving for t^* $(= R/V)$ and comparing t^* to p^* = t^{**}. The V required to yield a competitive return on the hookup is difficult to estimate, since t^* depends on p^*, and p^* varies across most markets. Further, estimating the average V for all markets is not meaningful because the t^* for those markets with a V less than the average V will be underestimated, indicating that the distance requirement has been met when, in some cases, it has not.

18. That is, we first identify which markets can support a 140-mile hookup. If market demand is small, however, the nearby supplier may bid to supply the entire market and fully replace all current suppliers. This will require additional divertible supplies, which reduces the likelihood of entry.

19. For a simple model of the interrelationships among wellhead, transportation, and end-use markets, see Russell (1983).

Using *FERC Form No. 11: Natural Gas Pipeline Company Monthly Statement*, which reports revenue and the cost of purchased natural gas for major interstate pipelines, the 1983 weighted average transport fee is 20 percent of the delivered price of gas.

For 1983, computerized tabulations of the monthly reports yield a weighted average annual sales price of \$4.14 per Mcf with the associated purchases of natural gas at the wellhead at a price of \$3.33 per Mcf. The difference of \$0.81 per Mcf represents the current transport fee or cost of service, which is 19.57 percent of the sales price. The annual tabulations of the monthly FERC Form 11 data were provided by FERC.

20. The basis for any price increase is the demand elasticity for *delivered gas,* which depends, in part, on the alternative suppliers of natural gas and alternative fuels that can be delivered to the market. Control of a transmission path does not create market power if there exist alternative suppliers of the delivered product or if there are substitutes for the delivered product. The relevant price increase is therefore the price increase of the delivered product--not the increase in the transport fee.

Defining the relevant product as natural gas delivered to the city gate, or consumer, also permits us to evaluate the corresponding welfare effects of a 5 to 10 percent price increase. An analysis of the welfare costs of continued regulation is provided in

Chapter 6.

21. The 1983 weighted average price of delivered gas in all U.S. markets is $4.23 per Mcf. DOE/EIA (1985b), Table 21, p. 54.

22. Given two years to generate sufficient divertible gas to serve the new market, it is assumed that potential entrants are able to procure gas from producers sufficiently close to the new market so that the transport costs from the wellhead to the origin of the new hookup are not significantly greater than the costs of current suppliers. In Arkansas markets, for example, the transport fee implicit in the $3.41 delivered price is $0.68 [= (.20)($3.41)]. We therefore assume that a potential entrant can transport gas from the wellhead, or upstream supplier, to the origin of the anticipated pipeline hookup at a cost of $0.68 per Mcf. Although this estimate may be too high or too low in some cases, it is not systematically biased in either direction. On this basis, we estimate the maximum costs per Mcf needed to build and operate a 140-mile hookup (between the potential entrant's trunk line and the new market) to equal the expected *increase* in the price of delivered gas in the new market.

The costs of transporting gas from the wellhead to the new market are difficult to estimate. Initially, the increase in the price of delivered gas in one market is likely to increase the demand for wellhead gas nearest to the market in question. Marginal pipeline purchasers may be priced out of the local wellhead market and turn to more distant producers. Ultimately, the wellhead price in more distant markets will also be affected. At the same time, potential entrants may reduce their demands for wellhead gas in areas where they plan to reduce service. The reduction in the wellhead price, however, allows the gas to be transported to more distant markets. The initial price increase in the end-use market is therefore likely to change the wellhead price of gas in different geographic areas. Estimating the changes in wellhead prices and the corresponding transport fees to each market is beyond the scope of this study.

23. The corresponding R_L values are ignored to avoid overestimating the number of markets in which potential entry is feasible. That is, using R_L will reduce V^* and tend to increase the number of entry markets.

24. Our analysis does not assume or require a 100 percent load factor (defined as the ratio of actual throughput to total capacity). Although we do not analyze peak and off-peak throughput rates, a pipeline diameter of 20 to 24 inches permits peak deliveries to be at least three times greater than off-peak deliveries, if necessary, and still earn a competitive return on the hookup.

For 11 of the 18 markets with annual sales over 120 Bcf, the load factor would approach 100 percent, and it would exceed 100 percent in the largest 7 markets. In all 18 markets, however, sales are so high that two 20-24 inch hookups would be profitable: the t^*, ranging from $0.01 to $0.06 per Mcf, is substantially below $p^* = $0.34. Since the costs of constructing a single hookup with a diameter greater than 24 inches would be cheaper than building two smaller ones with the same total capacity, our estimates are conservative.

25. Some of these 60 markets may have been inappropriately excluded. Since our sample of pipeline construction projects and operation costs are based on relatively large diameter pipe, these costs should be re-estimated for smaller markets. Given a 20-inch diameter hookup, for example, the corresponding load factor would be less than 10 percent in these small markets. If smaller-diameter pipe is more efficient, the

smaller hookup will decrease R and, in turn, V^* will decrease. The lower V^* will tend to expand the number of markets in which entry is possible.

26. For each of the 148 markets, $V > V^*$ implies $t^* < t^{**} = p^*$. Thus, if the minimum required transport fee (t^*) is less than the maximum allowable fee (t^{**}), the incentive of nearby suppliers to enter the market is given by $p^* > t^*$. The distance from the market is implicit in R, the required revenues to construct and operate a hookup of a specific length. Thus, if R is computed for a 140-mile hookup and $t^{**} = p^*$, the corresponding V^* represents the minimum throughput necessary to profitably construct a 140-mile hookup. Since current sales in 148 of the original 208 markets exceed V*, we find that suppliers within 140 miles of these markets meet the distance requirement (i.e., $t^* < p^*$).

27. The FERC Form 2 data are used to identify which pipelines deliver to each market and the counties outside each market. The distances between markets and between a market and its surrounding counties have been tabulated and computerized.

28. Some excess capacity may exist for some pipelines during peak periods. In this case, the pipeline can serve additional customers without reducing service to current customers. Data limitations preclude us from estimating excess capacity in such instances. Such an omission results in an underestimate of the ability of nearby pipelines to meet the size requirement.

29. The sample used in the 1984 EIA study of contracts between interstate pipelines and their customers was subsequently expanded by EIA and this larger sample was made available for our review. In the original EIA sample, three subsets of contracts were compiled: contracts for resale, industrial sales and transportation sales. For each subset, data on the 20 largest pipelines and their corresponding largest customers were collected. Contracts between smaller-volume pipelines and smaller customers are ranked and randomly chosen to round out the sample. For a complete discussion of the sample derivation, see DOE/EIA (1984b), Appendix A: "Survey Methodology."

30. The EIA contract information was checked and edited for accuracy and consistency. Notwithstanding our effort to retain all possible observations, approximately 10 percent of the EIA observations contained no expiration date or effective date and were therefore deleted from our sample.

31. If pipeline companies limit the amortization period of the new hookup to the term of the service contract, reductions in contract length will increase the required annual revenues (R) to justify a pipeline hookup. Although the reduction in the amortization period may reduce the number of "small" entry markets (see *infra*, p. 265, n. 38), it will not change the number of competitors in the remaining markets. If ten-year contracts are standard in Arkansas markets, for example, a 10 percent increase in the delivered price of gas ($0.34) would approach the $0.35 per Mcf necessary to construct and operate a 140-mile hookup to Texarkana, the smallest MSA in Arkansas. In most other markets, however, entry by suppliers within 140 miles of the market is highly likely because (a) the higher delivered prices in most other markets will yield price increases greater than $0.34 and (b) the larger volumes in most other markets will reduce the required transport fee below $0.35. Thus, ten-year contracts do not significantly change our original finding that suppliers within 140 miles of a new market are likely to meet the distance requirement.

Furthermore, if LDCs question the ability of a potential supplier to meet its contractual obligations, the contract period may be less than the payback period of the physical hookup. For example, if an LDC refuses to renew its contract with an incumbent supplier and switches to a new supplier, it may be costly to recontract with the incumbent on short notice if the new supplier fails to perform. Given its own service commitments, the LDC may be forced to purchase gas at relatively high prices on the spot market during peak demand periods. By amortizing the specific investment in the hookup over a longer period than the service contract, a new supplier can signal its intentions to meet its contractual obligations. For example, if the new hookup is amortized over 15 years but the delivered price of gas is based on a 20-year amortization, the supplier will earn a competitive return on the hookup only if the service contract is extended for five years. Thus, the LDC can impose a loss on the new supplier by refusing to extend the contract. For a case study of how investments in specific (nonsalvageable) production assets can assure contractual performance, see Gallick (1984a).

32. It is important to note that the remaining life of these contracts is not evenly distributed around the mean of 5.6 years reported in Table 5.3. Only six contracts have a remaining life greater than 5.6 years.

33. Table 5.3 suggests that the group of resale and industrial contracts negotiated before 1984 are expected to have a remaining life of five years or less.

34. Alternatively, the ability to consistently obtain gas deliveries at peak times under interruptible service contracts suggests that the likelihood of interruption is so small that such interruptible service is a good substitute for firm service.

35. Total peak day deliveries equal peak day interruptible plus peak day firm, or noninterruptible, deliveries. Using the Transmission System Peak Deliveries Schedule (p. 516), line 3 (Deliveries to Others) is divided by the sum of line 3 and line 2 (Deliveries to Customers Subject to FERC Rate Schedules).

36. On the FERC Form 2, sales for resale are reported on pages 310-11 and industrial sales are reported on pages 306-7.

37. Recall the discussion in Appendix C. Assuming a linear demand curve, the minimum output necessary to threaten a colluding group of current suppliers is 50 percent.

38. Operationally, we distinguish between small and large entry markets. If aggregate market sales are greater than V^* but less than $2V^*$, potential entry is feasible if the nearby supplier can bid to serve the entire market. This subset of entry markets is termed small entry markets. In contrast, a large entry market is defined as any market with sales greater than $2V^*$. Regardless of whether an entry market is classified as small or large (for purposes of computing divertible gas necessary to threaten a colluding group), the sales in each market exceed V^*, the minimum volume necessary to yield a competitive return on the pipeline hookup. In this sense, all these markets are entry markets.

In small entry markets, entry is limited, to a large extent, by demand. If the colluding group reduces market output to one-half the competitive level, a potential entrant may have to bid to supply the entire market in order to earn a competitive return on the pipeline hookup. That is, for a given p*, the volume (V) implicit in supplying one-half of a small market is insufficient to cover the required annual revenues (R). In small markets, therefore, the nearby supplier is assumed to bid to supply the entire market. In this case, the divertible supply necessary to earn a competitive return on the hookup is twice that required to threaten the colluding group.

In contrast, one-half of the quantity demanded in large entry markets equals or exceeds the minimum volume (V^*) necessary to justify a hookup. Since a monopolist or colluding group will reduce output to one-half its competitive level, a nearby supplier need only be able to supply one-half of the market to threaten the colluding group. Thus, in these large markets, divertible gas must at least equal one-half of current sales.

39. In addition, the pipeline may also be subject to legal action to enforce contractual performance or to recover damages suffered by the customer due to nonperformance.

40. That is, if b is the number of PE markets bid on, then

$$(1) \quad b \ = \ s/WR$$

where

$$s \ = \ (ER)(n) \ = \ \text{subset of PE markets that can be entered simultaneously,}$$
$$ER \ = \ \text{potential entry ratio,}$$
$$n \ = \ \text{number of PE markets, and}$$
$$WR \ = \ \text{win ratio.}$$

If ER equals WR, substituting ER = s/n into (1) yields

$$(2) \quad b \ = \ n$$

Since b can never exceed n, ER > WR also implies b = n. In the example above, ER = .20 > WR = .10, therefore implying that b = n = 10.

If, on the other hand, WR > ER, then b < n. That is, if the win ratio exceeds the potential entry ratio, the number of markets bid on will be less than the number of PE markets. In our example, WR = .33 > ER = .20 and s = 2 determine b = 6.0. Thus, the supplier will bid in only six of the ten PE markets. It will be important to note that as long as the pipeline does not expect to win every bid (i.e., WR < 1.00), b > s. Using s as an estimate of b will therefore underestimate b.

41. Although b can be determined if s and WR are known, there is no simple way to determine the subset of n markets that will be bid on. Continuing our example, given WR = .33, s = 2, and n = 10, we can solve for b = s/WR = 6. Hence, the potential entrant will bid in six of its ten PE markets. Time limitations preclude us from developing a method of estimating the specific six markets that will be bid on. Instead, we use the lower limit of b, which presumes that WR = 1.0 (i.e., the potential entrant expects to win every bid).

42. Since markets are not uniform in size, a higher ER (ER_H) may result if we assume that potential entrants bid on the smallest PE markets first. On the other hand, a lower ER (ER_L) may result if potential entrants bid on the largest markets first. We therefore computed the number of markets below a HHI = 2500 corre-

sponding to ER_L and ER_H. The results vary by less than 5 percent. In addition, given that the expected rate of return is the same in all markets and the win ratio is constant, the ER_H is more realistic.

Further, ER_L is difficult to interpret for incremental changes in divertible gas. For example, consider a potential entrant with divertible gas of 600 Mcf and four nearby markets with the following minimum volumes to enter: A = 700, B = 400, C = 200, and D = 100 (Mcf). Since there are three PE markets (B, C, and D) and two can be entered simultaneously (B and C), the ER_L is .67 (or 2/3). If divertible gas increases to 700 Mcf, however, market A (the largest market) will now be entered first, exhausting the total available divertible gas. Hence, the 100-Mcf increment in divertible gas reduces the ER_L to .25 (or 1/4). In contrast, the corresponding ER_H increases to .75 (or 3/4). Thus, the reason for a change in ER_L is sometimes counterintuitive.

For all of the above reasons, we prefer to use ER_H.

43. Nearby suppliers too small to enter a market on their own are not allowed to joint venture with other nearby suppliers. Recall the discussion at pp. 35-36, *supra*.

44. This is approximately equal to the highest WR reported in Table 5.4.

45. Increasing the cost-adjusted WR to 40 percent is equivalent to increasing the average WR from 20.53 (in Table 5.4) to 21.90 percent, a 6.67 percent increase.

46. Recall that b = s/WR.

47. Although 60 of the original 208 markets are not large enough to consider potential entry, they account for only 1.3 percent of the total output (see pp. 57-58, *supra*). Thus, our findings are quite general with respect to volume, but they are more limited with respect to the number of markets.

48. Compare the total number of markets with a HHI < 2500 in Tables 5.6 and 5.7.

49. The inclusion of potential entrants between 121 miles and 140 miles of the market, however, does increase the number of markets below the HHI of 1800 from 98 to 106. At 140 miles, 72 percent of the entry markets that suggested possible anticompetitive concern in the short run fall below the HHI of 1800.

50. The increase in contract length reduces divertible gas from 20 percent to 10 percent per year. Over a two-year period, this source of divertible gas would be reduced from 40 percent to 20 percent of current deliveries. If interruptible service contracts account for 10 percent of deliveries, total divertible gas is 30 percent. Except for 11 markets, the HHI distribution in Table 5.7 is unchanged for HHI < 2500 despite the 40 percent reduction in divertible gas from 50 percent to 30 percent. The number of competitive markets is more sensitive to reductions in divertible gas over 60 percent.

51. The number of entry markets with a HHI < 2500 would have decreased from 129 to only 125 in response to the higher cost-adjusted WR. Note that the cost-adjusted WR = 40 percent implies a WR = 21.90 percent (= 40.00 - 18.10). Thus, increasing the WR from 21.9 to 41.9 represents an increase of 90.32 percent. It is this increase in the WR that corresponds to a 50 percent change in the cost-adjusted WR (from 40 percent to 60 percent).

52. Hookup lengths greater than 140 miles are not considered in this study. Since a 5 to 10 percent increase in the market price of delivered gas is more than sufficient to justify a 140-mile hookup to large markets, more distant suppliers should be identified in any subsequent research.

These results are not particularly sensitive to even a doubling of the cost of constructing the hookup into a local market. Most large entry markets would be expected to be served by a new entrant if local prices rose 5 percent, even if the cost of building pipeline hookups were much greater than our estimates indicate.

53. The four MSAs and their corresponding foreign suppliers are (1) Algeria and Nigeria to Boston, MA (33,662,169 Mcf); (2) Germany to New York, NY (1 Mcf); Algeria to Beaumont, TX (110,454,308 Mcf); and Japan to Los Angeles, CA (236 Mcf). Source: *Tariff Schedules of the United States Annotated (1984)*, Annex A, p. A-2 and p. 8276.

54. Without accounting for gas imports, potential competition from domestic suppliers near these four markets (or LNG ports) and near all markets within 140 miles of these four ports is sufficient to reduce the HHI below 2500. Thus, the competitive effect of domestic and foreign suppliers is reinforcing and substitutable. Given our analysis of domestic suppliers, the impact of foreign suppliers on the HHI is expected to increase the number of markets with a HHI below 1800.

55. At this stage of our analysis, price regulation is assumed to be perfectly efficient. Thus, the regulated prices in the current market produce the competitive output. As will be shown in the next chapter, however, the social costs of regulation dramatically increase if regulated prices are even 5 percent above or below the competitive level.

56. The same general result is found for the HHI distributions at 100 and 120 miles.

57. In our example, WR = .33 > ER = .20 and s = 2 determine b = 6. Using s to estimate b results in an underestimate of b by 200 percent [= (2 - 6)/2]. See n. 40, p. 265, *supra*.

58. This size requirement limits potential entrants to only those suppliers who, acting independently, can prevent the colluding group from setting a price 5 to 10 percent over cost. Our approach underestimates potential entry, since smaller potential entrants would further reduce the monopoly profits of the colluding group. (See also pp. 35-36, *supra*.) We use this conservative measure of potential entry because it provides an intuitive understanding of how to adjust the HHI to account for potential entry. Simply stated, since each firm in the colluding group is large enough to eliminate monopoly profits at prices 5 to 10 percent over cost, the sales and profits of the colluding group are shared equally among its members.

59. In some cases, a pipeline may prefer to abandon service in less profitable markets in order to generate the divertible gas necessary to serve a new market.

In the absence of federal regulation, a similar qualification may apply in the form of environmental and right-of-way issues. Under the Natural Gas Act (Section 7h), FERC-regulated pipelines that cannot successfully contract with landowners are granted eminent domain. Since this study considers suspending only regulations that restrict price, entry, and exit, changes in the right of eminent domain are not considered. One possible change, however, is to allow states to administer the right of eminent domain. Furthermore, in cases where the potential entrant is currently operating a crude oil pipeline, it may be possible to construct a natural gas pipeline parallel to the crude oil pipeline, using the existing right of ways. Other common alternatives include buying the right of way in advance and using alternative routes.

60. The competitive supply of transportation will constrain the *delivered price* of gas. That is, the ability of a colluding group to raise the delivered price of gas will be constrained by the ability of the LDC to purchase gas from an alternative supplier and transport it via a Section 311 transportation pipeline.

61. This study considers only the output subject to federal regulation. Recall that our original sample of 208 markets excludes 106 markets that receive no FERC-regulated pipeline deliveries. (Appendix A lists the 314 MSAs.) Since these 106 markets are not subject to federal regulation, however, federal deregulation would have no impact on the exercise of market power in such markets. We therefore believe that the relevant output to examine is the output of the 208 markets subject to federal regulation. The 148 entry markets account for 98.7 percent of the total output in these 208 markets.

CHAPTER 6

1. Thus, only the winning bidder or bidders incur the actual pipeline hookup costs. It is also possible that an existing hookup (or a segment of the hookup) owned by the former supplier may have a higher-valued use if sold to the new supplier. In this case, the construction of a new hookup may be avoided.

2. See Demsetz (1968) and Goldberg (1976).

3. Competition does not pit buyers against sellers. Sellers compete against sellers. For each opportunity to serve an LDC under contract, for example, the "conflict of interests" among alternative suppliers to win the contract will be resolved in favor of that supplier who offers the most favorable terms. As long as the buyer faces alternative sellers, the offer by one seller is best evaluated relative to the offers of alternative or competing sellers. See Alchian and Allen (1969).

4. In the long run, all current suppliers are potential entrants. There are no fringe suppliers. The HHI for the market therefore serves as a proxy for the coordinating and policing problems facing the colluding group.

5. Recall the discussion in Chapter 3 at p. 32, *supra*.

6. Granted, the cost of producing a given output tends to decline (up to a point) as the production period increases. The cost savings on a pipeline hookup, however, are assumed to be insignificant. As explained in the preceding chapter, construction costs are initially estimated for the intermediate run. The short run does not allow sufficient time to build a pipeline hookup. Since the hookup can easily be constructed within the two-year period allowed in the intermediate run, no cost savings are expected for construction extended over longer periods.

7. Recall that an entry market is a market large enough to yield a competitive return on a 140-mile pipeline hookup if the market price increases by 5 to 10 percent.

8. In our model, a bidder must be a potential entrant. A bidder, therefore, is not just any nearby supplier. If there are four bidders, any one of the four can totally eliminate cartel profits at prices 5 to 10 percent over cost. (Nearby suppliers too small to qualify as potential entrants are considered fringe suppliers or nonbidders.) Recall the discussion concerning the relatively large size of potential colluders in Chapter 3 at p. 38 and in Chapter 5 at p. 69 and p. 71, *supra*.

9. Granted, the increase in the HHI from 1800 to 2500 may increase the market power of the colluding group. However, the increase in market power, if any, is considered insignificant relative to the *indirect* costs of continued regulation.

These indirect costs take the form of regulated prices that are set too low or too high relative to the competitive price. Regulated prices can therefore limit annual returns on pipeline investments to competitive levels and still be inefficient in rationing output at peak (i.e., set too low) and maximizing throughput off-peak (i.e., set too high).

10. This proposition refers to regulation at the federal level. State regulation may be warranted if the potential welfare losses in markets within the state exceed the regulation costs incurred by the state.

11. The cost-benefit analysis considers only the *direct* costs of regulation. The indirect costs of regulation (i.e., setting the regulated price above or below the competitive price) are used, in part, to justify the 2500 HHI threshold.

12. Since all 148 entry markets receive interstate pipeline deliveries, a HHI of 10000 suggests a single *current* supplier. Table 6.1 further suggests that there are no *potential* suppliers within 100 miles of any of the six markets currently served by a single pipeline. Otherwise, the HHI would fall to 5000 or less.

13. Electric utilities often operate generators fueled with natural gas. Transportation refers to any form of public transportation (e.g., city Metro and rail service) that operates on electricity generated from power plants fueled with natural gas.

14. DOE/EIA (1985a), pp. 5-9.

15. This is an overestimate, since all markets in Florida are not highly concentrated. Our sample of 148 entry markets contains two Florida panhandle markets with a HHI of 2500 or less: Pensacola and Tallahassee.

16. The size of the welfare loss can be shown to vary linearly (or directly) with the elasticity of demand. See Scherer (1980), pp. 459-60.

17. Deregulation of natural gas markets does not imply that the antitrust statutes will no longer be enforced. Pipelines that (1) attempted to monopolize or to maintain a monopoly in a deregulated market or (2) attempted to collude in the bidding for contracts to serve LDCs would therefore be subject to the antitrust laws. Consequently, if markets are deregulated, we assume a *maximum* price increase of 5 to 10 percent over cost is possible in a highly concentrated market without raising an antitrust concern.

18. That is, resources are assumed to be valued no more or no less in their next best use. If this assumption is unrealistic, the welfare loss estimates may be biased. *A priori* the direction of the measurement bias is indeterminate. See Scherer (1980), p. 463. Empirical studies of natural gas do not provide a reliable supply elasticity

estimate that is applicable to our study.

19. Additional welfare effects result if domestic supply is not infinitely elastic and foreigners supply part of the domestic market. See, for example, Gallick (1984b).

20. The area of a triangle equals one-half its height times its base.

21. Substituting $P_2 = 1.05P_1$ into $(P_2 - P_1)$ and simplifying yields $.05P_1$. Similarly, if $P_2 = 1.10P_1$, $(P_2 - P_1) = .10P_1$, which corresponds to a 10 percent price increase above cost.

Although the actual demand elasticity for residential users has been estimated to range between .27 and 1.01 (Chapter 3, Table 3.1), we use the upper-bound estimate of 1.0, which will tend to produce greater welfare losses and make the case for deregulation more difficult to support.

22. We use the weighted average price of natural gas sold in the state. MSA-specific prices that correspond to our MSA-specific quantity data are not available.

23. Consumption in the Florida markets has decreased over the same time period. Aggregate consumption has also declined in all the non-Florida markets with HHIs over 2500, allowing for potential entrants within 140 miles. [DOE/EIA (1985b), p. 38; and DOE/EIA (1987), p. 77.] The reduction in consumption would also tend to reduce the potential welfare loss.

24. The welfare analysis assumes a 10 percent price increase rather than a 5 percent price increase because a 10 percent increase was required by the 5 smallest markets in Arkansas to qualify as entry markets. The remaining 143 entry markets require a price increase of less than 10 percent. Since the larger price increase produces larger benefits from continued regulation, it biases the cost-benefit analysis in favor of continued regulation. Thus, a finding that continued regulation is not cost-justified is a strong finding.

25. Recall the discussion in Chapter 5 that explained the economic motivation to build a pipeline hookup. In brief, the costs of constructing and operating a 140-mile hookup can be recovered if the city-gate price increases by 5 to 10 percent. See pp. 56-58, *supra*.

26. Estimated by Donald Chamblee (assistant director of congressional liaison, Office of Congressional and Public Affairs, FERC) and reported in NERA (1983), Table II-6: "Industries Regulated by the Federal Energy Regulatory Commission," p. 37. The $26.0 million estimate of FERC direct expenditures was reduced by $0.5 million to account for filing fees and miscellaneous charges assessed by FERC and paid by FERC-regulated pipelines. Without this adjustment, these fees would be double-counted, since they are reported as private regulatory commission expenses by the pipelines and are also included in the estimate of FERC direct expenditures. Chamblee has estimated FERC expenditures for 1986 at $34.5 million.

Since the 148 entry markets account for 98.7 percent of the federally regulated output (see pp. 57-58, *supra*), we use total direct public (private) expenditures on natural gas pipeline regulation as our estimate of direct public (private) regulation costs in the 148 entry markets. Alternatively stated, given the total cost of federally regulating the pipelines that provide 98.7 percent of the output, the marginal cost of regulating many of the same pipelines that provide the remaining 1.3 percent of the output is not likely to be significant. Thus, our estimate is quite reasonable.

27. Computed from the 1983 FERC Form 2: "Regulatory Commission Expenses," p. 351, columns (h) plus (k). See also n. 26, *supra*.

28. The potential welfare loss associated with the original 208 markets (including the 60 small markets where entry is not profitable if prices increase no more than 10 percent) is $5.4 million if suppliers within 140 miles of each entry market are considered.

29. The 11 entry markets and their potential welfare losses are shown in Table 6.6 (column 4). Given that 7 of the 11 markets are in Florida, state regulation may be warranted.

Although the 11 markets represent 7.43 percent (11/148) of the entry markets in our sample, most markets differ in size. The finding that these 11 entry markets account only for 2.14 percent (160 Bcf/7,481 Bcf) of output suggests that they are relatively small entry markets. Thus, counting the *number* of possibly anticompetitive markets is misleading, since in this case only the smaller markets appear to represent potential competitive problems.

30. The potential welfare losses from monopoly pricing are lower in 1986 because natural gas prices and consumption have both tended to decline since 1983. At the same time, public expenditures on pipeline regulation have risen from $26.0 million to $34.5 million. Thus, unless private expenditures on regulation fall enough to offset the $8.5 million increase in public expenditures (which is highly unlikely), the net social gain from deregulation will actually be greater in 1988 than in 1983.

31. Since area b = $(.10P_1)(.10Q_1)$ and area c reported in Table 6.6 (column 4) = $(.10P_1)(.10Q_1)(.5)$, we simply multiply the potential welfare losses of $3.0 million in Table 6.6 (column 4) by 18 to determine the redistribution effect associated with a 10 percent price increase over cost.

32. The same computer program used to compute and sum the individual welfare losses in the Florida and non-Florida entry markets (Table 6.6) was also used to compute the corresponding redistribution losses in each of the 148 markets. Market-specific sales across all 148 entry markets total 7.5 trillion cubic feet.

33. Given the magnitude of these indirect regulation costs, it seems reasonable to conclude that they are sufficient to offset both (1) the $54 million annual redistribution losses and (2) the increased market power, if any, due to the raising of the HHI threshold for market power from 1800 to 2500.

CHAPTER 7

1. Given that exchange deliveries represent one use of pipeline capacity, pipelines that make exchange deliveries could reduce such deliveries and use the associated capacity to serve new markets. Since we do not consider exchange transactions, our measure of annual gas deliveries is an underestimate. If total gas deliveries are underestimated, the corresponding divertible gas volume will also be underestimated.

2. See Table 5.3.

3. For example, Morris (1988, p. 13) finds that on average competition among three incumbents is sufficient to reduce prices to a level equal to that achieved by regulation. If true, a Herfindahl level of 3333 (consistent with three equal-sized firms) might be appropriate.

4. In the intermediate run, the lack of delivery data on a number of pipelines (which are not required to file FERC Form 2s) forced us to treat these suppliers as pass-through pipelines instead of nearby suppliers. Without delivery data, divertible gas could not be estimated. Consequently, 8 of the 19 markets with a HHI > 2500 in the intermediate run may be incorrectly classified. With more complete delivery data, it is possible that the intermediate-run HHI distribution in Table 5.7 would not significantly differ from the long-run HHI distribution (Table 6.3).

5. See Table 6.4.

6. For a discussion of the redistribution effects of deregulation, see p. 88.

7. Recall the discussion at p. 85 and p. 88.

8. See Leddy (1986), p. 2. According to the DOJ's Merger Guidelines, a postmerger HHI above 1800 is considered highly concentrated. The DOJ is likely to challenge mergers in this region under two conditions: that (1) the merger increases the HHI more than 50 points and (2) there is a lack of evidence that other factors such as ease of entry (which suggests that the HHI is overstated) are significant. See U.S. Department of Justice (1984b), p. S-5.

9. The five states and the associated welfare losses are as follows: Arizona ($1,256,330), California ($6,207,492), Florida ($1,818,835), Minnesota ($3,627,617), and South Carolina ($1,356,290).

10. With a HHI threshold of 1800, the total annual welfare losses are $16.6 million, allowing for potential entrants within 140 miles of the market. Arbitrarily limiting potential entrants to 100 miles of the market and continuing to assume a 10 percent increase in the price of delivered gas determines a maximum welfare loss of $19.4 million. The corresponding social costs of continued federal regulation, however, remain at $51.7 million per year.

11. See pp. 57-58 and Chapter 5, p. 266, n. 47, *supra*.

12. See p. 88, including n. 28, *supra*.

13. Although a pipeline may be subject to regulation in some markets but not in others, the case is no different than present regulations that control prices on nonbulk heat uses (i.e., small residential and commercial uses where cleanliness and ease of control are important characteristics) and allow unregulated prices on bulk heat uses (i.e., large industrial uses that can be performed with alternative fuels such as residual fuel oil, coal, and nuclear power) in the same market.

14. For example, when a pipeline applies to FERC for market-based rates in its destination markets, the pipeline should include an evaluation of the competition in each of these markets, including potential entry, to support its application.

15. Recall the other qualifications cited earlier, pp. xiii-xiv and p. 5, *supra*.

REFERENCES

Adelman, Morris A. *The Supply and Price of Natural Gas*. Oxford: Blackwell, 1962.

Adelman, Morris A.; Bradley, Paul G.; and Norman, Charles A. *Alaskan Oil: Costs and Supply*. New York: Praeger, 1971.

Alchian, Armen A., and Allen, William R. *Exchange and Production: Theory in Use*. Belmont, CA: Wadsworth, 1969.

Associated Gas Distributors v. Federal Energy Regulatory Commission, 824 F2d 981 (D.C. Cir 1987).

Atkinson, Scott E., and Halvorsen, Robert. "Interfuel Substitution in Steam Electric Power Generation." *Journal of Political Economy* 84, no. 5 (October 1976): 959-87.

Baker, Jonathan B., and Bresnahan, Timothy F. "Estimating the Elasticity of Demand Facing a Single Firm: Evidence on Three Brewing Firms." Research Paper no. 54, Stanford University Department of Economics (1984).

------. "The Gains from Merger or Collusion in Product-Differentiated Industries." *Journal of Industrial Economics* 33, no. 4 (June 1985): 427-44.

------. "Estimating the Demand Curve Facing a Single Firm." *International Journal of Industrial Organization* 6 (1988): 283-300.

Balestra, Pietro, and Nerlove, Marc. "Pooling Cross Section and Time Series Data in the Estimation of a Dynamic Model: The Demand for Natural Gas." *Econometrica* 34, no. 3 (July 1966): 585-612.

Barnes, Roberta; Gillingham, Robert; and Hageman, Robert. "The Short-Run Residential Demand for Natural Gas." *Energy Journal* 3, no. 1 (January 1982): 59-72.

Beirlein, James G.; Dunn, James W.; and McConnon, James C. Jr. "The Demand for Electricity and Natural Gas in the Northeastern United States." *Review of Economics and Statistics* 63, no. 3 (August 1981): 403-8.

Blattenberger, Gail R.; Taylor, Lester D.; and Rennhack, Robert K. "Natural Gas Availability and the Residential Demand for Energy." *Energy Journal* 4, no. 1 (January 1983): 23-45.

Braeutigam, Ronald R., and Hubbard, R. Glenn. "Natural Gas: The Regulatory Transition." *Regulatory Reform, What Actually Happened*. Edited by Leonard W. Weiss and Michael W. Klass. Boston: Little, Brown, 1986.

Broadman, Harry G. "Deregulating Entry and Access to Pipelines," in *Drawing the Line on Regulation: Report of the Harvard Study on the Future of U.S. Natural Gas Policy*. (forthcoming 1987), Draft: 36.

------. "The Elements of Market Power in the Natural Gas Industry." *Energy Journal* 7, no. 1 (January 1986): 119-38.

Broadman, Harry G., and Montgomery, W. David. *Natural Gas Markets After Deregulation*. Washington, DC: Resources for the Future, July 1983.

Bronsteen, Peter. "A Review of the Revised Merger Guidelines." *Antitrust Bulletin* 29, no. 4 (Winter 1984): 613-52.

Carney, E. M. "Pricing Provisions in Coal Contracts." *Rocky Mountain Mineral Law Institute*. Proceedings of the 24th Annual Institute. New York: Matthew Bender (1978): 197-232.

Carpenter, Paul R.; Jacoby, Henry D.; and Wright, Arthur W. "Natural Gas Pipeline Regulation after Field Price Decontrol." Massachusetts Institute of Technology, Draft. (November 26, 1982).

Coate, Malcolm B. "The Application of the Structure-Conduct-Performance Theory to Oligopolistic Industries." Collusion Project Working Paper no. 2, Federal Trade Commission, Revised 1985.

Coburn, Leonard L. *Petroleum Pipeline Deregulation: A Competitive Analysis*. Washington, DC: (May 1982). Reprinted in "Oil Pipeline Deregulation: Hearings on H.R. 4488 and H.R. 6815 before the Subcommittee on Fossil and Synthetic Fuels of the House Committee on Energy and Commerce." 97th Congress, 2nd Session. Washington, DC: U.S. Government (1983): 57-135.

Council of Economic Advisors. Annual Report of the Council of Economic Advisors in *Economic Report of the President*. Washington, DC: Government Printing Office, February 1986.

Danielson, Albert L. "A Specification Analysis of the Demand for Petroleum Products, Coal, and Natural Gas." *Review of Business and Economic Research* 13, no. 2 (Winter 1977-78): 3-20.

Demsetz, Harold. "Why Regulate Utilities?" *Journal of Law and Economics* 11 (April 1968): 55-65.

Department of Commerce, Bureau of Economic Analysis. *BEA Economic Areas: Component SMSAs, Counties, and Independent Cities*. Washington, DC: (1977). Stock no. 003-010-0060-1.

------, Bureau of Census. "Standard Consolidated Statistical Areas and Standard Metropolitan Statistical Areas." Washington D.C.: (October 1979).

Department of Energy (DOE), Energy Information Administration (EIA). *Annual Report to Congres*s 3, DOE/EIA-0173 (1979): 332-33.

------. "The Natural Gas Industry." *Natural Gas Monthly*, DOE/EIA-0130, (December 1982): 11-18.

------. *Natural Gas: Use and Expenditures*, DOE/EIA-0382 Prepared by Gerald E. Peabody. Washington, DC: (April 1983a).

------. *Natural Gas Monthly: December 1983*, DOE/EIA-0130, (December 1983b).

------. *Recent Market Activities of Major Interstate Pipeline Companies*, DOE/EIA-0440,

Washington, DC: (January 1984a).

------. *Competition and Other Current Issues in the Natural Gas Market*, DOE/EIA-0489, Washington, DC: (June 1984c).

------. *A Study of Contracts between Interstate Pipelines and Their Customers*, DOE/EIA-0449, Washington, DC: (July 1984b).

------. *Statistics of Interstate Natural Gas Pipeline Companies: 1983*, DOE/EIA-0145, Washington, DC: (November 1984d).

------. *Natural Gas Annual, 1983*, DOE/EIA-0131/1, (March 1985b).

------. *State Energy Data Report: Consumption Estimates 1960-1983.* Washington, DC: (May 1985a).

------. *Natural Gas Monthly: December 1985*, DOE/EIA-0130, (February 1986).

------. *Natural Gas Monthly: March 1987*, DOE/EIA-0130, (June 1987).

Department of Justice (DOJ). *Competition in the Oil Pipeline Industry: A Preliminary Report.* Washington, DC: (May 1984a).

------. "Merger Guidelines Issued by the Justice Department, June 14, 1984, and Accompanying Policy Statement." *Antitrust & Trade Regulation Report.* Special Supplement, no. 1169 (June 14, 1984b).

------. *Oil Pipeline Deregulation: Report of the U.S. Department of Justice.* Washington, DC: (May 1986).

Dillard, Fay B., and Levine, Ken. "Main Line Natural Gas Sales to Industrial Users, 1981." *Natural Gas Monthly*, DOE/EIA-0130, (1983): 3-9.

Elzinga, Kenneth G., and Hogarty, Thomas F. "The Problem of Geographic Market Delineation in Antimerger Suits." *Antitrust Bulletin* 18, no. 1 (Spring 1973): 45-81.

Federal Energy Regulatory Commission (FERC), DOE. *FERC Form No. 2: Annual Report of Major Natural Gas Companies.* Washington, DC: Government Printing Office, Revised December 1984.

Federal Trade Commission. "Federal Trade Commission Statement Concerning Horizontal Mergers." *Antitrust and Trade Regulation Report*, Special Supplement, no. 1069 (June 17, 1982).

Federal Trade Commission Staff. "Regulation of Natural Gas Pipelines after Partial Wellhead Decontrol: Comments by the United States Federal Trade Commission Staff," submitted to the Federal Energy Regulatory Commission. Docket no. RM85-1-000 (July 19, 1985).

Ferguson, Charles E. *Microeconomic Theory*, 3rd ed. Homewood, Ill.: Richard D. Irwin, 1972.

Fink, Donald, and Carroll, John. *Standard Handbook for Electrical Engineers*, 10th ed. New York: McGraw-Hill, 1968.

Friedman, Milton. *Price Theory: A Provisional Text.* Chicago: Aldine, 1962.

Gallick, Edward C. *Exclusive Dealing and Vertical Integration: The Efficiency of Contracts in the Tuna Industry.* Federal Trade Commission. Washingtion, DC: Government Printing Office, (1984a).

------. "Estimation of the Costs to the U.S. Economy and to Consumers of the Increase in Tariff on Imported Canned Tuna Not in Oil to Thirty-five Percent." Appendix A in Prehearing Brief by the Federal Trade Commission before the United States International Trade Commission: Certain Canned Tuna Fish, Investigation no. TA-201-53 (May 1984b).

Garbacz, Christopher. "Residential Energy Demand: A National Micro-Based Model."

Presented at the American Economic Association Meeting Session: Energy Demand and Supply, December 28-30, 1983.

Goldberg, Victor P. "Regulation and Administered Contracts." *Bell Journal of Economics* 7, no. 3 (Autumn 1976): 426-62.

Goldberg, Victor P., and Erickson, John. "Long Term Contracts for Petroleum Coke." Department of Economics Working Paper no. 206, University of California at Davis (September 1982).

Gonzales, Richard J. "Interfuel Relations Governing Natural Gas Demand and Supply," in Keith C. Brown, ed., *Regulation of the Natural Gas Producing Industry*, Washington, DC: Resources for the Future (1972): 56-62.

Halvorsen, Robert. "Energy Substitution in U.S. Manufacturing." *Review of Economics and Statistics* 59, no. 4 (November 1977): 381-88.

Hansen, John A. "Competitive Aspects of the United States Petroleum Pipeline Industry: Implications for Regulatory Policy." Ph.D. dissertation, Yale University, Department of Economics, 1980.

Helms, Robert B. *Natural Gas Regulation: An Evaluation of FPC Price Controls*. Washington, DC: American Enterprise Institute for Public Policy Research, 1974.

Horowitz, Ira. "Market Definition in Antitrust Analysis: A Regression-Based Approach." *Southern Economic Journal* 48, no.1 (July 1981): 1-16.

Hubbard, R. Glenn, and Weiner, Robert J. "Regulation and Long-Term Contracting in U.S. Natural Gas Markets." *Journal of Industrial Economics* 35, no. 1 (September 1986): 71-79.

Information Please Almanac: 1988, 41st ed. Boston: Houghton Mifflin, 1988.

Interstate Natural Gas Association of America (INGAA). "Issue Analysis: Carriage through 1987." 88-7 (May 1988): 1-4.

Jacoby, Henry D., and Wright, Arthur W. "The Gordian Knot of Natural Gas Prices." *The Deregulation of Natural Gas*. Edited by Edward J. Mitchel. Washington, DC: American Enterprise Institute for Public Policy Research (1983): 124-48.

Johnson, Frederick I. "Market Definition under the Merger Guidelines: Critical Demand Elasticities." Federal Trade Commission, Working Paper no. 142 (August 1986).

Joskow, Paul L., and Baughman, Martin L. "The Future of the U.S. Nuclear Energy Industry." *Bell Journal of Economics* 7, no. 1 (Spring 1976): 3-32.

Kwoka, John E., Jr. "The Effect of Market Shares and Share Distribution on Industry Performance." *Review of Economics and Statistics* 61, no. 1 (February 1979): 101-9.

------. "The Effect of Market Share Distribution on Industry Performance: Reply." *Review of Economics and Statistics* 66, no. 2 (May 1984): 358-61.

------. "The Herfindahl Index in Theory and Practice." *Antitrust Bulletin* 30, no. 4 (Winter 1985): 915-45.

Kwoka, John E., Jr., and Ravenscraft, David A. "Cooperation versus Rivalry--Price Cost Margins by Line of Business." *Economica* 53, no. 211 (August 1986): 351-63.

Landes, William M., and Posner, Richard A. "Market Power in Antitrust Cases." *Harvard Law Review* 94, no. 5 (March 1981): 937-96.

Leddy, Mark. "Recent Merger Cases Reflect Revolution in Antitrust Policy." *Legal Times* (November 3, 1986): 17-21.

MacAvoy, Paul W. *Price Formation in Natural Gas Fields: A Study of Competition, Monopsony, and Regulation*. New Haven, CT: Yale University Press, 1962.

Masten, Scott E., and Crocker, Keith J. "Efficient Adaptation in Long-Term Contracts: Take-or-Pay Provisions for Natural Gas." *American Economic Review* 75, no. 5 (December 1985): 1083-93.

Mead, David E. "Concentration in the Natural Gas Pipeline Industry." Federal Energy Regulatory Commission, Staff Working Paper, Washington, DC: (August 1984).

Miller, Richard A. "The Herfindahl-Hirschman Index as a Market Structure Variable: An Exposition for Antitrust Practitioners." *Antitrust Bulletin* 27, no. 3 (Fall 1982): 593-618.

Mitchell, Edward J. "A Study of Oil Pipeline Competition." Unpublished manuscript (April 1982).

Morgan, Joseph M. "Activity, Costs up in Competitive Market." *Oil & Gas Journal* 88, no. 3 (January 21, 1985): 81-85.

Morris, John R. "The Relationship between Industrial Sales Prices and Concentration of Natural Gas Pipelines." Federal Trade Commission, Bureau of Economics Working Paper no. 168 (November 1988).

Mulherin, J. Harold. "Specialized Assets, Governmental Regulation, and Organizational Structure in the Natural Gas Industry." Unpublished Ph.D. dissertation, University of California at Los Angeles, 1984.

Munasinghe, Mohan. *The Economics of Power System Reliability and Planning.* Baltimore: John Hopkins University Press, 1979.

National Economic Research Associates, Inc. (NERA). *Competition in Oil Pipeline Markets: A Structural Analysis.* Prepared by Robert E. Anderson and Richard T. Rapp. NY: White Plains, (April 20, 1983).

NETS. See U.S. Department of Transportation and U.S. Department of Energy.

Office of Management and Budget, Executive Office of the President. "List I: Metropolitan Statistical Areas," "List II: Consolidated Metropolitan Statistical Areas and Primary Metropolitan Statistical Areas," "List III: Metropolitan Statistical Areas Arranged by State," and "List IV: Definitions of New England County Metropolitan Statistical Areas (NECMAs)." OMB-83-20, 84-16, and 84-24, Washington, D.C.: (1983 and 1984)

Ordover, Janusz A., and Wall, Daniel M. "Understanding Econometric Methods of Market Definition." *Antitrust* 3, no. 3 (Summer 1989): 20-25.

Pautler, Paul A. "A Review of the Economic Basis for Broad-Based Horizontal-Merger Policy." *Antitrust Bulletin* 28, no. 3 (Fall 1983): 571-651.

Pindyck, Robert S. "Interfuel Substitution and the Industrial Demand for Energy: An International Comparison." *Review of Economics and Statistics* 61, no. 2 (May 1979): 169-79.

Plott, Charles R. "Industrial Organization Theory and Experimental Economics." *Journal of Economic Literature* 20, no. 4 (December 1982): 1485-527.

Rice, James O., and Rosaler Bob. *Standard Handbook for Plant Engineers.* New York: McGraw-Hill, 1983.

Rosenberg, Laurence C. "Natural-Gas-Pipeline Rate Regulation: Marginal-Cost Pricing and the Zone-Allocation Problem." *Journal of Political Economy* 75, no. 2 (April 1967): 159-68.

Russell, Milton. "Overview of Policy Issues: A Preliminary Assessment." *The Deregulation of Natural Gas.* Edited by Edward J. Mitchell. Washington, DC: American Enterprise Institute for Public Policy Research (1983): 3-32.

Salop, Steven C. "Symposium on Mergers and Antitrust." *Economic Perspectives* 1, no. 2 (Fall 1987): 3-12.

Salop, Steven C., and Simons, Joseph J. "A Practical Guide to Merger Analysis." *Antitrust Bulletin* 29, no. 4 (Winter 1984): 663-703.

Scheffman, David T., and Spiller, Pablo T. "Geographic Market Definition Under the U.S. Department of Justice Merger Guidelines." *Journal of Law and Economics* 30, no. 1 (April 1987): 123-47.

Scherer, F. M. *Industrial Market Structure and Economic Performance*, 2nd ed. Chicago: Rand McNally, 1980.

Schwendtner, A. "LNG Ocean Transportation Costs." *Pipeline and Gas Journal* 204, no. 10 (August 1977): 52-60.

Smith, Vernon L. and Williams, Arlington W. "On Non-Binding Price Controls in a Competitive Market." *American Economic Review* 71, no. 3 (June 1981): 467-74.

Smith, Vernon L.; Williams, Arlington, W.; Bratton, W. Kenneth *et. al.* "Competitive Market Institutions: Double Auctions vs. Sealed-Bid Auctions." *American Economic Review*, 72, No. 1 (March 1982): 58-77.

Stigler, George J. "A Theory of Oligopoly." *Journal of Political Economy* 72, no. 1 (February 1964): 44-61.

Stigler, George J., and Sherwin, Robert A. "The Extent of the Market." *Journal of Law and Economics* 28, no. 3 (October 1985): 555-85.

Tariff Schedules of the United States Annotated (1984).

Tiratsoo, E. N. *Natural Gas*, 3rd ed. Houston, TX.: Gulf, 1979.

Tucker, Elizabeth. "Firms' Battle to Bypass Natural-Gas Middlemen Heats Up." *Washington Post* (April 28, 1986).

Tussing, Arlon R., and Barlow, Connie C. *The Natural Gas Industry: Evolution, Structure, and Economics*. Cambridge, MA: Ballinger, 1984.

------. "The Rise and Fall of Regulation in the Natural Gas Industry." *Public Utilities Fortnightly* 109, no. 5 (March 4, 1982): 15-23.

U.S. Department of Transportation and U.S. Department of Energy. National Energy Transportation Study: A Preliminary Report to the President. Washington, DC: (July 1980); referred to as NETS.

Untiet, Charles. "The Economics of Oil Pipeline Deregulation: A Review and Extension of the DOJ Report." Economic Analysis Group Discussion Paper no. 87-3. Department of Justice, Antitrust Division, (May 22, 1987).

Weinstock, David S. "Using the Herfindahl Index to Measure Concentration." *Antitrust Bulletin* 27, no. 2 (Summer 1982): 285-301.

Wellisz, Stanislaw H. "Regulation of Natural Gas Pipeline Companies: An Economic Analysis." *Journal of Political Economy* 71, no. 1 (February 1963): 30-43.

Wolpert, George S., Jr. *U.S. Oil Pipe Lines*. Washington, DC: American Petroleum Institute, 1979.

INDEX

ABOUT THE AUTHOR

Edward C. Gallick is Director of the Division of Competition Analysis in the Office of Economic Policy at the Federal Energy Regulatory Commission (FERC). The Division is responsible for providing expert economic analysis in litigated and nonlitigated cases in the natural gas pipeline, oil pipeline, and electric utility industries. Dr. Gallick is the first Director of the Division which began as an experiment in 1988.

Dr. Gallick has eighteen years experience in developing and managing complex analyses of market power, antitrust, and competition issues in unregulated and regulated industries. He has conducted numerous competition analyses of market-based rates and mergers in the natural gas pipeline, crude oil pipeline, and electricity industries; he has developed litigation strategy and expert economic testimony; and he has managed an interdisciplinary staff of economists, operations research and financial analysts, accountants, and attorneys.

Prior to joining the FERC in 1988, Dr. Gallick was a senior economist in the Division of Industry Analysis and a Deputy Assistant Director in the Division of Economic Evidence of the Federal Trade Commission. Dr. Gallick has also served as an independent economic consultant.

Dr. Gallick earned his PhD degree in economics from UCLA in 1984. He has written a book on the efficiency of exclusive dealing arrangements and has written articles and presented papers on a wide variety of market power issues.